等值理论视阈下的
汉语歇后语翻译

侯　霞　何孟良　著

西北工业大学出版社

西　安

【内容简介】 对汉语歇后语及其英、俄译的研究不仅有助于中、英、俄跨文化交际的深入,而且对丰富外语语汇具有重要意义。本书利用什维策尔提出的等值模式,通过对比、分析汉语文学作品中的歇后语原文与英语、俄语译文,对译文实现的各类等值层面进行实证性研究,并在此基础上进一步分析影响歇后语翻译实现更高级别等值层面的语言和文化因素及译者翻译策略的选择。

本书适用于学习外语专业的学生、从事外语教学和对外汉语教学的教师,以及语言研究者、翻译工作者、文化研究者和其他爱好汉语、英语和俄语学习人士。

图书在版编目(CIP)数据

等值理论视阈下的汉语歇后语翻译/侯霞,何孟良著 . —西安:西北工业大学出版社,2023.2
ISBN 978 - 7 - 5612 - 6499 - 7

Ⅰ.①等… Ⅱ.①侯… ②何… Ⅲ.①汉语-歇后语-英语-翻译-研究 Ⅳ.①H315.9

中国版本图书馆 CIP 数据核字(2019)第 181162 号

DENGZHI LILUN SHIYUXIA DE HANYU XIEHOUYU FANYI

等值理论视阈下的汉语歇后语翻译
侯霞 何孟良 著

责任编辑:杨 睿	策划编辑:张 晖	
责任校对:雷 鹏	装帧设计:李 飞	

出版发行:西北工业大学出版社
通信地址:西安市友谊西路 127 号   邮编:710072
电　　话:(029)88491757,88493844
网　　址:www.nwpup.com
印　刷　者:广东虎彩云印刷有限公司
开　　本:787 mm×1 092 mm　　1/16
印　　张:15.625
字　　数:289 千字
版　　次:2023 年 2 月第 1 版　　2023 年 2 月第 1 次印刷
书　　号:ISBN 978 - 7 - 5612 - 6499 - 7
定　　价:78.00 元

前　　言

　　歇后语是广大人民群众在丰富的生产生活实践中创造出的一种极具民族特色的语言表达形式,堪称汉语中的奇葩异卉。歇后语作为汉语语汇的重要组成部分,以独特的结构、生动活泼的表现形式和妙趣横生的表达效果而为大众所喜闻乐见。歇后语通常由两个部分组成:前一部分是形象的比喻,像谜语中的谜面;后一部分则是对前一部分的解释说明,揭示语句本义,像谜底。歇后语不仅在社会各阶层口语中被广泛使用,而且在古典文学和现当代文学作品、文章中也随处可见。它通过使用比喻和双关的修辞手段来增添语言的艺术感染力。

　　大多数歇后语或包含着丰富的文化信息,或体现着汉语语言的个性特征,这是中英语言和文化交流的一大障碍。对汉语歇后语及其英译的研究,不仅将有助于汉语与英语跨文化交际的深入,而且对丰富英语语汇具有重要意义。本书试图揭示汉语文学作品中歇后语英译实现的等值层面及影响因素,并在此基础上探讨歇后语翻译策略和翻译方法的灵活选择。

　　在翻译文学作品中的歇后语时,译者首先基于自己的背景知识和文化意识来理解某条歇后语表达在特定语境中的含义。因此,笔者从语义学的角度分析歇后语的语义结构及释义问题,揭示歇后语在语言使用过程中其内部与外部语境的关系,分析引申义的实现手段,总结歇后语的修辞特点及在句中的语法功能,借此为歇后语的翻译研究扫除源语理解阶段的障碍。

　　等值理论在翻译理论中一直占有极为重要的地位,对翻译实践与译作评价有着理论指导与实用意义。本书借鉴了什维策尔提出的等值模式,通过对比分析汉语文学作品中的歇后语原文与英语译文,对译文实现的各类等值层面进行实证性研究,并在此基础上进一步分析影响歇后语翻译实现更高级别等值层面的语言和文化因素及译者翻译策略的选择。

　　关于翻译策略的选择,译界一直存在"异化"与"归化"之争。前者主张译文应以源语或原文作者为归宿,后者则认为译文应以目的语或译文读者为归宿。"异化"和"归化"是直译与意译争论的延伸和扩展,是两种并行不悖的翻译策略,各有利弊,均有其存在和应用的价值。文学作品中歇后语的翻译方法因作者意图、文本类型、翻译目的和读者要求的不同而灵活多变。总的说来,以源语为导向的翻译方法能较好满足源语文化传播的需要,而读者接受水平的个体性差异则决定了以目的语为导向的翻译方法在一定时期内的必要性。但是从历史的角度来看,异化必将成为文学翻译的主要趋势。

写作本书曾参阅了近年来出版的翻译理论书籍、英汉语言学专著和外语类核心期刊所载的论文以及从英译的文学作品中引用了相关译例,旨在用以示范说明,而无主观褒贬之意,并在此向其作者和译者深表谢意。

限于笔者学识浅陋,水平有限,书中错讹之处在所难免,诚望各位学者及读者指教。

著　者

2019 年 1 月

目　　录

第一章　汉语歇后语的科学分析

　　歇后语是汉语语汇的重要组成部分,它像谚语、俗语一样极富形象性和表现力,因而在人们的日常生活和曲艺、诗文甚至古今文学名著中被广泛地运用。不少歇后语具有丰富的想象力,语言诙谐幽默,"以游戏的态度,在嬉笑间把人事和物态的丑陋、鄙陋和乖讹当作一种有趣的意向去欣赏和批判"。

　　歇后语应该说是汉语中的一朵奇葩,其作为一种文学语言,长时间以来并不被大众所认可。究其原因,在中国漫长的封建社会里,"文言"作为"正统"的书面语被士大夫等文人群体所推崇。可以说,绝大部分的古典文学名著都是用文言完成的。歇后语被认为是所谓的俚语、鄙言,是"村夫野人"之言。① 这就决定了歇后语不可能进入文学作品这个"殿堂"。既然不能进入"正统"的书面语,歇后语就成了"旁门左道"。这就是歇后语为什么在封建社会很少被士大夫知识分子所赏识、运用的原因。

　　随着金元时期杂剧的盛行,很多歇后语渐渐出现于这个时期的作品中。因为杂剧的作者与广大人民群众保持着密切的联系,对他们的语言和文化生活较为熟悉。但直至中华人民共和国成立前,歇后语都被认为不够"典雅",或者说它只是一种文字游戏的偏见仍然没有彻底消除。

　　茅盾在 1953 年中国文学艺术工作者第二次代表大会上关于《新的现实和新的任务》报告中指出:"艺术作品中存在大量使用歇后语这种庸俗的俏皮语的现象。歇后语充其量只是一种文字游戏,它不属于文学语言。增加歇后语的使用不仅不利于丰富扩充我们的语汇,而且还会污染文学语言。"

　　茅盾认为,歇后语只是一种单纯的文字游戏,它不属于文学语言的这种观点引来了国内众多语言学家的反对。朱波士撰文《歇后语——文字游戏?》,表示反对将歇后语排除在文学语言之外,不赞成将歇后语视为仅是文字游戏的观点。他指出,很多歇后语不仅意蕴深厚,而且具有语言活泼、诙谐、形象的特

---

　　① 谭永祥. 歇后语新论[M]. 济南:山东教育出版社,1984:159.

点。合理使用歇后语能够润色语言,增强表现力,可给读者带来深刻的印象。中国文化革命的主将鲁迅先生在他的文章中用过歇后语,中国古典小说《水浒传》《儒林外史》《红楼梦》中也时常有歇后语的身影,事实充分说明:歇后语不是难登大雅之堂,而是早已登上大雅之堂了。因此,怎样对待和运用歇后语,不仅具有重要的理论意义,而且还有它的现实意义。

第一节　歇后语的语义特征

一、歇后语的双部结构

完整的歇后语由前后两部分组成。这种双结构是歇后语区别于其他谚语、俗语的典型外部特征。歇后语在口语中运用时,这种结构上的切分可通过语调来解决。歇后语的第一部分使用完结语调,第二部分通过短暂的停顿与第一部分相隔开,并且语调上与歇后语所在的句子语调保持一致。歇后语在书面中运用时可通过标点符号来区分前后两部分,通常可用"破折号"或"逗号",较少用"冒号"或"引号"。

此外,歇后语区别于其他语汇的另一显著特征是其典型的双语义成分。歇后语像谜语一样被划分为两个部分:第一部分像谜面,后一部分像谜底。歇后语的前一部分通常被称为"提示语",其意义在于引发人的思考,使人产生某种联想或想象。第二部分通常被称作"目的语",其实际意义根据所构建的具体语言场景来确定。

提示语		目的语
猪八戒照镜子	——	里外不是个人
裁缝掉了剪子	——	光剩尺(吃)了
瞌睡碰到枕头	——	凑巧得很

根据上述例子可以看出,歇后语的第一部分具有谜语的特点,语言表述富有形象性,能让人联想到某个场景。歇后语的第二部分则是对前一部分形象构想的解释说明,旨在揭示该形象的具体意义。换句话说,运用歇后语就好比说话人先给大家提出个谜语,而后他自己又为大家揭开谜底。使用歇后语时,一般具有完整结构,即带有前后两个部分,很少省略其中任一部分。根据相关文献著录,《红楼梦》《儒林外史》《西游记》《暴风骤雨》《李自成》等五百二十多部文艺作品中所用的 4 893 条的歇后语,后一部分"歇"去的只有 375 条,占不

到1/12。①

为何歇后语的后一部分一般不省略呢？这是因为组成歇后语的前后两个部分是密切相连的,且后一部分还是表达语义的重点所在,如果硬要"歇"去后一部分,就会影响表达效果。

首先,容易让读者感到费解。茅盾在分析歇后语的双部结构时指出,如果省略歇后语的第二部分将很难猜测其所指意义。例如:

却说那三个魔头,齐心竭力,与大圣兄弟三人,在城东半山内,努力争持。这一场,正是那"铁刷帚刷铜锅,家家挺硬"。(吴承恩《西游记》)

上例中"家家挺硬",原意是指两个东西都很坚硬,用在句子里引申指双方态度都很强硬,如果"歇"去,就不太容易让读者猜测出来。

其次,尽管歇后语的第一部分形象相同,但所指的意义不同,这样容易引起歧义甚至是误解。例如:

①这二三十年,一个运动又一个运动,沟沟坎坎,坑坑洼洼,他却鸭子过河——不沾水,一路平安,没有伤着半根汗毛。(刘绍棠《柳伞》)

②巧姑娘看了都摇摇头说:"价钱有限,难见真心。"结果都婉言谢绝了。所以,有的人叹口气说:"唉,真是人心皆同,巧姑娘也是鸭子过河——随大流的,变成了高价姑娘,我们是六尺跳板要过八尺洞——搭不够呀!"(吴仁龙《巧姑娘招亲》)

③一个卫兵正好走来,看到他在大发脾气,便默默地站在一边。尚军长问道:"你听说过'鸭子过河'这句话吗？什么意思？"卫兵笑道:"那是咱们家乡的土话,管那只会说、不会做的人就像鸭子过河——嘴上前。尚将军问这个做甚？"(蒋和森《黄梅雨》)

上述三例,前一部分都是"鸭子过河",后一部分分别作"不沾水""随大流""嘴上前",如果后一部分都省略,就很难捉摸也无法区别它们的确切意义。

再次,会损害句子的完整性,使句子失去表情达意的功能。这在前后两部分之间插入其他语言成分,或后一部分被拆开中间插入其他语言成分时,表现得最为明显。例如:

①(生)大王,则我今日学得个哑谜儿,试与俺兄弟们答问咱。你见关大王卖豆腐来？(众)见来,人硬货不硬哩。(生)你见尖底瓮儿来？(众)见来,少不得一撞便倒哩。(生)你问过哑姑姑做梦来么？(众)问来,如今都谁醒谁知哩!(明 王辰玉《郁轮袍》)

_____

① 温端正.歇后语[M].北京:商务印书馆,2000:2.

②合作社里一片嘈杂,老初的大嗓压倒所有的声音,他说:"这算什么合作社? 这家伙,布袋里买猫,尽抓咱们老百姓的迷糊。"(周立波《暴风骤雨》)

③现在是哑巴吃蚕豆——黎元洪心中有了数,他也慢慢地站了起来,边擦眼泪边踌躇,口气不同了:"谁同你们造反?"(李六如《六十年的变迁》)

例①前后两部分都插进了"(众)见来,少不得";例②后一部分"尽抓迷糊"被拆开,中间插进"咱们老百姓"。在这种情况下,后一部分是无论如何都不能"歇"去的,如果硬要"歇"去,不仅意思表达不清楚,连句子本身也不能成立了。

张古一在谈到歇后语在句中的使用特点时指出,歇后语的第二部分可以省略,并且也常常省略,但这需要一个前提条件,即是该歇后语的完整形式在大众中已是耳熟能详,读者能毫不费力地将省略成分复原出来。例如:

①施忠说:"今日应了俗语:大水冲了龙王庙咧! 没得说,今求众位赏我黄天霸点脸,大家笑合笑合,也免旁人耻笑。"(《施公案》)

②你是狗扑老鼠! 你有良心,把她抬到你家去。放进龛里供养起,我李家管不着!(刘江《太行风云》)

③姊姊! 这才是"狗咬吕洞宾"呢! 我常常听见人家说,做了官是用大秤称金子,小秤称银子的,我们这个番禺县,又是有好名的好缺,衙门里却是冰清水冷的,外面的人说起来,都说如今这个县官是个呆子,有钱不会用。(《九命奇冤》)

以汉语为母语者,谁不知晓"大水冲了龙王庙咧"即指"自家人不认自家人","狗扑老鼠"即指"多管闲事","狗咬吕洞宾"多指"不识好人心"的含义呢。因此,使用过程中将负载主要意义的第二部分省略,读者对省略成分心有灵犀,点滴交代,反而不妥,似乎作者将读者置于悟性差、文法低的境地。

二、歇后语的内、外部语境

Ю. Л. Кроль 对汉语歇后语的研究投入了极大的热情,发表题为《汉语歇后语分类经验和结构描述》的文章。他表示,歇后语在具体语句中使用时可以被划分为两个语境:伴随歇后语使用场景的变化而变化的外部语境;无论使用环境如何改变保持不变的内部语境。①

在内部语境中大部分歇后语的第二部分兼具字面意义和形象意义,该种

---

① Кроль Ю. Л. Опыт описания структуры и классификации пекинских поговорок сехоуюй. Жанры и стили литератур Дальнего Востока. Тезисы докладов научной конференции[M]. Наука:Ленинград,1966:268.

意义是始终保持不变的。当语言的外部语境发生改变时,歇后语第二部分的意义会随之发生必要的改变以适应语言交际的需要。歇后语第二部分的意义与内外部语境之间的关系可见图1.1。

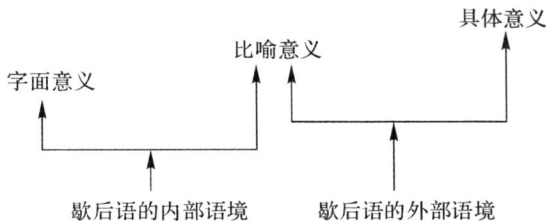

图 1.1 歇后语第二部分意义与内外部语境间的关系

为了充分解释这一点,下面通过具体事例来加以分析。

①水仙不开花——装蒜。

②小叶盯着前边的公路,只管说她的:"老实坦白,有了没有?"那姑娘故作不解:"什么有了没有? 有啥?"于小叶说:"水仙不开花——装蒜! 这有什么不好意思? 心上人!"(王东满《山月恨》)

通过观察可以看出,①中歇后语的第二部分"装蒜"显然只处在内部语境中。"装蒜"在此仅具有"装成大蒜的样子"的字面意义以及利用谐音构成"虚伪"的比喻意义。相比而言,歇后语在具体语言使用环境下,如在②中,歇后语的第二部分同时处于内部和外部语境中,因此第二部分拥有了具体的意义。在②中,歇后语的第二部分"装蒜"实际上表示的意思是"姑娘隐瞒有男朋友的事实"。

③人嘛,药材店里的抹布——甜酸苦辣样样都得沾点。(张贤亮《河的子孙》)

大部分情况下,歇后语第二部分在外部语境下使用时扮演"语义词"的角色。而在歇后语的内部语境下,它的这种语义统一被破坏,变为带有成语性质的词汇的自由组合,其中每个具有完整意义的词变成独立的语义单位。①

歇后语可以在没有具体使用语境的情况下孤立的存在。因此,歇后语无论是在意义上,还是在形式上(语法上)都是一种自足的语言形式。换句话说,

---

① Кроль Ю. Л. Опыт описания структуры и классификации пекинских поговорок сехоуюй. Жанры и стили литератур Дальнего Востока. Тезисы докладов научной конференции. [М]. Наука:Ленинград,1966:269 – 270.

仅从歇后语的内部语境来看,歇后语具有完整的结论,而这种结论是通过句子的形式表现出来的。① 有时,内部语境会为歇后语的第二部分增添新的感情色彩或者带来新的伴随意义,而这种增添的意义在言语的外部语境下是不会有的。例如,在内部语境下歇后语的第二部分有时具有贬低的意义,或者说是拥有戏谑的色彩,然而放到外部语境下,第二部分的语义色彩变得崇高了,或者达到中性的色彩,完全严肃化了。②

众所周知,歇后语的内部语境在句中的外部语境里缺乏交际功能。然而,由于内部交际层面的存在,歇后语可以具有表情功能。从这个层面上来讲,歇后语的第一和第二部分之间的功能关系具有独特的特点。这两者之间的关系可以视作歇后语语义结构的必需成分。歇后语的第一部分表述形象生动,第二部分揭示其寓意的具体特征。两者之间可以是结果、原因、条件或者时间的关系。③

三、歇后语的交际焦点

与谚语和俗语的意义完全由所有构成成分来确定的特点不同,歇后语是成语单位,其交际焦点取决于第二部分,这可以由下述几点来证明。

(1)如果交谈对象对歇后语的完整形式不够熟悉,在歇后语的使用时省略了后一部分,这会大大妨碍对歇后语的理解。

①恐怕有人要问:"四人帮"倒台三年,张寡妇还如此"二三四五六七八九——缺一(衣)少十(食)",简直难以置信。(《小说月报》1981 年 2 期)

②两个人一唱一和打得火热,把别的几位士绅代表冷在一边。这在张梅椿说来,他是吃笋子剥皮,一层层来。(柯蓝等《风满潇湘》)

③大家都在说市公所最近就要计划将伊的土地列入拓宽道路的范围。如此一来,若是伊房子给拆了,要在原地再盖房子,便是和尚看嫁妆,来世见啦!(王祯和《伊会念咒》)

---

① Прядохин М. Г. Китайские недоговорки — иносказания[M]. Москва:наука,1977:33.

② Кроль Ю. Л. Опыт описания структуры и классификации пекинских поговорок сехоуюй. Жанры и стили литератур Дальнего Востока. Тезисы докладов научной конференции[M]. Наука:Ленинград, 1966:269.

③ Прядохин М. Г. Китайские недоговорки — иносказания[M]. Москва:наука,1977:55.

显然,如果上述三例中在使用歇后语时将各自第二部分"歇"去,那么它们看起来和谜语没什么差别了。正如黄伯荣、廖序东主编的《现代汉语》对歇后语的解释:"歇后语是由近似谜面、谜底两部分组成的带有隐语性质的口头用语。"

(2)如果在句子表述过程中要用到歇后语时,将其第一部分即提示语省略而保留歇后语的第二部分,句子的意义保持不变。也就是说,从交际层面来讲,句义没有发生改变。我们对比以下例子。

郭全海一想,黄皮子给小鸡拜年,他还能安啥好肠子吗? 他不要。

郭全海一想,他还能安啥好肠子吗? 他不要。

(周立波《暴风骤雨》)

两头老人催着他们年前结婚,秀英一直没吐口,小强他爹娘就自顾自地忙活起来了。

(马春《龙滩春色》)

任何一句歇后语,当它进入具体句子以后,都是作为双关来用的,由于歇后语的后一部分都是双关语,表面上"说明"它的前一部分"话题",实际上是另有所指。因此,很多进入具体句子的歇后语,即使把它的前一部分"话题"拿掉,整个句子的基本语意并不受影响,不过修辞色彩减弱罢了。

(3)从语法功能角度来看,歇后语的第一部分类似主语,而第二部分类似谓语。因此,歇后语的第二部分具有双重意义,既要与内部语境中的主语保持一致又要与外部语境即在具体的句子中作相应的成分。换句话说,歇后语的第二部分同时处于内外部两种语境下。歇后语的第二部分这个"谓语"具有双关的特点,不仅能够跟它自己的"主语"相应,而且能够跟它所进入的具体句子的主语相应。歇后语在它作为待用语汇形式的时候,它只有一个"主语",但当它一旦进入具体的句子,歇后语的后一部分,即"谓语",马上就"一仆有了二主"。这两个"主",它都能够与之"相处其得"。所以,如果去掉了歇后语的前一部分,这不过是让歇后语的后一部分扔掉了自己原来的"主"(语),而换上了一个新的"主"(语)而已。[①]温端正把歇后语的前后两部分之间关系比作"引"和"注"的关系。"引"是主语部分,"注"是谓语部分,这在"引"是名词或名词性结构时,看得最为明显。[②] 如:

---

①　谭永祥.歇后语新论[M].济南:山东教育出版社,1984:113-114.

②　温端正.歇后语[M].北京:商务印书馆,2000:56.

　　臭豆腐——闻着不香吃着香

　　墙上的草——随风倒

　　强扭的瓜儿——不甜

　　拔节的竹笋——天天向上

　　阴沟里的泥鳅——翻不起大浪

　　属公鸡的——光啼不下蛋

　　属吕布的——有勇无谋

　　因此,歇后语的第二部分在具体句子中使用时同时具备两种功能。一方面,在歇后语的内部语境中第二部分揭示第一部分即提示语的内容;另一方面,作为成语性单位,歇后语的第二部分在语句即外部语境中发挥交际功能。因此,歇后语的第二部分可以看作是连接内外部语境的交点。

　　必须指出的是,歇后语第二部分在语句中表示的真实含义常与其在内部语境下的意义不相符合。不论在什么情况下,歇后语的基本意义都是由后一部分来表示的。歇后语后一部分所表示的基本意义有本义和别义之分。有的歇后语只有本义,没有别义。例如:

　　①他对小队长是一肚子不满意,特别是看到刚才突然进来一伙客商,更觉得住在这里是"鲁肃上了孔明的船"——错了!(孙景瑞《难忘的战斗》)

　　②"事倒没事,可有意见!"缪虎是个急性子,肚里藏不住话,"依我说呀,班长现在捣鼓这玩意,可是大热天穿棉袄——不是时候!"(程景楷等《新花似锦》)

　　③刘光禄这才又"唉"了一声,说:"不用提啦,王连生那小子,狗咬耗子多管闲事,就是他穷积极,专门和我过不去。"(胡正《汾水长流》)

　　上述例子里的歇后语,第二部分都只有本义,没有别义,无论是作为语汇形式单独存在的时候,还是运用到句子里面的时候,后一部分"错了""不是时候""多管闲事"都只有一个确定的意义。

　　可是,下述这些例子里的歇后语却不一样,除了本义之外,还有别义:

　　①没有这东西,你就什么也别想望办成。修房不给你批地基,埋人不给你辟坟基,结婚不给你开介绍信,想到外面找工作,更是"墙上挂竹帘——没门儿"!(崔巍等《爱与恨》)

　　②谁知,到了腊月二十八早上住在村西头最末一家的榆木老汉突然宣布:"他不能管说书的饭,也拿不出这五块钱的书资。"这真是大煞风景! 他这一手,马上成为饭场上的头条新闻:"水仙不开花——他又装蒜哩!"(徐慎《双桥》)

③大水说:"唉! 他说命太苦,头一回说亲说了个你,闹了一回子,谁知道柳树上开花,没结果。这一回说了个翠花儿,眼看要过门了,又飞来了横祸。"(孔厥等《新儿女英雄传》)

例①"墙上挂竹帘——没门儿",后一部分"没门"本义指没有门户,但用在句子里实际意义是指没有门路;例②"水仙不开花——装蒜",后一部分"装蒜"本义指装成蒜的样子,但用在句子里实际意义是指装腔作势,装模作样;例③"柳树上开花——没结果",后一部分"没结果"本义指没有结出果实,但用在句子里实际意义是指没有达到预期的目的。

歇后语的别义是怎样产生的呢? 大致上有以下三种情况。

第一种情况,由后一部分里一个或几个词派生出另一种意义而产生别义。这种由原义派生新义而产生的别义,叫作派生义。派生大体上可分成引申和换喻两种方式。引申建立在两种意义反映的现实现象具有某种相似之处的基础上,如:

① 打锡人这时真是疔疮长在喉头上,有痛不敢说。补茶壶吧,怕夜长梦多;拒绝呢,又怕引起怀疑,露了马脚。(颜广林、盛祖绳等《井冈烽火》)

② 小爷们真行啊,干活不藏奸躲懒,马上马下都能来两下子。咱大队长早就当着贫下中农的面夸你是"二齿钩子挠痒——是把硬手"。(郭先红《征途》)

③ 迎面传来唧唧咕咕的说话声:"咱这份差事算干够了,小黄集岗楼是包脚布围嘴——臭了一圈啦!"(晋庆玉《英雄的乡土》)

例①后一部分里的"痛",本义指肉体上的疼痛,用在句子里引申指精神上的苦衷;例②后一部分里的"硬手",本义指坚硬的手,用在句子里引申指在某个方面有过硬本领的人;例③后一部分里的"臭",本义指气味难闻,"臭了一圈"指嘴的周围都有臭气,用在句子里,"臭"引申指不好的名声,"臭了一圈"指臭名传遍了周围一带地方。

换喻的基础,是两类现实现象之间存在着某种联系,这种联系或由于它在人们心目中经常出现而固定化,或由于在一定的上下文中显示出来,从而为人们所理解。由此可见,尽管它们之间并不存在什么相似之点,仍然可以用其中一类现象去指称另一类现象。例如:

①装甲车上的机枪手骂起来道:"水筲没梁,都是饭桶,怎么就叫人进来了?"(杨朔《中国人民的脚步声》)

②你这个人什么都好,就是嘴快,水盆里扎猛子,也没个深浅。(杨朔《三千里江山》)

③有新老汉走到灰灰脸跟前,拿起拐杖指住他的眉眼五官说:"哈巴狗带串铃,你充什么大牲口! 你说了为什么不算数?"(刘江《太行风云》)

④还有个老头说:"你们跟我们合哪! 是胖老婆骑瘦驴——肥瘦相搭呗!"(李准《李双双小传》)

例①后一部分"饭桶",本义指盛饭的桶,用在句子里比喻只会吃饭,没有实际用处的人;例②后一部分里"深浅",本义指水面到水底的距离,用在句子里比喻做事或说话的分寸。这两例,本义和派生义之间的联系原已固定,容易为人们所理解。例③后一部分里的"大牲口",用在句子里比喻装出很有气派的人;例④后一部分的"肥瘦",用在句子里比喻能力强的和能力弱的。这两例,本义和派生义之间的联系,是根据上下文才看出来的。

第二种情况,利用后一部分里一个或几个字形、音、义上的相关,通过谐音而产生别义,这种情况产生的别义叫作假借义。

(1)利用同音异形异义字。例如:

①而今,这场不比寻常的考试,老孙当了主考官,未过门的女婿要闯头一关:这可是铁鞋上掌——要见砧了!(李锐、权延赤等《摇楼记》)

②我们干事,不能像用五眼枪打兔子,光有响头没有准头。(曼生《玉龙的眼睛》)

③方兴士看罢当场就退还他,说道:"什么指挥部,它认识我,我还不认识它呢!"给他来个自行车下坡——不踩!(福建省军区政治部编《闽海激浪》)

例①"砧"借作"真",例②"响"借作"想",例③"踩"借作"睬"。

(2)利用近音异形异义字。例如:

①我嘴里嘟囔了一句,心里不由地想:这里几百万砖呢,几块次品有什么了不起。这明明是秋后上地——专找茬儿。(马骏等《松青旗红》)

②他使劲拍了拍龙阿四的肩头,说:"老四呀,你给我老母鸡抱鸡蛋——一边孵着去吧!"(曼生《玉龙的眼睛》)

③康顺风和刚从区上放回来的康家败,……跑到民兵家属跟前,假装怜悯地说:"这些娃子真可怜,看打成什么样子啦! 咱说一句不好听的话吧,正规部队都打不走日本,靠你们民兵可抵啥哩? 那是茅石板上的打滚,寻的往屎坑里跳哩嘛!"(马烽、西戎《吕梁英雄传》)

④朱店镇这地方不比一般的伪乡公所,他是牤牛耳——离角近,鬼子抬脚就到,不能死打硬拼。(山东省军区政治部编《沂蒙红缨》)

例①"茬儿"借作"岔儿",声母韵母相同而声调不同;例②"孵"借作"伏",也是声母韵母相同,声调不同;例③"屎"借作"死",韵母声调相同,声母不同;

例④"角"借作"家",声母相同,韵母声调不同。

（3）利用同音同形异义字。例如：

①说党团骨干,说互助合作基础,也不是我老鼠爬称钩——自称自,我团沙湾也不比别地差呀!（吴梦起等《杨春山入社》）

②于春保以教训的口气对钟卫华说："副业抓不上,春耕备不好,脑门上长瘤子——净搞些额外负担,到年底算总账分红的时候,叫大伙儿喝西北风去呀?"（李锐、权延赤等《征途》）

③王金堂脸上热辣辣的,胸脯上长草——荒（慌）了心啦。（肖英俊《山村风雨》）

例①里的"称",本是称东西的"称",借作"称赞"的"称";例②里的"额",本是"额头"的"额",指人眉毛之上、头发之下的部位,借作"数额"的"额",指规定的数量或范围。例③里"荒""慌"同音异义,产生幽默风趣,使人顿生新奇之感。

第三种情况,通过后一部分里两个词的搭配产生新词,从而使意义发生转换。这种情况产生的别义,叫作转换义,如：

①你说行,我就派人,你说不行,咱就脚后跟拴绳子——拉倒。（张恩忠《龙岗战火》）

②大队长谈到鬼子侵略中国,他说："你们别看他们现在灶王爷放屁,神气不小,可是他们迟早是要垮台的!"（李锐、权延赤等《到敌后去》）

③陈二端子紧紧地跟在李大嘴的屁股后边,为了讨海骥马,一步也不放松,苦苦地哀求着,说着小话。"我这个残废端子,跟着你转抹抹,连脚脖子都走疼了。""土豆子搬家——滚你姥姥家的蛋吧!"（马加《江山村十日》）

例①里的"拉倒","拉"本义指用绳子拉,"倒"本义指身子倒下,用于句中,合成一个新词,转指"算了""作罢"的意思。例②里的"神气","神"本义指神灵、神明,"气"本义指气体,用于句中时,合成一个新词,转指一种傲慢的神态。例③里的"滚",本义指滚动,"蛋"本义指球形的东西,用于句中搭配成一个（被拆开使用的）合成词,成为要别人走开时责骂的话。① 从以上例句可以看出,歇后语的第一部分多为形象比喻,第二部分大抵是对比喻的解释或揭示,是语义重点。所以,对后半部分的释义,有时需要读者悉心体会和领悟。

----

① 温端正. 歇后语[M]. 北京：商务印书馆,2000:56.

第二节 歇后语的修辞特征

作为一种特殊的语汇形式,歇后语具有其自身的特点。很多语言学家对歇后语的特点都进行了一定的总结,归纳起来歇后语的典型特征无外乎俚语性、形象性、谐趣性三种。

一、俚语性

歇后语是人民群众智慧的结晶,来源于口头创作,主要依靠口头来代代相传,因此歇后语的特点之一,便是口头性。虽然书面上也常常可以看到歇后语,特别是中华人民共和国成立后几十年来,歇后语被广泛应用于文学作品中,但就歇后语总的出现频率来看,书面上看到的远远赶不上口头上听到的多。即使在书面上看到的歇后语,根据对《红楼梦》《儒林外史》《新儿女英雄传》《艳阳天》这几部小说的粗略统计,绝大部分都是用在人物的对话里。这也间接并准确地说明了歇后语的"口头性"的特点确实存在。歇后语的口头性这一特点,决定了它是一种"引车卖浆者言"。习惯于使用"雅言"的封建士大夫文人,囿于阶级偏见,不屑也不敢大胆采用这种"鄙俗"之语。歇后语的口头性是通过语音、词汇和语法规则这三方面表现出来的。

歇后语口头性的特点在语音层面的表现在于构成歇后语的词汇具有灵活自由的发音规则,允许与标准普通话正音规范有较大出入。例如,音节中元音和语调可以简化;如果存在两个或两个以上发音方案,可以选择最为简单的那种。请看以下示例:老鼠跳在秤盘上——自称自在(赞)[zìchēngzìzài(zàn)]。在标准汉语中"在"和"赞"这两个字不是同音异义字。但是在口头语,尤其是在北方方言体系中,如在东北话、山东话和安徽话中,这两个字的发音动作部位接近,并且发音也很相似。另外,构成歇后语的词汇,其发音规则灵活性的特点还表现在歇后语中经常使用不同语调的近音异义词。例如,裁缝掉了剪子——光剩尺(吃)[guāng shèng chǐ(chī)]。

歇后语口头性的特点在语法层面的表现在于歇后语中大量使用无连接词来表达复杂的语法关系,倾向于使用无前置词结构来表达动宾、时间及地点等语法关系。例如:刮风扫地,下雨泼街——假积极。在这个歇后语第一部分中,我们可以看到此处没有像标准书面语法规则要求那样严格使用"刮风的时候扫地"和"下雨的时候泼街"。由此可见,歇后语的第一部分语法上整体是按照口语性的特点构建的。

歇后语口头性的特点在词汇层面的表现最为明显。这种口头性首先表现在构成歇后语的词汇虽然不同源,但都有共同的修辞特征。例如:狗咬刺猬——无处下嘴。显然此处歇后语的后半句——"没处下嘴"是对书面语"无从下手"或"无从着手"的简化说法。

二、形象性

歇后语的前一部分,在表义上只起辅助作用,在语法上多数情况也是起辅助作用,但在修辞上却处于很重要的地位。歇后语最基本的修辞作用,就在于通过它前一部分所表示的形象、感情等色彩,使后一部分所表示的语义形象化,如:

①他是梁化之的红人,外号霍三孙,平日里抓人杀人,敲诈勒索,坑害百姓,坏透了。(程秀龙等《解放太原之战》)

②这东霸天真是头顶长疮,脚底流脓——坏透了。从敌人占领岛子以后,他整天价不是收税收捐,就是杀人倒算。(姜树茂,程秀龙等《渔岛怒潮》)

③三十几个敌军官大眼瞪小眼,谁也不说话。(程秀龙等《解放太原之战》)

④"村南……桥……这桥叫什么呢?"他结结巴巴地问同伴。可是他的同伴被问得像"张飞穿针——大眼瞪小眼",答不上腔来。(福建省军区政治部编《海疆儿女》)

例①"坏透了"是一般说法;例②在"坏透了"之前加上"头顶长疮,脚底流脓",成了歇后语,比较一下就可以看出,后者通过"头顶长疮,脚底流脓"把"坏透了"形象化了。例③"大眼瞪小眼"指干着急说不出话来,本来就是一种形象的说法;例④改用歇后语"张飞穿针",语言诙谐幽默,增添了作品的生活气息达到生动活泼的修辞效果。

在文学创作中巧妙运用歇后语,通常是采用如下修辞手法,获得形神兼备的艺术效果。

(1)故意言过其实。对事物作扩大或缩小的描述,相当于修辞上的"夸张",故意夸大的,如:

冬瓜大的茄子——嫩不了;

丈二宽的长袍——大腰(摇)大摆;

一张纸画一个鼻子——好大的脸面。

故意缩小的,如:

两分钱开当铺——周转不开;

三个钱买条毛驴——自夸骑得；

九两线织布——想的稀奇。

（2）运用反问修辞。在歇后语的第二部分中运用反问的修辞格，如：

一个人拜把子——你算老几；

半边铃铛——咋响（想）的。

（3）运用借代法。用与人或物本身的特点或与人和事相关的事物代替本体事物，促使语言形象化、生动化，如：

戴着斗笠亲嘴——差着一帽子；

王大妈的裹脚布——又长又臭；

豁牙子吃西瓜——道儿多；

矮子上楼梯——步步高升。

上例中"豁牙子"代替缺牙齿的人；"矮子"代替矮个子的人。

（4）利用重复加强语势。运用重复可以加强语势，抒发强烈的感情，增强语言节奏感，如：

铁匠当军师——打、打、打；

三个土地堂——庙（妙）！庙（妙）！庙（妙）！

（5）使用拟人手法。拟人，凭借客观事物，充分展开想象，使人与物，此物与彼物，在习性和特征上，相互沟通，促使读者产生联想，如：

泥菩萨洗脸——越洗越难看；

老鼠替猫刮胡子——拼命地巴结；

夜明珠喘气——活宝。

上例的比喻都是赋予物（包括动物）以人的感情，语言格外生动、活泼，加之充当比喻的事情比较典型，所以更富有表现力。

（6）合用双关手法。双关，借助词语同音和多义的条件，使一个词语或句子同时兼有字面和字外两层意思，并以字外意思为重，如：

三九的萝卜——冻（动）了心；

棺材板上画老虎——吓死人。

（7）利用回环手法。回环不仅能揭示事物间相互依存、相互制约或相互对立的辩证关系，而且使语言有节奏感和循环往复之趣，如：

小孩供神佛——你哄我，我哄你；

挑了两筐鸡蛋上集——人敢碰咱，咱不敢碰人。

（8）利用倒装语序。倒装，语序是语言重要的语法手段之一，不同的语序排列会引起结构、意义和表达效果的变化，借此达到协调音律、突出重点的作用，如：

上茅坑吃瓜子——进的少，出的多；

披着蓑衣嚼茅草——吃的不行，穿的也不怎么样。

（9）巧用对比手法。对比，把两种对立的事物或者同一事物的两个不同方面，进行比较，使对立事物的矛盾鲜明突出，给人深刻印象，如：

棺材后头跟花轿——哭的哭，笑的笑；

骑着骆驼牵着鸡——高的高，低的低。

在歇后语的汉英翻译过程中，需要充分考虑歇后语的上述修辞特点，并具备扎实的汉语修辞功底，否则很难达到预期的效果。

三、谐趣性

谚语以洗练、形象、生动的语言，概括了生活斗争中的种种经验规律，表达了人民群众朴素健康的思想感情，闪耀着智慧的光芒。与谚语不同，歇后语是一种极具形象性的语言，可以称其为人民群众幽默的结晶。[①] 歇后语这种俏皮话，有时说来可以增加语言的活泼性，体现说话者的风趣幽默，有时听来却是一种嘲讽和挖苦。由此可见，歇后语可以赋予言语某种特定的感情色彩，或戏谑，或讽刺，或挖苦。歇后语的诙谐性和讽刺性是在前后两个部分的巧妙配合下形成的。诙谐跟讽刺既有联系又有区别。诙谐是指言语中对事物所表现的一种轻松愉快的态度，而讽刺则着重于揭露和指责。按照著名的美学家朱光潜的说法，它是"以游戏态度，把人事和物态的丑拙、鄙陋和乖讹当作一种有趣的意象去欣赏"。例如：

①李四道："我一向在学道衙门前。今有一件事，回来商议，怕三爷不在家，而今会着三爷，这事不愁不妥了。"潘三道："你又什么事捣鬼话？同你共事，你是'马蹄刀瓢里切菜——滴水也不漏'，总不肯放出钱来。"李四道："这事是有钱的。"（《儒林外史》）

②……过了半天，他咬着牙，虎起眼，站起来吼道："嘿！破风箱改棺材，风流了半辈子，你倒装起人样来了！"（《小说月报》1980 年第 11 期）

例①"马蹄刀"是一种马蹄形的弯刀，用它切菜，又是放在瓢里，别说撒不出来了，连水也不会漏出来一滴。"滴水也不漏"明指"马蹄刀瓢里切菜"不会泼洒，实际上是说李四的手紧，不大方。这句歇后语既挖苦，又幽默、风趣。

---

① Прядохин М. Г. Китайские недоговорки — иносказания[M]. Москва：наука，1977：116.

例②"破风箱改棺材,风流了半辈子,你倒装起人样来了!""风箱"一拉,里面空气流通,就产生了风,别解为"风流";"风箱"已"破",说明年代久了,别解为"半辈子";"棺材"是装人的,别解为"装起人样来",意即装得像个人样子。以上所列举的歇后语用比喻再加上解说构成一种幽默风趣的语句。

歇后语的诙谐性是怎样形成的呢?主要有以下三种情况。

(1)前一部分描述的是一种新奇的想象,场景是构思的,现实中可能并不存在,这样使人顿时感到莫名其妙,后一部分用一个贴切的注释,使人听了以后恍然大悟,从而产生妙不可言的感觉。例如:

①"守活寡,见你的鬼。没的我不知道,你跟老头子,高山上倒马桶,臭气冲天啊。破驴对破磨,你们凑合着混吧!"他夺开她的手。(李英儒《还我河山》)

②"这条老毒蛇,它放人,不是看在蔡伦先师面上,是看到我们工农义勇队还有力量。他在想新的毒计!"……众人纷纷议论,"老虎挂上念佛珠,想变着法子来吃人。棋盘蛇的诡计多着哩!"(杨佩瑾《霹雳》)

③老郝头慢吞吞地说:"我有个啥?孤人一个,'腿肚子贴灶王爷——人走家搬'啦!"(纪宁《洮河飞浪》)

"高山上倒马桶""老虎挂上念佛珠""腿肚子贴灶王爷"都是一种想象,人们一听便会惊愕,引起揣测,及至百思不解时看到后一部分注释,始悟出它的用意,不觉得哑然失笑。

(2)有的歇后语前一部分描述的虽然不是一种想象,而是现实生活中存在或可能出现的事物,但由于后一部分的注释别有风味,也能产生妙趣横生的效果。例如:

①遂林笑着说:"买下算了。这叫要饭的借算盘——穷有穷打算。他们买高头大马,咱就买这些老古董。十七还能常十七,十八也不会常十八。只要有这股干劲,将来咱也买好马。"(李准《两匹瘦马》)

②晚上指导员宣布:"二牛抬杠犁地四亩,'闺女穿她奶奶的鞋——老样'。"引起了一场哄堂大笑。(新疆建设兵团政治部编《天山战歌》)

例①"要饭的借算盘"算是现实中可能出现的事情,后一部分用了一个惯用语,其中"穷"字同"要饭的"呼应,"打算"同"借算盘"呼应,配合得非常巧妙。例②"闺女穿她奶奶的鞋"本来也不足为奇,但由于后一部分"老样"二字出人意料,结果"引起了一场哄然大笑"。

(3)后一部分既和前一部分密切配合,又通过运用双关把意思进一步引向深入,使人感到含蓄、幽默而又饶有兴趣。例如:

①凤姐笑道:"我说他们不用人费心,自己就会好的,老祖宗不信,一定要我去说和;赶我到那里说和,谁知两个在一块儿对赔不是。倒像'黄鹰抓住鹞子的脚'——两个人都'扣了环了'!那里还要人去说呢?"说的满屋里都笑起来。(曹雪芹《红楼梦》)

②凤姐儿笑道:"外头已经四更了,依我说,老祖宗也乏了,咱们也该'聋子放炮仗——散了'罢。"(曹雪芹《红楼梦》)

③众老问:"是那一位高徒去拿?"行者叉手道:"是我小和尚。"众老悚然道:"不济!不济!那妖精神通广大,身体狼犺。你这个长老,瘦瘦小小,还不够他填牙缝哩!"行者笑道:"老官儿,你估不出人来。我小自小,结实,都是'吃了磨刀水的,秀气在内'哩!"(吴承恩《西游记》)

例①"扣了环了"表面上指黄鹰和鹞子的爪子相对扣紧,不易撒开,实际上比喻贾宝玉和林黛玉亲密得不肯分手,通过双关的两重意义,说得很含蓄,听起来很有风趣,结果博得一场欢笑。例②聋子听不见炮仗声,只看见炮仗爆炸时炸散了。用在此处,委婉地表示时间不早了,大家也该早些回去休息了。例③"秀气在内"里的"秀"是"锈"的谐音,照应前一部分说肚里有刀的"锈"气,实际上指自己外表虽不怎样但有内秀,逗趣的同时又耐人寻味。

第三节　歇后语的语法功能

歇后语在句子结构中的地位相当复杂,一方面它可以作为一个完整的语法单位出现,另一方面它又可以被拆开来成为两个语法单位。

歇后语作为一个完整的语法单位出现,有时充当一个句子或复句里的一个分句,有时充当句子里的一个构成成分。当它被拆开成为两个语法单位时,便分别承担不同的语法成分。本节依次加以叙述。

一、歇后语独立成句

①"……贪生怕死,留恋家业,或是跟朱家朝廷割断恩情的,滚他娘的去。大年初一逮兔子,有它过年无它也过年!"(姚雪垠《李自成》)

②我变得跟屯子里的落后娘们一样了。火烧眉毛,光顾眼前。本位主义,实际上是个人主义的扩大。(周立波《暴风骤雨》)

由以上例子可知,歇后语充当句子时,往往是作为一句"现成话"被引用的,多见于对话中。

二、歇后语充当复句里的一个分句

①我忍不住对他说:"班长,得考虑考虑决心书的事儿了,顶好早交党支部,抢在各班头里,打响头一炮。再不抓紧,就大年三十看皇历——没期啦!"(济南部队政治部宣传部编《雨涤松青》)

②工人们群情激愤,怒不可遏。工头一看,众怒难犯,便鞋底擦油——溜了。(山东省军区政治部编《泰山风云》)

由以上例子可知,歇后语充当复句里的一个分句时,主语一般不出现。即使歇后语的前一部分有主语,其也不再起主语的作用。真正的主语或者是因对话而省,或者是因上下文而省。

三、歇后语作为一个语法单位充当句子成分

(1)作谓语。在句中作谓语,是歇后语的一个常见用法。例如:

①老孙头冲着他脸说:"谁推你为主任的? 你们几个狐朋狗友,耗子爬秤钩,自己称自己。你们三几个朋友,喝大酒,吃白面饼,吃得油渹渹,放的屁,把裤子都油了,这使的是谁的钱呀?"(周立波《暴风骤雨》)

②大队仓库保管员赵有成……挥动着两手大声地嚷道:"这回饺子破了皮——露馅啦! 他二秃子还说粮食是俺偷的,想吓唬俺,不让俺说,俺才不怕呢!"(王忠瑜《惊雷》)

(2)作宾语。在句中作宾语,也是歇后语常见的一种用法,例如:

①崔麻子老是骂他粗鲁,嫌他不善用计谋。此番又当了护路队长,死活想狗戴礼帽——装出点大人物的款儿来。(张恩忠《龙岗战火》)

②八戒点头道:"我理会得。但你去,讨得讨不得,趁早回来,不要弄做'尖担担柴两头脱'也。"(吴承恩《西游记》)

例①"狗戴礼帽——装出点大人物的款儿来"作动词"想"的宾语,例②"尖担担柴——两头脱"作动词"弄做"的宾语。

(3)作定语。歇后语在句中作定语,起修饰后面名词的作用,它和名词之间一般要加助词"的"。例如:

①去他妈的吧,往后,这些鸡毛炒韭菜乱七八糟的事情,马连福再也不沾边儿了。(浩然《艳阳天》)

②柳大筐是祖传的编筐匠,父亲一辈子,是窗户眼吹喇叭名声在外的老实人。(杨大群《西辽河传》)

（4）作状语。歇后语在句中作状语，着重描写动作的情态，它同后面的动词之间一般要加助词"地"，例如：

两头老人催着他们年前结婚，秀英一直没吐口，小强他爷娘就老头儿拉胡琴，自顾自地忙活起来了。（马春《龙滩春色》）

（5）作补语。歇后语在句中作补语，通常表示动作的结果，它和前面的动词之间一般要加助词"得"或量词"个"。例如：

①几句话，把个马连福说得张飞穿针——大眼瞪小眼，后脊梁苏苏地直冒凉气。（浩然《艳阳天》）

②在这鲜明对比之下，这两位富裕中农愈加感到：当初参加中农社本想捞点油水的，由于看错了人，投错了门，结果弄得长秃疮害脚气——两头不落一头。（浩然《闪光的年华》）

③胖得出奇的胡凤凤，飞着风沙眼，瞟了喜气洋洋的男人一眼，撇了撇嘴说："看你乐的，不要闹个猫咬猪尿泡，空欢喜一场。"（谷丰登《奔腾的大黑河》）

（6）作主语。例如：

秦文吉觉着很奇怪了："你这个灶王爷的横批——一家之主，怎么也这个心眼儿呀！"（浩然《金光大道》）

歇后语在句中充当各类成分，对此，译者唯有了然于胸，才能更好地进行语际间转换。

第二章　歇后语的可译性限度

　　歇后语是经过中华文明五千年历史沧桑沉淀、淬炼、凝聚而成的绝妙的汉语言艺术,反映了中华民族特有的风俗传统和民族文化。那么,其他地区的民族如何领会和欣赏歇后语的魅力呢? 首先我们谈谈其在英、俄语言中的命名。

第一节　"歇后语"一词的英、俄译名

　　汉语的歇后语,属于俗语的范畴,是汉语习语的重要组成部分。绝大部分的歇后语发源并流传于民间,称为民间歇后语,并在日常生活中为广大群众所喜闻乐见。歇后语通过比喻、谐音、双关等修辞手法,形象鲜明、立意新奇,常常意出言外。因此,歇后语在文学作品中的运用也极为频繁,它以其生动的比喻、丰富的联想、诙谐风趣的风格大大增强了作品的艺术感染力。而歇后语在英文中却一直未有较为统一的译名,影响了外国人对中文这一语言瑰宝的认识。在英、俄文中提到中文歇后语时,有以下几种情况:第一,有的译法失之偏颇,如有人用 Chinese enigmatic folk similes① 称呼中文歇后语,但歇后语不完全是比喻;还有人用 quiz-cracks 译之,但歇后语不完全是隐语或谜语,有的从字面就能引申出它的喻义,如:"竹篮打水——一场空",实际运用当中注重的是歇后语后半部的意义,而不是让读者或听者猜谜;第二,有的译法局限于解释性的说明,不适合作为命名(naming),如英文名:"a two-part allegorical saying, of which the first part, always stated, is descriptive, while the second part, sometimes unstated, carries the message"。② 第三,有的将其笼统地归入中文成语或习语的范畴,以汉语"歇后语"或音译"xiēhòuyǔ(英)、cexoyюй(俄),称之。因此为了更好地将数目庞大(《中国歇后语》的编者提到

---

① John S R. A Chinese-English Dictionary of Enigmatic Folk Similes[M]. Arizona: The University of Arizona Press,1991.

② 汉英词典(修订版)[M]. 北京:外语教学与研究出版社,1996.

共收集到 15 万条歇后语)、特点鲜明、极富感染力的这一语言形式介绍给对中
文感兴趣的英语国家的人士,有必要确立一个既符合歇后语本身内涵、又符合
英文命名惯例的英文译名。

　　歇后语在汉语中的本义是使用时常歇去(省略)它的后半部分,最早是文
人之间的一种文字游戏,故俄文名《речение с усекаемой концовкой》,即"后半
部分被截掉的话语"。现在一些常见的比喻性歇后语也经常歇去后半部,如:
周立波的《暴风骤雨》中,"怪道郭全海老问:你家有几口人? 够吃不够吃? 娘
们儿多大岁数呐? 原来是黄鼠狼给鸡拜年。"文中省去了妇幼皆知的后半部分
"没安好心"。但绝大多数情况下歇后语是两部分一齐说出的。其实从本质上
说无论是比喻性歇后语,还是谐音双关性歇后语,大多可以归入隐语一类(中
歇),或语义双关,或谐音双关,如不给出后半部分,经常会引起理解困难。如:

　　　刚下锅的饺子——有点生(语意双关);

　　　房顶上种麦子——刺激(脊)(谐音双关)。

　　从这个意义上来说,与英文中的 Pun(双关语)类似,但不能将歇后语与
Pun 等同起来,因为英文中的双关语,是指用同形异义词(homonym)或同音
异义词(homophone)来增强文字表现力的修辞手段,并不包含中文歇后语的
前半部分,如:We must all hang together, or we shall all hang separately. 我
们必须团结在一起,否则我们将一个个地被绞死(同音异义词)[①]。

　　比喻性歇后语与英文中的 simile 相通,谐音双关性歇后语与 quiz, puzzle
或 riddle 相通。Chinese enigmatic folk similes 对应的是比喻性歇后语,而
quiz-cracks 对应的是谐音双关性歇后语,两种译名都不全面。所以英文命名
应另辟蹊径——从歇后语的本质内容出发,找出一个定性的英、俄文译名(类
似英文习语中 proverbs, slang, sayings 等的命名方法)。

　　汉语的歇后语,比喻新奇、形象丰富生动,前半是形象,后半是喻义或双
关,要明白它的意义,往往要经过思索,才会达到理解上茅塞顿开、豁然开朗的
意外之境。许多歇后语给人的感觉既诙谐风趣,又辛辣刺激,如"麻脸瞧麻脸,
观点一致"或"阎王开会,都不是人"。中文歇后语这种表达意义的特点,其实
与英文的 wisecrack 具有异曲同工之妙。请看英文词典中对这一单词的
定义:

　　　wisecrack n.（informal）smart or clever（often unkind）saying or

---

　　① 范家材.英语修辞赏析[M].上海:上海交通大学出版社,1992.

remark. 俏皮话，（常指）风凉话[①]；或 wisecrack n. a clever or sarcastic remark[②] 名词：一种机智或讽刺的言辞。

再联系到《中国俗语大词典·序》谈到歇后语时所说的"最先叫作'俏皮话'而现在通称'歇后语'的说法，我们可以大胆地将中文歇后语英文译名定为"Chinese folk wisecracks"。加上"folk"（民间的）一词，是表示现在的中文歇后语绝大多数是流传于民间，说明它的语体色彩。这种译名避免了前述译法的偏颇，与英文习语（idioms）分类中的"quotations"或"sayings"等定性（qualitative）式的命名方法相通，易于被英语读者接受。

此外，郭建中在《汉语歇后语翻译的理论与实践》中支持罗圣豪教授把歇后语译作"enigmatic folk similes"。何为 similes？ 如前面所分析的，歇后语一般由"喻体＋本体"前后两部分组成，其修辞手段又是采用隐语的结构：folk，表明歇后语起源于民间，在日常口语中用得尤多；enigmatic，表示这种表达方式具有谜语的性质和特点，也可以说是由"谜面（喻体）＋谜底（本体）"两部分构成的一个谜语。也有人赞成歇后语的英语直译："rest-ending sayings" or "post-pause expressions"。根据其意义结构，还有人译作"example-explanation-sayings"。分析比较有关歇后语英文定名的观点，"Chinese folk wisecracks"和"enigmatic folk similes"更为广泛采用，前者着重从歇后语的语义功能方面考虑，后者偏向从歇后语的结构形式方面翻译，但两种方法基本上反映了汉语歇后语的特殊结构和本质特征。

俄语中的 Пословицы（谚语）是民间流传的言简意赅而又具有训诫意义的箴言，通常包括形象叙述和道德告诫两部分；Поговорки（俗语）也是一种民间创作，是比较短的、多半不成句的妙语；Выражения（习语、惯用语）是一种固定词组，其各个组成部分的词汇意义，或者发生了变化和转义，或者完全失去原义而表达另外的意思；Изречения（名言警句）或 Цитаты（名言）和 Афоризмы（格言），多半是著名作家、诗人的文学作品中的引言或杰出社会活动家、学者们所说的某些精辟而有教诲意义的语录。俄语修辞格中的 Тропы（为了形象生动地表达某种思想，不使用其直义、而使用其转义的转喻）和 Каламбуры（在特定语言环境中，利用语音和语义条件，使某些词语获得双重意义的双关）。凡此种种，它们与汉语歇后语都存在不尽相同之处。俄语用

---

① 牛津高级英汉双解词典［M］. 北京：商务印书馆，牛津大学出版社，1997.

② Merriam Webster's Collegiate Dictionary(Tenth Edition) ［M］. 北京：世界图书出版公司，1996.

Недоговорка、Недомолвка(半吞半吐、意犹未尽的话语)加以表达,其"歇后语"命名本身,就反映了翻译的某种无奈。

第二节　翻译的悖论

"翻译即译意",但在具体翻译时,需要处理的则是几个方面的意义,如奈达划分的词汇意义、语法意义、修辞意义、指称意义以及内涵意义。巴尔胡达罗夫划分的所指意义、实用意义和语内意义,或如刘宓庆划分的概念(主题)意义、语境意义、形式意义、风格意义、形象意义和文化意义等。通常情况下,只有其中某项或某几项意义能够得到全面的翻译,其余的意义则不能全面翻译出来。歇后语翻译更是如此。例如:

"没良心的,狗咬吕洞宾,不识好人心。"(曹雪芹《红楼梦》)

俄文译文:Бессовестный вы! Вы похожи на 《собаку, которая, кусая Люй Дун- биня, не понимала, что делает! 》(перевод Панасюка)

通常,两种语言文化之间的差异越大,其等值转换就越难,等值程度就越受到影响。吕洞宾是国人家喻户晓的道教八仙之一,加上歇后语是汉语中独有的语言现象,要做到各类意义的全面等值表达,几乎是翻译的梦想。试比较英语译文:

"You ungrateful thing! Like the dog that bit Lü Congbin — you bite the hand that feeds you. "(杨献益、戴乃迭译)

虽说如今大都用"狗咬吕洞宾,不识好人心"的转义,但翻译时兼顾形象和意义的表达,多有力不从心之感。为了更好地探讨歇后语翻译问题,我们首先对翻译理论研究中争论不休的"可译性限度"问题进行梳理。

翻译是一个悖论迭出的领域。在诸多悖论中,可译与不可译是一对二律背反的命题。几千年的翻译史告诉我们,人类对可译性的认识经历了漫长的历史过程。在西方翻译的初期,也就是说以古希腊语翻译《圣经·旧约》的逐字翻译时期,由于人类对语言的认识尚处在幼稚时期和出于对圣经文字的迷信与虔诚,人们错误地认为各语言之间没有多大差异,因而可以使一种语言机械地翻译成另一种语言。

罗马帝国灭亡后,分裂成多个国家,民族地域逐渐划定,民族要求也日趋强烈,民族语言也相继形成和受到重视。翻译的范围也不再局限于清一色的宗教书籍。文艺复兴早期,意大利诗人但丁在其著作《飨宴》里,盛赞俗语的优点,还对翻译问题做了明确论述。他对《圣经·诗篇》的拉丁语译文进行了认真的研究,发现原文中有许多的诗的特征在译文中走失了,从而首先提出了

"文学作品不可译"的观点,这对摆脱语言的幼稚看法而言无疑是一种进步。

15—16世纪,文艺复兴运动波及西欧各个国家,涉及文化领域的各个方面,"复古"之风悄然盛行,古代语言受到重视,古代作家受到推崇。逐字翻译渐失去了其主导地位,人们越来越清楚地意识到翻译的困难和许多现有译作的不够完善。例如,约翰·赖希林认为原作的形式与原语紧密融合,无法在译语中得到保留。他指出,荷马的作品只在希腊语中读来才具有活力,译成其他任何语言都会有损于文学作品的美学价值。而西班牙作家塞万提斯在《堂吉诃德》一书中,借矮子桑丘之口把翻译比作"佛拉芒挂毯的反面",意为图形轮廓固然可见,但正面那清晰、平整与斑斓的色彩则全然不见了,说出了与但丁颇为相仿的翻译悲观论调(... it seems to that translating from one tongue into another... is like viewing Flemish tapestries from the wrong side, for although you see the pictures, they are covered with threads and obscure them so that the smoothness and the gloss of the fabric are lost)。类似的观点(Cervantes,1615),与中国六百多年前宋高僧的"如翻锦绮"一说如出一辙。

反对逐词译又极易造成"自由译"。到了17—18世纪,这种倾向发展到了登峰造极的地步,特别是当时法国的作家与翻译家主张要使外国文学作品符合法国的"高雅鉴赏力"原则,因而对外国文学作品进行随心所欲地增删与改写。面对这一现象,法国启蒙运动先驱者伏尔泰发出了"翻译增加了一部作品的错误并损害了它的光彩"的感叹。

拿破仑发动战争之后,欧洲自由运动广泛兴起,人民要求了解本民族及其他民族的历史和现状的心情非常迫切,因此对违背原作的译作大为不满。于是力求传达和表现原著的特点,使读者或观众仿佛置身于另一个国家、另一个时代,强调原著中所独特的和异乎寻常的东西,成了这一时期译者遵循的共同原则。由于提高了对翻译的要求,追求翻译在意思与艺术上的准确,因此对翻译困难的认识更加深刻,从而导致了不可译观点的加强。其代表人物就是德国著名语言学家威廉·洪堡特。他在1776年7月23日写给奥古斯特·施莱格尔的信中说:"我认为,任何翻译毫无疑问都是试图完成不能完成的任务,因为每个译者必然要撞到两个暗礁之一,译者由于过于遵守原作而损失本国人民的审美习惯和语言,或者要么过于照顾本国人民的特色而损害了原作。要找到某种折中的办法不仅困难重重,而且简直是不可能"(Всякий перевод представляется мне безусловно попыткой разрешить невыполнимую задачу. Ибо каждый переводчик неизбежно должен разбиться об один из двух подводных камней, слишком точно придерживаясь либо своего подлтнника за счет вкуса и языка собственного народа, либо своеобразия собственного народа за счет своего подлинника）。另一位德国古典语言学家弗里德里希·施莱尔马也谈道：各种语言在结构上的特征是不容抹杀的。而与洪堡特同时代的另一位德国语言学家和翻译家施莱格尔则表示："翻译好比两人决斗，总有一方必死无疑，不是原作者，便是译者。"19 世纪，俄国语言学家波铁布尼亚认为，由于不可能翻译各个词的全部意义和形式特征，因而也不能翻译这些词的组合。而德国的语文学家豪普特则说得更加绝对"翻译是理解的死亡"。意大利的哲学家克罗齐更是一语惊人："翻译就像女人，忠实的不漂亮，漂亮的不忠实"。

在我国翻译史上，有关不可译的说法也比比皆是。早在佛经翻译时期，思想家老子的"美言不信，信言不美"就在译界广为流传。东晋时期的道安洞察到翻译的种种困难提出了"五失本""三不易"的原则，其实就是对翻译中"不可译因素"的一种处理办法。后秦的译经大师鸠摩罗什曾有言："但改梵为秦，失其藻蔚，虽得大意，殊隔文体，有似嚼饭与人，非徒失味，乃令人呕哕也。"这是在中国翻译史上第一次提出了风格不可译的观点。对于翻译，宋代高僧法云说道："音虽似别，义则大同"，如锦绣背面之"左右不同耳"，意为翻译的东西失去了原有的光彩，这似乎与《堂吉诃德》书中所述不谋而合。即便到了近现代，可译性问题仍然受到人们的质疑。例如，金岳霖先生在谈到诗歌的翻译问题时，就感慨道："诗差不多是不能翻译的。"周煦良先生则认为原文的风格是无法转译的。他奉劝某些翻译家不要对原文的风格多费脑筋，那些认为风格可译的人，只不过是"英雄欺人语"，因为翻译的媒介是语言，就等于用铅笔或钢笔临摹水墨画。而王以铸先生在《论诗之不可译》一文中指出：诗歌的神韵、意境或说得通俗一些就是"诗味"是万万不能翻译的。因为诗之所以为诗的东西，在很大程度上有机地溶化在诗人写诗时使用的语言之中，这是无法通过另一种语言来表达的。

古今中外竟有如此多的哲学家、文学家、语言学者和评论家在不同的时代和不同的国度里，对翻译的可能性提出质疑。这确实是一个值得思索和深入探讨的问题。我们认为，不可译论的产生有着宗教、哲学和语言学三方面的背景。

（1）宗教背景。在《圣经》和佛经的翻译中，神职权威们认为圣言不可有任何变动，挑选何种语言表达圣意是圣者自己的安排，改变了语言就会改变圣意。正如《旧约全书》的首卷所示，上帝与人类之间的中介是语言，但不是任何语言，而只是希伯来语；上帝希望把他的奥秘通过希伯来语告知凡人。因此，每一个愿意解释《圣经》的人,必须首先熟悉希伯来语的语法,以便能懂得《圣经》中每一个词的真正含义。据此,文艺复兴时期的德国人文主义作家约翰·赖希林认为:没有一个说拉丁语的人能不先懂得《旧约》的用语而能准确地解释《旧约》的。因为希伯来语原著中包含的"精神实质",在译文中必然会有所走失。按照他的观点,翻译的目的在于将读者引回原作,因为原作的完整思想在任何翻译中都表达不出来。

(2)哲学背景。这可概括为以下两方面。第一,受亚里士多德的二元论,即范畴分离性理论的影响,认为事物要么绝对可译,要么绝对不可译,而绝大部分情况下是不可译的。把可译与不可译看成两个绝对分离和不相联系的独立的范畴,而不是一个范畴中的两个方面,即矛盾的统一体。第二,从主观唯心主义的立场出发,把思想意识置于客观现实之上,否认超出单个语言范畴的概念体系和支配超语言现实的普遍法则的优先存在。在此基础上,针对17—18世纪在德国广为流行的一种半哲学半功利主义的观点——认为语言符号可以完全互换。洪堡特认为语言反映了一个民族的世界观,是民族精神的外在表现。不同的民族对世界的看法也不同,所以不同的语言之间没有通约性,而标志不同语言特征的原则之一就是其非对应性。于是便有了"暗礁"这一说法。而笃信"直觉"在人的意识中起主导作用的唯心主义哲学家克罗齐把翻译比做"漂亮的女人不忠实,忠实的女人不漂亮"也就不足为奇了。在唯心主义的世界"不可知论"这一论调的影响下,19世纪西班牙唯心主义哲学家奥尔特加·伊加塞特则提出了一种颓废的翻译观。他认为"人所从事的一切都是不可实现的",因而翻译是"乌托邦无望的努力"。

(3)语言学背景。如基南认为,没有任何事物是能够翻译的。这是因为人类自然语言本身具有不确定性、模糊性。德国哲学家和语言学家莱布尼茨认为,世界上没有任何一种语言能够势均力敌地传达另一种语言,哪怕是采用相似表达也难(俄文译文:Нет в мире языка, который был бы способен передать слова другого языка не только с равной силой, но хотя бы даже с адекватным выражением)。也就是说,只有具有这种不确定性和模糊性,我们才能在无限情境中向无限的受众谈论无限现象。而自然语言本身内在的模糊性具有模糊的功能,往往造成了不同语言集团之间的语义的非对应性,从而也就限制了翻译转换的可能性。无怪乎许多才智之士、唯物主义者(如法国著名的唯物主义哲学家狄德罗等)和近现代许多具有先进世界观的知名学者,也对翻译的可能性与具直性提出了种种的异议和质疑。

虽说如此,数千年的翻译史及人们通过翻译得以交流和交往的事实却是不容抹杀的,也是翻译的可能性的有力明证。诚然,不可译的悖论也并非空穴来风或故作玄虚,它是植根于民族语言与文化在语际转换中必然产生的矛盾与困难之中。当代美国翻译理论家尤金·奈达说得好,翻译是一项充满悖论的活动,它最为复杂困难又非常简单迷人,它的一切悖论源于语言和文化的悖论。只要深入地考察一下,就可发现可译性之中包含着对不可译的思考,不可译性中兼容着对可译性的承认。它们相辅相成,共同推动着翻译研究不断向前发展。正如苏联的评论家费道罗夫所说:"可译性观点已经相当成熟,以至于研究不可译性已成了翻译科学的迫切问题。翻译理论的进一步发展在很大程度上取决于这一问题的解决"。

第三节　可译性的理论依据

从总体上看,语言是可以翻译的,语言或语言意义的所谓不可译性是就局部而言的。我们一方面认为任何两种语言之间都可进行翻译,另一方面又看到每一种语言或每一篇话语中都可能存在一些难以传译到另一种语言的复杂成分。因此,可以说,语言的可译性与不可译性是互为矛盾而又互为依存的两个概念。就翻译的实际工作而言,重要的并不是翻译究竟是可能还是不可能,而是某个具体话语究竟可译到什么程度,或不可译到什么程度。

一、人类认识的同源性

一个显而易见的事实是,人们虽然居住在不同的地域,却可以观察到相同的自然现象,如日月经天,四时轮转、电闪雷鸣、冰雹雪雨等;接触到相同的事物,如金、木、水、火、土、花草、虫鱼、劳动工具等;有着同样的生理和生活需要,如七情六欲、吃穿住行等;产生同样的感情,如喜、怒、哀、乐等。可以说是人同此心,心同此理。人的认知心理,不仅古今相通,而且中外相通。

法国当代翻译理论家乔治·穆南在现代语言学对共相现象的研究的基础上对其进行了认真的分析与归纳,期望对这一事实做出解释并试图从理论上证明翻译的可能性。他指出,宇宙共相是不容忽视和置疑的。因为所有人都居住在同一个星球上。四海之内皆有金、木、水、火、土,日与月,冷与热,风与雨,天与地,动物界与植物界,即整个生态共相的领域。换言之,人类的认识都源自于同一客观的现实世界。例如:水(water,вода)虽说在不同的语言中有不同的名称,却都是指称自然界中的一种无色无味、化学成分为 H_2O、流动而透明的液体物质。马克思曾经说过:物的名称,对于物的性质,全然是外在的。

按照辩证唯物主义的观点,物质是决定意识的,是先有物质,才有意识的,也就是说物质是第一性的,而意识是第二性的。没有物质,就没有意识。根据马克思主义关于意识能够反映存在的原理,并且人面对的是同一世界,并且语言是思想的物质外壳,是对物质的描述,那么我们可以期望在各种"民族语言中,发现一定的相似性"。可见,世界的同一性即是人类认识的同源性,人类的共性使翻译成为可能,这就是可译性理论的基本前提。

二、逻辑思维的同一性

众所周知,人与动物最大的区别在于生产劳动。生产劳动决定了创造语言的需要,同时又促进了人类思维的产生。但即便是思想的东西也有自己的物质基础,即生命物质的最高形式——大脑。因而作为同一物种的不同民族,必然有着相似的生理结构,即生理共相。而思维作为人脑的一种机能,是人脑反映客观世界的过程。由此可知,凡是正常的人,无论他属于哪个民族,他们的大脑都具有相同机能。因而思维能力及思维规律是全人类性的,而不是民族性的。

翻译活动并不单纯是语言活动,更重要的是思维活动,是逻辑分析的实践活动。翻译中的思维活动和语言活动是不可分割的。思维和语言是互为依存的条件。两种语言文字的转换是以逻辑为基础的。事物间的基本关联,时空的基本推移,是不可更易的客观实际,也是形诸任何语言的客观基础。

从思维的形式,即思维借以表现内容的手段、方式及有规律的活动过程来看,说不同语言的人也大体相通。按照逻辑学的观点,思维形式都可分为概念、判断和推理三种类型。比如,说汉语的人运用汉语的语法概念,从演绎直言推理将某一句子判断为"简单句"。这种结论与说俄语的人运用俄语的语法概念以演绎推理形式对同一句子做出的判断不会互相矛盾和抵触,其原因就是操不同语言的人的思维逻辑形式存在着相同性。同样,归纳推理也可以使操不同语言的人对同一现象得出相同或相近的推论。比如,无论汉语还是俄语,句子都有主、谓、定、补(宾)、状的语法成分,句与句的连接方式都有因果关系、假设关系、条件关系、转折关系和修饰关系等。"因"与"果"尽管可能有表达上的先后之分,但不可能有性质上的差别,说汉语的人心中的"因"不可能成为说俄语的人心中的"果"。"因火生烟"不可能在俄语中就成了"因烟生火"。可见,这种思想逻辑方式是源于人的认识本性,它是由人们认识活动的需要,由实践的需要所决定的。人类不论说何种语言,任何正常的思维活动都不可能违背这些形式规范。因此,当各民族语言源起时,虽然处在各自不同时间和空间,但对客观事物本质认识的思维是一致的。也正是这一同一性,构成了语言之间可以转换的客观基础。

三、语义生成的共核性

任何一种语言的意义都打下了人类的实际经验即人类认识客观现实的印记。用马克思和恩格斯的话来说,就是"无论是思想,还是语言都不会自己形成特殊的王国⋯⋯它们只能是真实生活的反映。"可见,任何一种语言的语义都是反映人类周围整个外部世界及人类自己的内部世界,也就是把操该种语言的集团的全部经验固定下来。乔治·穆南认为,语言的共相或各语言间存在相似性是宇宙、生态、生理和心理等共相现象存在的必然结果。据此,我们可以认为,既然说不同语言的集团周围的现实本身的一致之处大大超过了它们的不同之处,那么不同语言中的意义(意义本身,而不是表达这些意义的语言单位)的一致之处也应该大大超过了它们的不同之处。这正如萨丕尔所说:世界各语言中没有比它的普遍性更惊人的特殊性了。如在颜色研究领域,许多人认为不同的民族因有不同的"世界映象",因而在语言上表现了极大的差异,但仍有不少语言学家指出,即便如此,它们中仍然存在着恒定的东西。如加里弗认为"没有理由假定人的视网膜或皮层组织会因人种和所处的地方不同而有不同的功能。"弗利奥查特在与汉学家热尔内的谈话中,也指出"当您说中国人看色彩与我们不同,我猜想您是指他们看的色彩与我们还是一样的,只是他们具有不同的命名罢了。"这是因为在色彩的辨别中,存在着那些先于任何命名事实的生理共相基础,即存在看一个参照(参照生理学的共同的辨别事实)意义核,即使并非所有的内涵价值在不同的语言之间都可自动加以传达,但这一意义核至少可以使所指概念的意义得以交流,因为词的概念意义就是词义的核心,是全部意义转换的基础、轴心和主体。所以,虽说意义在不同语言中可以有不同的切分、分类和组合,但有了语义生成"基础"的共核性后,翻译在原则上是可能的。

当前翻译理论界新近从科学界引入的"同构"这一概念作为可译性的理论依据。这一概念表明:所有人类的生存环境和认知对象都是同一个客观世界,都具有相似的生物基础和思想基础,相似的生活经历和社会活动,因而具有一些关于客观世界的共同认识,所以在操某种语言的人们头脑中关于客观世界的概念不会与操另一种语言的人们的概念本质上相违背。这是因为他们共同的认识依据即物质基础是同一的。这种同一性可以使他们在各自的头脑中构成一个粗略的、但基本相同的概念系统框架,从语言学的角度来说就是语义系统。其实,这是从另一个角度阐述了"语义生成共核"这一问题。

形式各异的语言之所以能互译,还在于语言具有"异构同质"的符号特征。在语言内部,结构与意义之间普遍存在两种关系:一为"向心"关系,即相异的结构可以表达相同的意义;一为"离心"关系,即同一结构也可以有不同意义。在语言的外部,世界的同一性,促成了思维上的共性,而这一共性通过语言表现出来就是语义生成的共核。由于语言与思维有着密不可分的联系,不同的语言和人类共性之间构成了一个巨大的异构同质的向心结构,从而也就可以实现语际转换的可能性。

四、语言描述潜力的无限性

洪堡特说:"可以放心大胆地说,没有任何事物是语言表达不了的,即使是我们还不太了解的原始人类的语言也可以表达一切……例如说,什么是最高的、最低的、最强硬的或最柔软的等。"这就是说任何语言都有对任何事物及其性质、运动等进行描述的无限潜力。但是有人认为,具有无限描述能力的语言仅限于"发达"语言,如费道罗夫在论证可译性时就曾写道:"每种高度发达的语言都是一种强有力的手段,足以传达用另一种语言的手段表达的与形式相统一的内容。"其言外之意就是"不发达"的语言则不能做到这一点。然而,现代语言学告诉我们,这一观点是完全错误的。任何语言都有其复杂的语音、语法和词汇体系,都有生成新话语的无限潜力。例如,玛雅语中虽没有"四季"之分,只有"干、湿"两季,但当他们了解这一自然现象后,仍然可以表达这一概念。再以俄汉两种语言为例,虽说汉语中名词无单、复数之形式和时态的语法范畴,但决不能据此认为汉民族的思维中没有时和数的概念。翻译时可以通过添加修饰语和虚词等办法表达出俄语的这些语法意义。词汇是记录使用某种语言的人们意识中反映的现实的,因而同一现实可用不同的语言来描述。奈达指出:语言具有同等的表达力。说话人只要掌握一定数量单词或语义单位,就能谈论各种各样的生活经验,其中包括无数的事物、思想、概念、信仰等极其抽象的东西。可见语言是不应有"发达"与"不发达"之分的,而是具有相同的描述潜力的。巴尔胡达罗夫说得好:"任何一种语言都能描述其使用者所碰到或将碰到的任何实物、概念和情景,使用某种'原始'语言的集团,只要知道了某些实物、技术设备、政治制度、科学概念等,他们的语言中立刻就会出现标志这些实物和概念的相应的词语。"

列宁的《反映论》指出:认识是思维对客体的永远的、没有止境的接近。意思是说人类的认识潜力是无限的,既然如此,那么当语言作为思维的物质载体和表现手段时,我们就有理由认为,语言对于人类认识的描述潜力也是无限的。因为认识作为思维的过程是可以用语言来描述的。洪堡特还说:"语言是人所共有的天性,所有的语言都持有可以理解其他任何语言的钥匙。"因为人类面对的是同一个物质世界,又有着相同的逻辑思维,所以只要译者有足够的驾驭译语文字的能力,只要拥有利用语言的规律不断地更新和丰富组织语言的手段的能力,那么他就能够用译语准确而完整地表达他所接受的全部原语信息。

综上所述,尽管不同语言之间存在着结构上的种种差异,但任何语言都具有无限的描述潜力,用一种语言表达的东西就可以用另一种语言来加以描述和再现。正如沃尔夫拉姆·威尔斯所说:"翻译乃是一种解释性的过程,而且说到底,所有语言,包括原始语言,都具有差不多相类似的表达意思的潜在能力,这种潜在能力可以向多方面发展,并具有很大的'生成'条件,足以使言语集团用自己的语言充分表达外界的一切事物,包括那些超出自己社会文化经验的事物。"

五、语言、文化之间的可通约性

众所周知,不同民族有着不同的文化,不同文化之间既有联系又有区别,既有普遍的共性又有各自的个性。正是这种共性为一种文化与另一种文化进行交流提供了可行性的依据和基础。

L. A. 怀特曾说:语言是文化的载体,每个民族的文化在其语言中表现得最为全面和完美。语言总是在文化发展的各个阶段完整地、协调地反映文化,并将其固定下来,世代相传,成为民族文化和知识的载体和集体经验的共储藏器。

(一)语言文化的共质、趋同性

人,作为区别于大自然中其他生灵万物的生命体,有着基本相同的生存需要、生活模式和思想感情。因此,有些文化几乎同时发生和存在于不同的地域。这种文化是超越了特定区域的非特定文化,而成为诸多区域的共同性文化,即人类性文化。这种共同性或人类性文化也必然反映在各自的语言之中,使不同的语言中存在着大量的对等、对应或相似的成分,从而使跨文化、跨语言的交际成为可能。一种语言所表达的思想内容可以用另一种语言重新表达出来。例如:当中国古代思想家老子(前550—前470)提出"道"这一哲学概念,指出"道生一,一生二,二生三,三生万物",用"道"来说明宇宙万物的演变时,古希腊哲学家赫拉克利特(前550—前470)也提出了"Logos"(理论、理念)

这一概念,指出它是永恒的、普遍的,为宇宙万物生成变化所遵循的规律。而"道"与"logos"两个概念基本对应。在古代缺乏文化交流的情况下,中西两个完全独立的思想体系竟会有此相似的发展轨迹,实在是令人惊叹的。而今,随着对比语言学和跨文化交际学的兴起和发展,人们看到的不仅是它们的个性,而是它们的共性。人们发现,不同语言中的对等、对应和相似的成分也不胜枚举。例如,在俄语、英语、汉语的成语库中存在着完全对等的现象。如汉、俄、英对比:

"趁热打铁"——"Куй железо, пока горячо";"strike while the iron is hot."

"祸不单行"——"Беда не прцходит одна";"Bad luck comes in threes."

"浑水摸鱼"——"В мутной воде рыбу ловить";"fish in troubled water."

"晴天霹雳"——"гром среди ясного неба";"a bolt from the blue."

此外,还有例如汉英对等,"熟能生巧"——"Practice makes perfect"等等。而"пустиль козла в огород""Ни рыба, ни мясо""Паршивая овца стадо портит""сидеть меж двух стульев""брать быка за рога"与"引狼入室""非驴非马""害群之马""脚踏两条船""擒贼先擒王"的字面意思虽相去甚远,但喻义却是对等。也就是说,虽然它们的表面词语各异,但是深层语义是对应的。

(二)语言文化的兼容、渗透性

文化具有相互兼容、渗透的特征。这一特征为语际转换创造了条件。由于民族之间在经济、政治、文学等各方面的交流,一个民族独有的事物及其概念逐渐为别的民族所熟悉和了解,从而渐渐融入使用另一种该语言的民族的文化之中,扩展了各语言文化之间的共性,因此民族之间能够信息相通。例如,前些年,俄罗斯人对中国的武术和气功很不了解,他们只觉得新奇和神秘,连个名称也叫不出来,到底是"功夫"还是"中国拳术"? 到底是"呼吸运动"还是"瑜伽"? 随着中俄之间民间文化交流的深入,如今,有关武术和气功的书籍译成俄语后十分走俏,甚至"武术协会会长"的头衔也在俄国人的名片中出现。同样,英、法语言的发展史也充分证明了这一点。1066 年诺曼人入侵大不列颠,使当时先进的基督教文明深深植根于英国,英国因此从人种、语言到文化得以与欧洲大陆相融并进。据一项统计资料表明,诺曼人的侵入使大量法语渗入英语而被英语所吸收,特别是在中古英语(1100—1450)中,法语词语占全部英语词汇的近 43%。而如今,英国人在使用这些词汇时并不觉得它们是"舶来品",可见时间其实是一扇未被给予足够重视的洞开之门。随着两种语言之间接触、交流的历史不断延续,由于不同文化之间的相互兼容、渗透,不可译与可译之间的转化也在悄然进行。原先无法互通的某种文化现实,因为该文化本身被认知和被接受而使传译变为可能。如:"替罪羔羊""武装到牙齿""鳄鱼的眼泪""闯进瓷器店的牛""以牙还牙,以眼还眼"等等一些外来词汇已完全进入了汉语词汇库,其所特有的民族文化语义,即使不加注,不仅没有构成理解的障碍,反而丰富了汉语的表现力。同样,汉语特有的表达法,如"百闻不如一见""纸老虎""第三世界"等也逐渐为俄、英、法等语言所吸纳。

①"百闻不如一见"

俄译:"Лучше один раз увидеть,чем сто раз услышать."

英译:"One eyewitness is better than ten hearsays."

②"纸老虎"

俄译:"Бумажный тигр."

英译:"paper tiger ."

③"第三世界"

俄译:"Третий мир."

英译:"the Third World Country."

大体上讲,不同文化系统的开放性程度虽有差别,但它总要与外部异质的文化系统进行各个层次上的交流。文明是一条长长的河,不断有细流渗去和汇入,我们在"输入"西方文化的同时,也是在"输出"中国博大精深的文化。

第四节　可译性限度的存在

盖天下语言所以称作语言,原因在于:①语言是人类结群活动的产物,同时又是活动赖以延续的工具;②语言的功能是相同的;③语言在语义层面上是基本一致的;④语言都受着自然界中其他系统的影响和制约;⑤语言产生的生理机制和心理机制是基本相同的;⑥语言都是渐变和发展的;⑦语言都有自身的内部系统。这些都是语言的共性。语言研究理应研究这些共性,然而辩证法认为,共性寓于个性之中,故此,我们说语言学研究除了研究语言的共性,还要研究个性,而且共性的研究应当建立在不同语言个性的比较研究之上,与此同时,还要研究人类思维、人类社会、人类文明发展史之间的关系等。①

人类思维是客观世界的反映。不同语言中的概念之间存在相关的等值成分或相关的语境特征。人类思维逻辑形式也存在广泛的同一性,人类思维在

---

①　金惠康.跨文化交际翻译[M].北京:中国对外翻译出版社,2003:5-6.

概念内涵、情景、逻辑三个范畴中存在同一性,当概念被组织起来以表达一个完整的思想即句子时,不同的语言也往往具有大体同一的模式,并不因语言之不同而逻辑各异。但是语言是一种十分复杂的思维交际手段,它的复杂性首先表现为每种语言都有自己不同的民族历史、民族文化和民族心理背景。特定语言的特定的结构形式以及这一语言的特定的社会和历史背景,往往导致使用这种语言的人会形成某种特定的思维方式。人类认识所指与思维活动形式的同一性构成了语际转换信息通道相同的两个最重要的条件,人类思维的内容与基本形式是同一的,在转换中的语言是可译的。然而,可译性不是绝对的,它有一定的限度,在语言的各层次中并不是处处存在着信息相通的通道,这就限制了有效转换的完全实现,即存在着可译性的限度翻译不仅是一种跨语言的,还是一种跨文化的交际活动。翻译活动面对的是语言和文化的双重障碍。就语言而言,最大的障碍莫过于独特的结构形式;就文化而言,莫过于独特的民族内涵。因此,可译性限度的存在,虽然其原因是复杂的、多方面的,但主要是语言和文化差异所造成的。在西方翻译理论中,首先提出"可译性限度"及"不可译性"概念的是语言学派的理论家,例如,卡德福特提出不可译性可以分为"语言上的不可译性"与"文化上的不可译性"两方面。

可译性限度也存在着哲学因素。从语言哲学讲,意义也是不可确定的。意义受文化和主观因素的制约,作者和译者的主观性都极大地影响到意义的准确传递。写作是一个复杂的过程,跟作者的文化背景、世界观、语言能力及创作心理都有密切关系,有些因素难以衡量,无法予以准确描述。而译者既要注意分寸的把握,又受自身文化背景和经历等因素的影响,加上语言能力的限制,翻译达到绝对对等就完全不可能。

世界上任何两种语言、文化之间都存在着许多共同点,它们是人类文化共性的表现,也是翻译可行性的依据所在。然而,世界虽具有统一性,但同时又具有多样性。各民族由于存在着不同的社会结构、思想观念、宗教信仰和文化传统等,造成了众多领域里的差异,而这些差异又无不反映在各自的语言当中。既然是不同的语言,那么他们肯定有所区别。所以说"语言是民族的,不同民族存在着不同的语言。"①德国语言学家洪堡特认为:"人类语言与民族语言的关系是一般与个别或本质与现象的关系。人类语言是全人类的共同财富,反映了人类统一的本质。另一方面,语言是一种民族现象,各民族的语言结构形式、意义内涵上有所不同,一定的民族语言与一定的民族性和文化特征

---

① 陈宗明.现代汉语逻辑初探[M].上海:三联书店,1979.

相维系。"换而言之,语言文化之间的共质性是本质的、广泛的,而异质性则是深刻的、不容忽视的。

梅纳德·麦克曾指出:"当我们通过一篇优秀的英语译文阅读塞万提斯、蒙田、马基雅维利或者托尔斯泰的作品,我们已经获得了与西班牙人、德国人、意大利人或者俄罗斯人大致相同的感受,而'大致'这个词是恰如其分的。"美国翻译理论家尤金·奈达也指出:"如果读者对译文所作出的反应与原文读者对原文所作出的反应基本一致,那么便可认为翻译是成功的。"在他看来,绝对一致的翻译是不存在的,因而只求反应"基本一致"。无论是梅纳德·麦克还是尤金·奈达的观点,都明确提出翻译之所以只能求得"大致""基本一致"的感受和反应,是因为两种语言之间有距离和差异,从而导致了翻译的障碍。而距离与差异的存在是因为各语言所具有的区别于其他语言的独特的个性,即异质性。

我国学者许钧在《翻译的哲学与宗教观》一文中谈及"译本与原本是否含有同一真理"这一问题时指出:"关于这个问题说到底,是个表象能否反映本质的哲学命题。语言和语言所表述的现实之间,还不仅仅是个表达与被表达的关系,不是简单的镜子与映照的关系,里面还有许多因素值得深入探讨。"他的这段话也表明,翻译之所以不能百分之百的等值,是因为有"许多因素"干扰着翻译的进行。这诸多因素中,语言文化的异质性因素占据主要地位。

刘宓庆先生在其《当代翻译理论》一书中对可译性、可译性限度进行了理论上的架构,提出了可译性的四点理论依据,即:"认识所指的同一性及语义结构的'同构'原理""思维形式的同一性""语法差异的规律性及语义系统的对应"和"文化的相互渗透性"。该理论从认知、思维、语言和文化四个维度对语际转换中的源出语的可译性限度进行了论证,其结论为"从理论上说,语际间存在着基本的、广泛的意义转换条件和手段,我们可以称之为'信息转换通道'(the channel for message transferring)。正是信息转换通道,提供了语际转换的可译性,而在信息通道不存在或不完全存在时,就产生了可译性限度。"继而刘宓庆又提出可译性限度的两点理论依据,即:"同构的相对性及语言的模糊性""语际转换中的障碍",包括语言文字结构障碍(the linguistic structure obstruction)、惯用法障碍(the usage obstruction)、表达法障碍(the expression obstruction)和语义表述障碍(the semantic obstruction)及文化障碍(the cultural obstruction)。[①] 同构的相对性有两个主要原因:第一,源出语

---

① 刘宓庆.当代翻译理论[M].北京:中国对外翻译出版社,1999:99-104.

所反映的外部世界是源出语作者用头脑"加工"了的世界,这种"加工"往往带有主观局限性;第二,译者对源出语的理解、对其蕴含意义的领悟以及对其风格的体会与源出语有误。

由于人们对外部世界的描述只有相对的真实性,思维结构的同构关系也具有相对性。作为思维的载体——语言,也具有一定的差异。英语词义与思维表述方式比较灵活、抽象、含糊;汉语词义与思维表述方式比较执着、具体,有时过于明确、凝滞。因此,由于分属两种不同的语系,英汉语言确实存在很大差异,英汉语言中存在着可译性限度。英汉语无论在语音方面,还是在语义方面,也无论是在语法表达、句子结构方面,还是在文体、修辞方面都判然有别。

一、语言上的可译性限度

(一)语音的可译性限度

语音是语言的重要表达形式,是口头语言中表情达意的重要手段,英、汉语语音规律上迥异,某些语音现象在另一种语言中不存在对应的形式,致使其成为翻译中的可译性限度。如:

What keys are too big to carry in your pocket?

A monkey, a donkey, and a turkey.

例句中,英语利用了发音上/ki:/与/ki/的相似性和词形"key"的相同性,点出了答话人的机敏与幽默风趣。这种由语音相似所构成的韵谐美和词形后缀相同的形式美在译成汉语时是难以达到"等效"效果的。虽然可以通过变换语序,达到押韵之目的,如"猴子,火鸡还有驴",但是原文中所蕴含的诙谐与幽默就荡然无存了。

(二)音韵节奏的可译性限度

英国作家斯提芬·斯彭德(Stephen Spenser)曾说过:"有时,在写作中我感到遣词造句犹如谱写音乐,这个音乐性对我的吸引,远远超过词语本身。"语言内在的音乐性主要体现在语言的音乐感和音韵上,从而加强语言的表现力和感染力,因此语音修辞一直是语言修辞的重要手段,这也是翻译的重要课题。英语中常用的语音修辞形式有四种,头韵、半谐音、谐音和拟声。它们彼此相近,但各有不同。先以最常用的压头韵为例:He is all fire and fight,译为"他怒气冲冲,来势汹汹"。例句中由于都使用了首音韵的语音修饰手法,起首辅音的重复,配以明快悦耳的节奏,明显增强了语言的形象感和音乐感,给读者留下深刻印象,但从翻译的角度看,译文也是词比句对,寓意贴切。但原文的头韵已消失,因为无法根本体现上述英语压头韵的效果,从而造成了音韵节奏上的可译性限度。

(三)语言模糊性导致的可译性限度

有时译语没有在意义上和原语完全相同的对等词,这种不完全的对等词,或对等范围大小不同,或对等意义不甚确切。如:英语 wife 一词可用来表达汉语的妻子、夫人、爱人等。cousin 相当于汉语的堂兄、堂弟、表哥、表妹等八个词。双关语的可译性限度也很大,很多双关语实际上是"不可译"的。如:

Professor of Physics：What is matter?

Student：Never mind.

Professor：Then what is mind?

Student：It does not matter.

这段话是利用 matter 和 mind 这两个词的双关语,matter 指"物质"又指"事情",What is matter? 可理解成"什么是物质?"也可理解成"有什么事?"mind 指"心理"又指"介意","反对",Never mind 可理解成"不要紧",也可理解成"绝不是心理"。由于这个对话用了好几个双关语,使之成为可译性限度的一个重要问题。

(四)语法的可译性限度

英汉语分属不同的语系,在音、形上不可能形成同源对应（cognate equivalence),在字(词)形的结构方面也必然存在着很大的差别,特别是英语乃至拼音文字,每一个单词都是由字母按一定规律排列组合而成,字母的变动就会构成新的单词,从而词义也相应发生变化;汉语中的许多合体字也可以拆分,拆分后的偏旁或部首有的也能独立成字,从而具有新的词义。翻译中遇到既有词(字)形变化,同时又有词(字)义变化,词(字)形与词(字)义融为一体的内容时,往往成为不可译的难题。如:"我叫张斌,弓长张,文武斌。"这是中国人在介绍姓名时常用的一种方式,在某些情况下也是一种拆字游戏,是汉字所具有的独特的构词规律的体现。

例 1：What word can be made shorter by adding something to it?

——short

例 2：Why are the letter g and the letter s in gloves close to each other?

——Because there is love between them.

以上两例的译文,对于不懂英语的汉语读者来说,如果不加注释是无法理解的,因为句中的 short,shorter 和 g,s,gloves 不仅起着组词成句的形式作用,而且他们的词义也都是剧中重要的内容,词形和词义是构成句中双关幽默的重要组成部分,缺一不可,这种特定语境中的词形和词义的翻译,在一文中要达到同样的效果也是不可能的,于是造成语法上的可译性限度。

二、文化上的可译性限度

翻译的表象是语言与语言的沟通,而实质则是文化与文化的交融。文化的经典定义是 1871 年由英国人类学家泰勒(Edward Tylor)在《原始文化》(*The Primitive Culture*)一书中提出的:文化是一个复合的整体,其中包括知识、信仰艺术、法律、道德、风俗,以及作为社会成员而获得的任何其他的能力和习惯。翻译不仅要克服语言上的障碍,更要克服文化上的障碍。如果遇到无法逾越的障碍,造成信息根本无法传达,就出现了不可译现象。文化具有鲜明的地域性,而这正是文化不可译性存在的前提。各种文化因素为翻译工作者设置了数不清的语言文化障碍,因而造成翻译过程中不可避免的限度问题。

林肯在《葛底斯堡演讲》中的第一句为:"Four score and seven years ago, our fathers brought forth on this continent a new nation, conceived in liberty, and dedicated to the proposition that all men are created equal."在这一庄严的时刻,林肯想到了《圣经》中一个重要的日子,即 Abraham(基督教《圣经》中犹太人的始祖)生第一个孩子时,是"four score and six years old"。利用这样一个互文结构的短语,林肯可以有力地感召笃信基督教演讲课题的听众,激发他们为南北战争的胜利贡献自己的一分力量,达到了"振臂一呼,应者云集"的效果。但恰恰是这样一个貌似简单的短语"Four score and seven years ago",在将其翻译成汉语时就出现了难以跨越的障碍。因为对于没有读过《圣经》的汉语读者而言,这一短语无法使他们产生共鸣,当然也就达不到原文读者心目中可能产生的那种效果。加之汉语并无"score"这一词的对应词,我们只能译为"87 年前"。不得不承认这种译法丢失了原文的韵味,译文读者很难体会到原文读者读原文时所感受到的强烈的文化震撼,这也证实了翻译的相对可译性。

以中国的"文房四宝"为例,它指的是"笔墨纸砚"。作为物品,它们是可译的:"笔"可译为"writing brush","墨"为"ink stick","纸"为"paper","砚"为"ink slab"。但对没有接触过中国文化的外国人来说,是很难理解汉语"笔""墨"和"砚"的文化意义和功能的。当中国人说"挥毫泼墨"时,这里面包含着一些独特的文化背景:为什么"挥毫"呢?因为中国人写字、画画用的毛笔,是用狼毫、羊毫、兔毫等制成的,这与英国人说的"drive the quill"(挥笔写字)并不一样,"quill"是鸟类的羽毛管。因为过去英国人的笔是用羽毛管制成的,所以对他们来说不是"挥毫",而是"挥管"。至于"泼墨",差距就更大了:中国书画家所用的"墨",也是最具特性的文化用品。这是一种用松烟等原料精制,并经过特殊工艺处理的黑色颜料,它与英语文化中的对应物"墨水"更是截然不同。至于"砚",作为文化用品,英语文化中更属阙如。这就是上文所说的文化内涵上的障碍所在。总之,在一种语言文化里人人都懂得的事物或情感表示,在另一种语言文化里不加解释便难以理解。

第五节　歇后语翻译的限度

一般来说,语言和文化差异导致可译性限度。而歇后语体现着汉语语言独有的个性特征,包含着丰富的文化信息,具有鲜明的民族特色,浓郁的生活气息,幽默风趣,耐人寻味。这些特征无疑会构成语际转换、文化交流的一大障碍。

一、语符表层形态的不同而产生的可译性限度

(一)歇后语语音体系特征及其翻译

同音异义字广泛地应用在歇后语中。由同音异义字制造双关意义才能最终达到幽默的效果。同音异义字包括同音异义和同形异义。关于同音异义字,在汉语言中,字符是单音节(单一的字符有一个发音和一个意思),有着少数的音调种类,字符也是非曲折的(动词形式不改变人称和时态,同时,名词无论单复数都保留原形)。这就为大量同音异义词的产生提供了条件,进而涌现无数通过两部分关键词语的谐音而显示寓意的歇后语。这就是为什么歇后语大都是些同音字的口头游戏。

汉语能够更惬意地玩转于同音字中并且让其艺术性的表达更加规则化,这一切都要归功于汉语的单音节字符和可变的语法。由于英语是受"词性""性别""格"等约束的建筑化语言,所以如果歇后语中频繁使用同音字,歇后语的汉英翻译就会有巨大的困难。对那些坚持歇后语是不可译的人来说,汉英语间这道无法逾越的鸿沟是他们的主要论点。然而,要以达到最终交流目的的观点,也可以说只要能从翻译信息表达出潜在意义,任何东西都是可译的。

"双关语"指在一定的语言环境中,利用词的多义和同音的条件,有意使语句具有双重意义,言在此而意在彼的修辞方式。双关可使语言表达得含蓄、幽默,且能加深语意,给人以深刻印象。法国大文豪雨果也说:"双关语是飞舞着

的灵魂的产物。"双关一般可分为谐音双关和语意双关两种。一是谐音双关，指利用一个词义同或音近而兼顾两种不同事物言此指彼的修辞手法。它又可以分为四种类型：音形皆同的谐音双关，即所用词与深层次的词不仅读音相同而且形体也相同，如"我失骄杨君失柳，杨柳轻飏直上重霄九"中的"杨"实际上是指杨开慧，"柳"实际上是指柳直荀；同音不同形的谐音双关，这种谐音的表层词与要表示的深层词只是音同而字形不同，如李商隐《无题》"春蚕到死丝方尽，蜡炬成灰泪始干"中"丝"即"思"的意思，以此来表达男女之间的爱情；隐语谐音双关，这种音的深层含义是指一种不能明言的事件或人物命运等，这种双关多用于文学作品中，如《红楼梦》第五回："可叹停机德，堪怜咏絮才。玉带林中挂，金簪雪里埋。"诗中的"林"中挂的"玉带"，"雪"中埋"金簪"，加上前面两句诗，暗示了林黛玉、薛宝钗的命运；曲解谐音，即通过谐音使词的意义扩大，一音多词，如"谈笑有鸿儒，往来无白丁"中"鸿"谐"红"故能与"白"相对。再如"水春云母碓，风扫石楠花"中"楠"谐"男"，才能与"母"相对。二是语意双关：是一种根据词的多义条件而故意导致言在此而意在彼的修辞方式。如："借问瘟君欲何往，纸船明烛照天烧。"（毛泽东《送瘟神》）。这种修辞在歇后语中经常出现。如"茶壶里煮饺子——心里有嘴倒不出"，再如"老太太抹口红——给你点颜色瞧瞧。"

英汉语中的双关语，都是指同形异义或同音异义词的妙用，因此双关语分为谐音双关语和谐意双关语两类。如：It's a long, long way to Siberia and a long, long wait at Moscow airport.（去西伯利亚的路，千里迢迢，在莫斯科机场候机，遥遥无期。）句中 way 和 wait，语音相谐，long, long way 和 long, long wait 相迭，更增添了人们路途遥远、几无盼头的感觉。谐音双关语一般是不可译的，因此原句中的双关修辞格形式在译文中无法再现，只能通过"迢迢""遥遥"叠字形式补偿原文双关语所负载的语义。

可是，当同音异义字用在归结子句中时，歇后语会让听者觉得更加难以理解。"何仙姑嫁给了姓郑的，郑何氏（正合适）"就是一个很好的例子，字面翻译就是：The immortal lady, He is married to a person by the surname of Zheng and becomes Mrs. Zheng, nee He. 对于说英语的人来说，这仅仅是关于一个女人结婚后名字的变化的一个合乎逻辑的陈述，所以他们对这番说辞不会留有任何印象。可是，要是中国听众的话，听到这句，他/她也许会爆笑出声。因为在汉语中，"郑何氏"的发音和"正合适"正好完全一样，在英语中就是："it fits perfectly."

如果是用同音字的歇后语，要想理解其潜在意义，就要考虑更多的因素，它也假定同音字是给听众提供更多的认知程序以求找出最佳的假定,而不是越过同音字来处理歇后语。歇后语中采用同音字是对智力的挑战,对翻译者来说不能称之为例外。似乎同音字使得汉英字面翻译变得极其的困难,因为如果同音字只是字面的翻译了,就会失去其潜在的深层意义,或者这个翻译在英语中就变成了废话。这是由于一对对的词汇和短语虽然在这种语言里发音一样,但在另外一种语言里却不尽相同。

在翻译过程中,能不能在传达了歇后语的相同意思的同时,又创造了相同的双关效果,显然用直译的方法几乎是不可能的,只能采取再造和间接翻译。

第一种方法是再造英语双关:先提炼主题;查出它们的所有同义词;从中找出可作双关的词语;具体到这个连环谐音双关,还得在三个入选的双关词语之间审视建立连环关系的可能性;找出意境,造出一句或多句连环俏皮话。也就是说,找出所有与潜在意义相对应的词或者同义词,接着试着模仿原始措辞的效果。举个例子,"绱鞋不使锥子——针(真)好!"可以译成"A sherbet in a midsummer night's dream:cool!"即使这不是个字面的翻译,它在保留双关效果的情况下传达了相同的意思。"Cool"在这儿既可以解释成冰冻果子露的温度,也可以是那种在大热天喝上一杯冰冻果子露的凉爽感觉。又如"狗撵鸭子呱呱(刮刮)叫!"可译成"Jill milking Jack, what for? cream of the cream!(玉女为金童挤牛奶,图个啥? 精化之精华!)"虽说意境粗俗,和原文的风味还是不相上下的。

第二种方法是间接翻译,也就是仅翻译它的潜在意义,这也是口译人员最常用的方法。因为日常会话的特点就是简单有效,冗长的解释就显得不那么重要了,也没有必要为译文语言重新创作一个对等的谐音双关语,这类歇后语的意义往往非常简单明了。如"和尚打伞无法无天"实际就是"unruly"的意思,一词解决问题。"猪鼻子里插葱——装象",如果是口译,也只要一个词就行:"pretentious"或"vain";而"老太太靠墙吃稀饭——卑鄙(背壁),无耻(齿),下流!"就带上了对老龄妇女的侮辱,光用中文都有损形象,别谈翻译了,直接用"base, shameless and dirty"得了,根本不值得绞尽脑汁生造对应的英文谐音双关语;"何仙姑嫁给了姓郑的,郑何氏(正合适)"就可以译成"fit perfectly";"人家给个棒槌,我就拿着认真(针)"可以译成"Always getting hold of the wrong end of the stick";"外甥打灯笼——找舅(照旧)"可以译成"Things will be back to what they were before"。在译文里用事理逻辑意义较为抽象、笼统的词或词组代替原文中较为具体的形象比喻,译者必须就其交际行为重要程度来处理歇后语的语义重点。

(二)歇后语的词汇特征及其翻译

在词汇的层面上,最典型的歇后语就是用名词来描述普通大众脑海里最熟悉的动物和人物的形象,这些形象都反映了中国人的思维方式和感知。根据统计分析,歇后语中使用的人物形象,大部分用的是神话人物、出名的虚构人物和历史人物,例如,张飞(三国时期的名将),猪八戒(《西游记》里的人物),还有阎罗王(死神);这些形象中有年轻的、老的、有病的、虚弱的和那些与众不同的形象。如"张飞穿针——大眼瞪小眼""猪八戒照镜子——里外不是人""狗咬吕洞宾——不识好人心"等。

将汉语从字面上翻译到英语时,与这些形象相关的观念是要考虑的诸多因素当中的一个,特别是那些诸如神话人物、历史人物和虚构人物的形象。一般情况下,由于对理解的实验性原则的缺乏会给跨文化翻译造成一定的难度。在翻译歇后语的过程中,翻译者不仅仅是在翻译这句话,更是在传播中国的文化和历史。以下面这句歇后语的翻译为例,"张飞抬曹操,一举两得(德)",译文是"In the case of General Zhang carrying Cao Cao, there will two 'De' – with only one doing the lifting (in one action)."然而,这个译文对于说英语的人是没有任何意义的,因为这些说英语的读者不仅对这两个人物没有相当的认识,就更不用说理解这两个人的称呼(两个人的字中都有"德"字,张飞字"翼德",曹操字"孟德"),而"德"与"得"恰好构成谐音双关意义。这也是为什么尤金·奈达在他的作品《语言和文化——翻译的上下文》中指出对翻译者来说,最困难的情形就是处理被译文章的潜在意义。

由那些没有相应英语对等物的汉语观念所造成的文化空白可以有两种可行的策略来填补。一种是直译加注解。例如:"三个臭皮匠,合成一个诸葛亮"可译成"Three cobblers with their wits combined would equal Chukeh Liang the master mind";"狗咬吕洞宾,不识好人心"可译成"Like the dog that bit Lu Tung-pin, you bite the hand that feed you"。另一种是对等翻译,也就是找寻有相似意思的英语俗谚。按照这种途径,"张飞抬曹操,一举两得(德)"译文就该是"killing two birds with one stone"。在两种语言里有很多意义相近的俗谚可以配成对,例如:"猫哭耗子,假慈悲"和"Shed crocodile tears.";"毛驴上马掌,小蹄(题)大做"和"(to)make a mountain out of a molehill";"张飞请李逵,黑吃黑"和"One robber robs the other."

毫无疑问,第一种译法可以帮助传播中国优秀传统的文化。而第二种译法的翻译是非常有效果的,想要表达的意义也更容易被理解;可是也会让英语读者失去了欣赏中华智慧的良机,同时丢失了原汁原味的中国文化特色。我们只能根据具体需要和强调来选择两种译法之一。

(三)歇后语的句法特征及其翻译

作为一种俗谚,歇后语靠着独一无二的句法特征将自己和汉语谚语区别开来。歇后语由两部分组成,较少只有第一部分(条件从句)说出来而留着第二部分让听者自己领悟。通常,第二部分补充或进一步修饰第一部分,因此组成了一个自由的句子结构。这种结构有助于为交谈营造一个轻松从容的氛围。

如果将两部分结合起来,我们可以看出歇后语是一种复杂化的自由结构,其中,主句打头,从句跟着,而且通常第一部分比较沉重,第二部分不仅活泼,还提供了新的信息。自由的句子结构能够营造轻松的氛围,只要让说话的人有更多的时间补充更多的详细资料和信息。有了这个优点,歇后语可以帮助说话人制造紧张和悬念,保留潜在意义一直到最后,或不吭声或接连处暂停一下都会更吸引听众。

由于以下几个原因,歇后语的暂停效果是很难翻译好的。第一,从经过字面翻译的第一部分来推断归结子句中的潜在意义基本是不可能的。第二,由于不同种语言的本质,经翻译后的歇后语就没什么悬念了。对于这样的情况,如果要强调歇后语中这种独特的暂停效果,可以采用这样的方法:将第一部分转化成从句而第二部分则变成主句,就这样句子变得有周期性了。这一转变的标志就是"if""when""as""just as"或"in case of"引导的状语从句,或者是"-ing"形式的伴随状态,又或者是开头的不定状语。例如:"城门楼上吊嗓子,唱高调"译成"If one practices scales on top of the tower of a city gate, the tune sung will be high";"头顶生疮脚底流脓,坏透了"译成" As the ulcer is growing on the head and the pus is flowing from the sole — the system has become rotten through and through. "

这种翻译方法尽管克服了歇后语松散的结构特点且它的条件从句也被翻译了出来,但归结子句的语气不够有力。当然,也有成功的翻译,我们可以忽略歇后语的松散结构,根据语境的需要程度来翻译它。如:"猫哭耗子,假慈悲"译成"A cat weeps over the death of a mouse — pretence of being sympathetic.""死鬼要账,活该"可译为"The ghost of a dead person comes to demand repayment of a debt — a sum owed to him when he was alive"。

二、文化差异与翻译的限度

翻译是运用一种语言把另一种语言所表达的思维内容准确而完整地表达

出来的语言活动。人类的共性决定各民族语言文化间的共性,只有重视文化内涵,才能克服翻译过程中的语言障碍,真正达到文化交流的目的,因此文化差异对翻译的影响不可忽视。这里特从以下几方面谈谈理解文化差异对翻译所起的至关重要的作用。

(一)词汇对应现象

语言和文化密不可分,语言是文化的载体,也是文化的一面镜子,透过一个民族的语言层面,展现在我们眼前的乃是这个民族绚丽多姿的文化色彩。从语言的社会功能看,文化差异在词汇层面上体现得更为突出。德国语言家雅格布·格林有一著名的论点:"关于各民族的情况,有一种比古迹、工具和墓葬更为生动的证据,这就是他们的语言。"语言像一面镜子反映着民族的全部,又像一个窗口,揭示着该文化的一切内容。"语言反映着文化,文化决定着语言"。作为语言的基本构成要素的词汇所体现出的文化差异是最为突出和广泛的。

从人的构造机能来看,任何人都有着共同的感知客观世界的心理器官——大脑。相同的心理特征和类似的生存经验决定了人类各民族的语言结构、思维和文化有许多相同或相通的地方,这种不同文化类型间相互迭盖的共性部分是跨文化交际的基础。同时,这种宏观共性赋予词汇相同的概念意义和一致的联想意义。

在任何语境中,head(头)和 heart(心)分别有其相同的概念意义,英汉两种文化语境也未能例外。如:from head to foot(从头至脚),over the heads of others(出人头地),put our heads together(交流思想),set one's heart at ease(放心),black-hearted(黑心的),from the bottom of one's heart(从心底里),heart and soul(全心全意)等。此外,汉语里的"心"可对应英语中的两个概念,即 mind(思考)和 heart(心)。如:记在心头(keep in mind),心不在焉(absent-minded),有心事(have something in one's mind)等。显然,英语的词汇量远远大于汉语,而且概念细微,表达准确。同时在思维方式上也反映了西方人重演绎,长于线性逻辑,层层推理,追求对客观世界的明晰认识,而东方人正好相反,重归纳,长于模糊思维。

在日常生活中,人们根据某些动物的生活习性而把它们同一定的品质或特性联系起来,这些品质或特性又往往使人产生某种反应或情绪。例如:狐狸(fox)在英汉两种语言中的所指意义相同,都指普通的、野生的食肉犬科动物,生性狡猾多疑。汉语中有"狡猾的狐狸"之说,英语也有 as sly as a fox 之喻;英语用"a fox in a lamb's skin"来描绘伪善的人,用"to play the fox"来表示

"耍滑、装假"。显然,狐狸一词的联想意义在英汉两种语言中都沿着贬义(derogatory)的方向发展,而且都基于狐狸生性狡猾多疑这一习性。同样,驴会让人想到"愚笨"(as stupid as an ass),蜜蜂使人联想到"辛勤、忙碌"(as busy as a bee),鹦鹉则是"学舌"的象征(to parrot what other people say)。这些例子反映了不同文化语境中人们对客观世界认识的契合点。

(二)词汇的半对应现象

词汇的社会文化意义牵涉到社会经验、思想态度、风俗习惯、价值观念等方面。这种社会文化意义最难把握。如:英语语言中的否定词"No",从词汇意义上讲,与汉语中的"无""没有"对等,然而从社会文化意义上讲,却又不尽相同。按英美人士的习惯,当一个朋友到另一个朋友家去做客,主人会问:"Would you like something to drink?(你想喝点什么吗?)"朋友回答:"No, thanks.(不,谢谢)"这意味着朋友确实不想喝什么。但中国人则不然,一个中国人首次到一个英国朋友去做客,如果主人问:"Would you like something to drink?"中国人出于传统美德自谦,则会说:"No(不喝)!"但实质上,若把饮料端上来,他也许会喝的。这样,许多英美人刚到中国就被这个简单的"No"搞糊涂了——是英语的"No"呢?还是汉语中的"No"?再如:英语中的"fat"一词,从词汇意义上讲,可与汉语中的"胖""丰满"对等。然而从社会的文化意义上讲,却截然不同。按中国人的习惯,朋友见面有时会说"你发福了",意思为身体健康,是恭维语;而英美则不然,他们对体重和体型非常敏感,许多人注重节食和减肥。因此,当面谈论别人胖是不礼貌的。又如:家庭(family),在汉语中,它的内涵较广,主要指以婚姻和血缘关系为基础的社会单位,包括由父母、子女组成的核心式家庭和其他共同生活的亲属在内。家庭还可以指一个家庭的上下几代,甚至整个家族。在中国,起核心作用的是"家",这点在语言中也有反映,如称自己为"自家",别人为"人家",全体为"大家",全国为"国家"。家给人以宁静、温暖、安全,尽享天伦之乐的联想。英语中,由于20世纪50年代讲英语的白人在美国所有社会机构和学校中占主导地位。78%的家庭由已婚夫妇组成,所以"典型"的family形象是白人,中产阶级,讲英语,住在以父亲为户主的核心家庭中,母亲买菜,打扫房间,为全家做早餐。这说明词义的文化差异与价值观念的差异有密切联系。根据"语言与文化共变"的规律,词义的演变伴随着文化的发展而产生。如刚才谈到的"family"一词,在美国的今天有四分之一的人口是非白人血统或是拉美血统人(此数字正在急剧增加);"核心家庭"正在消失;三分之一以上家庭以离婚告终;越来越多的未婚妇女怀孕后愿意留下孩子,因而单亲家庭急剧增加;四分之一以上有七八岁以下孩子的家庭由未婚女子担当户主,已婚夫妇家庭只占所有家庭的二分之一。这样,"family"一词的内涵又增添了"single-parent family"以及"blended family"等意思。

(三)词汇的非对应现象

不同的民族在不同的生存环境下建立了自己的文化系统,形成了他们独有的心理特点。因此,在不同的文化和语言中,同一客观事物可能包含不同的含义,具有不同的内涵,引起不同的联想。罗伯特·奈德说过:"我们把生活经验变成语言,并给语言加上意思是受了文化的约束影响的,而各种语言则由于文化的不同而互为区别。有的语义存在于一种语言中,但在另一种语言中却不存在。"这种词汇的非对应称之为词汇空缺(lexical gap),由此也就有了"联想意义空缺"(associative meaning gap)现象。

在西方,狗既可用来看门或打猎,也可视为人的"忠诚伴侣"和宠物。因此,英美人对狗一般不抱恶感,反倒有爱怜的感情,常用来比喻人或人的关系。因此,与狗有关的谚语多是褒义。而在中国,狗是用来保护人和家的,但它并不如它的同类在西方那么宠爱,传统意义上中国人对狗的看法多是厌恶和鄙视的。因此,汉语里多数与狗有关的谚语含有贬义。如,"狗眼看人低""狗仗人势,雪仗风势""狗嘴里吐不出象牙""狗改不了吃屎""救了落水狗,反被一口咬""狗咬吕洞宾,不知好人心"等。学生首次在英汉词典中发现"Love me,love my dog"被译成"爱屋及乌"时,它在中国学生头脑中引起的联想与原文中的联想是大相径庭的。这个译语在中国学生头脑中产生的联想是:爱我,也爱我身边最讨厌的东西。我们在弄清"狗"这个词在西方的文化含义后,就能正确接受与狗有关的英语句子的社会文化信息,而不犯文化差异方面引起的错误,从而实现真正意义上的跨文化交际。汉语语言中的"虎"形象勇猛、威武,把"虎"视作百兽之王;而英语语言中,狮子取代了老虎的地位,12世纪后期英王查理一世因勇武、大胆而被誉为"King Richard the lion-hearted(狮心王查理)",以此说明他的勇猛超群[①],难怪英国人选狮子作为自己国家的象征了。英语中的"dragon lady"是"母夜叉""母老虎",而不是中国的"龙女";在汉语语言里,"龙"是吉祥之物,是中国古代皇帝的象征,是中华民族的图腾,经常使人联想到"成功""生机勃勃""权贵",如"望子成龙""生龙活虎""攀龙附凤""真龙天子""龙袍"等。然而英语里的"dragon"是邪恶的象征,认为龙是凶残肆虐、兴风作浪、杀人放火的怪物,给人们带来的是"灾难""邪恶""恐怖",应予

---

① 陈金荣.英语谚语民族特点分析[J].云梦学刊,1992(2):83-85.

以消灭。因此,在中西方文化中,"龙"和"dragon"有着截然相反的联想,使英语国家的人很难想象中国人说的"我们是龙的传人"这一说法。而"亚洲四小龙"在英语里常译成"Four little tigers of Asia"以避免由于"dragon"所引起的文化差异。因此,弄清这些关系是我们学习和交流的前提。又如,汉语中有许多尊称,如"××先生""×翁""×公",英语中几乎没有与之对应的尊称。汉语中还有很多谦辞,如:"敝姓""寒舍""贱内",这是汉语民族"满招损,谦受益"的民族心理在汉语词汇层次上的反映。英语中则没有这些谦辞,因此,"敝姓"只好说成"my name","贱内"只好说成"my wife"。又如竹子(bamboo),英国没有竹子,汉语中的"笋"只能译成 bamboo root(竹芽)。而中国传统文化却赋予竹子丰富的联想意义。历代文人墨客赏竹、咏竹、画竹,邵谒有"竹死不变节,花落有余香"的名句,郑板桥的竹画更是享誉世界,而竹子也逐渐成了中国人坚强、高风亮节的性格之象征。同样,英语中的一些词在汉语里也是空缺的,如 privacy,汉译是"隐私、私密、私事",但这些译词都没能把真正的意思表达出来。原因在于中西方人的价值观念不同,历史传统各异。我们对于privacy 不像西方人那么重视,因此也就没有一个词能包括 privacy 所表达的那些意思。

(四)宗教信仰的差异与翻译

在《宗教百科全书》中,宗教的定义是这样的:"总的来说,每个已知的文化中都包含了或多或少的宗教信仰,它们或明了或令人疑惑地试图完美解释这个世界。当某些行为典范在特定的一个文化中得到确立时,它就将在这个文化中打下深深的历史烙印。即便宗教在形式、完整度、可信度等都因不同文化而异,但人在社会中还是不可避免要受到宗教影响。"西方人多信奉基督教,认为上帝创造了世界,世上的一切由上帝主宰;而中国主要有三大教派:佛教、道教、儒教。在我国的文化里,有道教的"玉帝",有佛教的"阎王",有神话中的"龙王",而这些概念在西方人的心中都不存在。在颜色方面,西方的葬礼一般由牧师主持,参加者身着黑色的衣服或佩戴黑纱,以示对逝者的哀悼,有悲哀、绝望、死亡之意。这一特征在词汇中的体现例如:a white day——吉日;black sheep——害群之马。

此外,与宗教信仰有关的习语也大量出现在汉英语言中。佛教传入中国时间已久。人们相信有"佛祖"在左右着人世间的一切,与此有关的习语很多,如"借花献佛""闲时不烧香,临时抱佛脚"等。在西方许多国家,特别是在英美,人们信奉基督教,相关的习语有"God helps those who help themselves"。(上帝帮助自助的人),也有"Go to hell"(下地狱去)这样的诅咒。歇后语中也不乏有关中国宗教典故和教条教理的体现。例如:和尚吃猪头——破戒;泥菩萨过河——自身难保;观音菩萨——年年十八;八仙过海——各显神通。了解宗教文化,有助于歇后语翻译。

(五)文化象征的差异与翻译

同一客观事物,在不同文化里有不同的文化象征,会引起不同的联想。就文学作品而言,作者常常有意或无意地赋予他的作品多重意义,用王国维的话说:"以我观物,故物物皆着我之色彩。"中外杰出文学作品讲究创造含蓄深远的艺术意境,重在言外之意,文学作品既"能状难写之景如在眼前",更要"含不尽之意,见于言外。"作为特殊读者的译者,必须借助语言文字的暗示、象征等特点,寻求在言外含有不尽之深意的文化象征意义。

(1)动物。在基督文化里,绵羊是驯服的象征;在中国文化里,老鼠是胆小懦弱的象征。英语中把 bat 看成是邪恶的象征,因为它外观古怪丑陋,居住在阴暗的角落,而且还有吸人血的 vampire bat,提起来就令人恐惧。因此,英语中有 as crazy as a bat, as blind as a bat 等。然而,汉语中"蝙蝠"的形象与英语中完全不同:"蝠"与"福"同音,蝙蝠被认为是幸福的象征。蝙蝠作为一个吉祥物,经常出现在民间的许多图案上。红蝙蝠的"红蝠"与"洪福"同音,更是象征着大吉大利。

另外,狗在汉语中是一种卑微的动物。汉语中与狗有关的习语大都含有贬义:"狐朋狗友""狗急跳墙""狼心狗肺""狗腿子"等。在歇后语中存在很多用狗来做贬义的表现形式。

1)狗啃骨头——天生喜欢吃硬的。用于责骂人不知趣,偏要给自己找麻烦或敬酒不吃吃罚酒。例如:

阎鬼婆骂道:"……好言好语难商量,再不给你点颜色瞧瞧,你就不知道老娘是马王爷三只眼。你们这些人,真是狗啃骨头,天生喜欢吃硬的。"(房群等《剑与盾》)

2)狗脸亲家——三日好,两日臭。用来形容随对方钱财权势变化而改变态度的人。讥讽人或责骂势利眼,对人时好时坏。例如:

这是,正好又叫小俊听见,便挨着嘴讽刺似地说:"哼,布谷鸟早都不叫了,还发明什么,真是狗脸亲家,三日好,两日臭,还嫌人批评哩!"她说这话,主要是想报复哩。因为前天叫光勤大骂了一顿。(程向照《布谷鸟又叫了》)

3)狗屎作的鞭子——闻也闻不得,舞也舞不得。这里的"闻"与"文"同音相谐,"舞"与"武"同音相谐,用于讥讽人既不能文,也不能武,哪一行都干不了。例如:话说清朝末年,鲍起是四川巫山县城里的一名烂秀才。此人从小喜

欢舞文弄墨,玩枪耍棒,但年近三十,还是一条狗屄作的鞭子,闻也闻不得,舞也舞不得。(刘长贵《豹子升官记》)

4)狗尾巴上的露水——经不起摇摆。本指狗尾巴一摇,上面的露水就会被抖落,转喻人的话里水分很大,经不起推敲、斟酌。例如:

只不过这只是一刹那,张财的话已经在精神上彻底将他击溃。他想,张财的话是狗尾巴上的露水,经不起摇摆,决不可听信。(莫伸《生命的凝聚》)

5)狗戴帽子——硬充人。讥讽坏人硬要充当好人。例如:

阿妈妮心里骂道:"狗戴帽子装人了,你怎么不说你当年给江家当'炮手'穿着府绸短褂,古铜色呢子毡帽,腰间扎着子弹袋,嘴里叼着烟卷儿,跟在钱氏后边,像个护腚狗,神气透了,哪个穷人敢靠近前啊……"(高梦龄《血土》)

诸如此类用狗来做歇后语形象的例子不胜枚举。而在西方英语国家,狗被认为是人类最忠诚的朋友。英语中有关狗的习语除了一部分因受其他语言的影响而含有贬义外,大部分都没有贬义。在英语习语中常以狗形象来比喻人的行为。如"You are a lucky dog"(你是个幸运儿),"Every dog has his day"(凡人皆有得意日),形容人"病得厉害"用"sick as a dog","累极了"是"dog — tired"。

而中国人喜爱用"馋猫"比喻人贪嘴,常有亲昵的成分,而在西方文化中,"猫"被用来比喻"包藏祸心的女人"。猫也常被用来作为歇后语的形象素材。

6)猫抓黏糕——脱不了爪爪。此句本指猫的爪子被粘住脱不开,转喻人陷入困境,脱不了身;或受到牵连,推脱不了责任。例如:

"不要猫儿抓黏糕,脱不了爪爪。"马义山说,"即使能杀他们几个,也不如杀几个当地人震动大。"(黎汝清《万山红遍》)

7)猫扒甑子——给狗赶了膳。甑子:蒸米饭等的炊具,形似木桶,有屉无底。膳:饭食。比喻奋斗来的成果被别人夺走。例如:

我们闹了几个月风潮,死了一铺缆子人,却为何来?唉!唉!老话讲得好:猫扒甑子,给狗赶了膳了。(李劼人《大波》)

8)猫见了鱼——真想求荤(婚)。荤:猫爱吃的鱼类等荤腥食物,与"婚"同音相谐。指人想求婚。例如:

"呵,你有个妹妹,多大岁数了?"张福全假装惊讶地说,随又故意露出赞叹的神气,"字写得那样好,人一定生得漂亮。"另一张桌上吃饭的李吉明……立即接口嘲弄到:"看你那个样子,猫儿见了鱼,真想求婚哪。"(艾芜《百炼成刚》)

另外还有关于"乌龟"和"猫头鹰"的歇后语,这两种动物在英汉两种语言文化系统中的联想意义也不一样。例如:乌龟遭棒打——缩头缩脑;王八碰桥墩——不敢露头；坟头上的夜猫子——不是好鸟；猫头鹰叫唤——名（鸣）声不好。

尤其是"龙"的含义，在英语中，dragon 是一种长有翅膀、身上长鳞、有爪子的能够喷火没有地位的爬行动物，它常常跟邪恶联系在一起，在西方人心目中是凶恶而丑陋的象征。而在汉语中，"龙"对中国文化有着特殊的意义，是民族文化的一部分。"龙"自古以来就是"神圣、高贵、吉祥"，是我们民族精神的象征。因此，在古代，皇帝被称为"真龙天子"，子孙被称作"龙子龙孙"，还有"龙袍""龙床"等词。我们中国的父母"望子成龙"，但是翻译成英语应说成 to hope that one's son will become an excellent person，并没有出现 dragon 这个词。汉语中的亚洲四小龙到了英语中则成了"four Asian tigers"。关于"龙"的歇后语也有许多，例如：阴沟里的蚯蚓——成不了龙，鲤鱼跳龙门——碰碰时气，把龙袍当蓑衣——白糟蹋，这些象征形象的差异给英文读者的理解造成了很大困难。

（2）颜色。颜色与我们的生活息息相关，人们无时无刻不在与颜色打交道，颜色的文化象征意义由于民族风俗、地理位置、宗教信仰、历史文化背景及审美心理的不同又存在差异。在英汉语言中，表示不同颜色或色彩的词语都很丰富，如红、橙、黄、绿、青、蓝、紫、黑、白等颜色词在很多语言中都是相通的，但由于文化差异，不同国家对色彩词汇的理解也不尽相同。

中国人以红色为贵，逢年过节的喜庆日子要挂大红灯笼，红中国结，贴红对联，红"福"字，放红鞭炮。传统婚礼上新房中要贴红喜字，点红蜡烛，新郎戴大红花，新娘穿红装，画红妆，戴红盖头，不仅给婚礼带来喜庆的气氛，而且希望婚后的日子会越过越红火。在形容人精神极佳，春风得意为"红光满面"，把促成他人美好姻缘的人叫"红娘"，得到上司宠信的人叫"红人"，运气和机遇很好称为"走红"，分到合伙经营利润叫"分红"，逢年过节老人常给小孩发"红包"。所以我们翻译汉语的"红"时要选择喜庆的词。比如：开门红 get off to a good start、满堂红 success in every field。颜色在歇后语中常随日常物品一同出现。

1）红萝卜——红皮白心儿。红萝卜：又称水萝卜，表皮红色，里面白色。比喻表面上伪装革命或进步，实际上思想反动或落后。例如：

"依我看，也不甚难。"他摸着几根稀零零的黄胡子轻蔑地一笑，"这大能人你别看他咋呼得凶，他这种党员儿不过是红萝卜——红皮白心儿。你瞧他这几年闹了个小家业，一听成社就慌了神了。还搂着他的骡子哭哩，说他那'阶级弟兄'要吃他的'肉疙瘩户'！"（魏巍《东方》）

2）红头绳拴豆腐——美得就别提了。红头绳：传说月下老人用来系有情人的绳子。用来拴豆腐，提不起来，故说别提。指得意之神态不必说了。例如：

那个座呀前边的人看电影都往前瞧，后头又没人，凡是专拣那种座号的，不是为看电影，而为相对象，那是"恋爱专座"。一对小青年往那一坐，真是红头绳拴豆腐——美得就别提了。（任飞《买大衣》）

3）红漆马桶送人情——外面红光光，里面黑屎汤。比喻人外表伪装得很好，内心却险恶歹毒。例如：

石刚说："依我说，这个人当民兵不够格。夏乡长说他斗地主积极，我看那是红漆马桶送人情，外面红光光，里面黑屎汤！"（丁令武《风扫残云》）

在西方文化中，红色主要指鲜血和火焰的颜色，常带有"危险""血腥""暴力"和"侵略"等的联想和伴随意义，是一种颜色禁忌。如：①a red battle 血战；②red alert 空袭警报；③a red waste of his youth 他那因放荡而浪费的青春；④red with anger 气得满脸通红；⑤be in the red 负债。

白色（white）在西方象征"纯真""崇高""吉祥""幸福"，"A White day"更是表示"良辰吉日"或"大喜之日"；"They treated us white"表示他们对我们很公正；"He is the white — headed boy of the new generation"表示他是新一代的宠儿。由此可见，"White"所表达的意义在西方文化中是高雅纯洁，积极向上的。因此西方国家至今新人的婚礼一般都在教堂举行，新娘总是身披白色的婚纱，取其圣洁美好之意。在汉民族文化中，白色常象征死亡，凶兆。如"红白喜事"中的"红"指喜事，"白"指丧事。中国人称带给男人厄运的女人为"白虎星"；把智力低下的人称为"白痴"；费力不讨好的叫"白忙""白费""白干"；奸邪、阴险的人称为"白脸"；平民百姓为"白丁""白衣"。

4）白脸狼戴草帽——假充善人。比喻坏人乔装打扮，冒充好人。例如：

红眼进了屋，并没有追问打王凤子的事，而是假惺惺地和爹爹套起了近乎来："大兄弟，腿好点了吧。得想个法子赶紧治一治呀。"玉宝心里骂道："这个黑心肝的东西，是白脸狼戴草帽，假充善人。"（高玉宝《宝玉宝》）

5）城隍老爷戴孝——白袍（跑）。城隍老爷：又称城隍、城隍爷，迷信传说称主管某个城池的神。白：双关，本指白色，专指徒然，白白地。袍：与"跑"同音相谐。指白白地跑了一趟。也泛指白费劲。例如：

和我一样，嘿嘿嘿，不瞒你们说，别看我没有工作，可是在这东半球（东城）都是我的哥儿们，钞票嘛，容易得很！就你们这两头蒜，还让我跟着你们干！嗨嗨，城隍老爷戴孝——白跑（袍）！（王州贵《一个要被逮捕的姑娘》）

6)白了尾巴尖的狐狸——老奸巨猾。例如：

"评委们赞扬你的演讲感情真挚、大方自然，尤其是以自己的亲身体会来反映学生思想上的弊端，真是独出心裁呀!"孔夫子真不愧是白了尾巴尖的狐狸——老奸巨猾，先以大局出发大加赞扬。(二丫头《我的水晶我的梦》)

在英语中,"yellow"还使人联想到背叛耶稣的犹太所穿衣服的颜色,所以黄色带有不好的象征意义。它除了表示低级趣味或以耸人听闻的方式报道新闻的报刊,如 yellow press"黄色报刊"外,还表示胆小、卑怯的意义。如:

I dislike Tom for he is a yellow dog. 我讨厌汤姆,他是个卑鄙小人。

He is too yellow to stand up and fight. 他太胆怯,不敢奋起战斗。

He has a yellow streak in him. 他有点胆小。

然而,中国的黄帝为祖先,华夏文化的发源地为黄土高原,中华民族的摇篮为黄河,炎黄子孙的肤色为黄皮肤,黄色自古以来就和中国传统文化有着不解之缘。汉代的星象学家还把五行学说与占星术的五方观念相结合,认为黄色为土,象征中央;青色为木,象征东方;红色为火,象征南方;白色为金,象征西方;黑色为水,象征北方;又因为黄色位居五行的中央,是中和之色,居于诸色之上,最为贵,定为天子之服色。当时丞相佩有金印紫绶,也就是金黄色的印章和紫色的系印绶带,它是皇帝一人之下,万人之上的最高权力象征,这最初奠定了黄色与紫色在中国传统文化中的重要地位。宋太祖赵匡胤陈桥兵变时,诸将给他披上黄袍,便代表拥立为帝,成为一国之君,可见当时人民对黄色的重视。明清两代,北京成为首府,黄色更成为皇家专用色彩,平民百姓不得以黄色为衣。九五之尊的皇帝,穿黄袍,坐的御车叫黄屋,走的路叫黄道,出巡用黄旗,包扎官印用黄色织物,故黄色引申为权力的象征。只有皇亲国戚才能在红墙黄瓦的建筑中居住,百姓的建筑只能是青砖青瓦。人们常说的"飞黄腾达""黄金时代"都象征着富贵、光荣的意义。

(3)植物。在人类社会发展中,植物与人类关系非常密切。除了植物的实用价值,其独特形态特点和习性唤起了人们无限的美感,使人们产生了种种联想,并借其来表达思想,寄托感情和抒发理想。在中国绚丽多彩的花草树木一直是文人墨客歌咏的对象。汉语中的许多花木也因此具有了极丰富的联想意义和文化内涵。英语国家受西方古典神话和历史文化影响,花木情结悠久而强烈。由于观察角度和侧重点及所处的社会文化背景不一样,汉英民族对同一花木联想到的特征和所引起的情感也不尽相同,这样某种植物在一种文化中具有丰富的联想意义,而在另一种文化中却无任何联想意义,可能仅仅是一个语言符号。

中国的传统花木,松、竹、梅、兰、菊和牡丹等的联想意义最为丰富。松(pine),四季常青,寿命可逾千年,在中国传统文化中,松树可用来比喻志行高洁、不畏强暴、不屈不挠的君子,真可谓"岁寒,然后知松柏之后凋也"。松树千年不凋,人们又用它的顽强的生命力象征长寿,故有"福如东海长流水,寿比南山不老松"之说。

(1)百年松树,五月芭蕉——粗枝大叶。百年的松树,枝干很粗;五月的芭蕉,叶子肥大。本指枝干粗、叶子大,转喻做事不认真细致。例如:

卢长河口问心里:"内中还有些曲折? 看来我的工作,却像俗语说的:百年松树,五月芭蕉——粗枝大叶。"脸上不禁有点发烧。(严亚楚《龙感湖》)

(2)花盆里栽松树——成不了材。例如:

有些警句甚至分不出是来自蒙古族的口传,还是来自作者的独创:"花盆里能栽松树吗? 晃头上能养骏马吗? 箭镞没有纯钢,厶皂够够射透盔甲吗?"似乎是两者的融合。因此在小雁教劳的身上,我们看到了作者的人生体验与蒙古族性格的融合。(周作人《陀螺》)

此外,还有,例如:

毛竹扁担做桅杆——担风险;今年竹子来年笋——无穷无尽;腊月里的梅花——傲霜斗雪;正月里的梅花——阵阵香;九月菊花逢细雨——点点入心等。

上述花草树木的文化联想意义,仅在汉语中存在。

(六)传统习俗的差异与翻译

斯大林曾指出,世界上的任何一个民族,或大或小,都有着区别于其他民族的一些本质特征。传统习俗可以说是其中的一个显著方面。传统习俗是指人们在社会生活中逐渐形成的,从历史沿袭而巩固下来的,具有稳定的社会风俗和行为习俗,并且已同民族情绪和社会心理密切结合,成为人们自觉或不自觉的行为准则。传统习俗的内容是复杂的,存在于一个社会的传统习俗大体上分两部分。一是历史遗留下来的,其源远流长,时代久远,具有社会性、集团性、民族性的特点。不同地区、不同集体、不同民族都具有不同的传统习俗,如不同民族的民风习俗。二是适应现实社会历史条件而产生的,如新中国成立后所倡导的新的生活习俗。

节俗是随着人类社会的进步而逐渐发展完善起来的。传统节俗作为历史的积淀物,其特点在歇后语中得到了鲜明的反映。隐含在节俗中的社会历史的发展轨迹、人类意识的演变轨迹,在歇后语中得到了生动的体现。中国岁时节俗的形成和防范邪祟的需要有密切的关系。而驱邪防范是人类在生产力不发达的条件下，面对大自然无能、恐惧的心理产物，是以原始崇拜为基础的。一般认为中国岁时礼俗萌芽于先秦时期，当时就有春节、上巳、端午、仲秋、冬至等节日。但是那个时候人们过节，并不是娱乐玩耍，而是要在这样的日子里集中搞一些驱邪、防范的活动，所以节日里不是充满喜庆气氛，而是被神秘的原始宗教气氛所笼罩。可见，当时的节日一般是需要禁忌的日子。

例如，除夕春节这个汉族和部分少数民族最重要的岁时节日，其基本是为躲避、防范山魈恶鬼而设置的。早在西周时期就有岁终"逐疫"的习俗了，人们"常以腊除夕饰桃人，垂苇茭、画虎于门，皆追孝于前事，冀以御凶也。"御凶，从另一个角度来说就是为了求福，御凶和求福是一致的。而春节还和原始社会的腊祭有关，"腊，岁终祭众神之名。"（西晋杜预为《左传·僖公五年》中"虞不腊矣"所注）也就是在过去的一年农事结束的时候，通过祭祀感谢众神的恩赐，祈求众神的赐福。随着时间的推延，除夕春节的活动形式有所变化，但是御凶求福的性质没有变，到了宋代，度岁成了年终大事，是夜家家户户都要换门神，挂钟馗，钉桃符，贴春牌，祭祀祖宗等。①

（1）传统节俗在歇后语中的体现。正月十五贴门神——晚了半个月。门神：旧俗除夕或正月初一贴在门上的神像，以为能驱逐鬼怪保平安。指行动迟缓，错过了时机。

例如：待老松田陪同津美联队长，带领四五百名鬼子，坐着土黄色的卡车，风是风，火是火地从保定城里赶来增援时，已是正月十五贴门神——晚了半个月啦。（冯志《敌后武工队》）

这条歇后语涉及中国的传统节日庆典。大年三十或年初一，各地各家都有张贴门神、春联的习俗。古代民间认为，门神是正气和武力的象征，既阻挡、缉拿鬼神，又迎接祥瑞、福祉。最初的门神为桃木所刻人形，挂在大门旁，后来画成门神像张贴于门。最古老的门神是神荼、郁垒兄弟，二人专门统管鬼魅，凡有他们驻守的门户，大小恶鬼、凶煞一概不敢入门为害。唐代以后，多以唐朝猛将秦琼、尉迟敬德二人像为门神，也有画关羽、张飞像为门神的。又有祈福门神，专为祈福而用，中心人物为赐福天官。供奉、张贴者多为商界人物，希望从祈福门神那儿得到功名、利禄、财富。贴门神不仅有上述寓意，而且为春节增添喜庆色彩。一般地，正月十五闹完元宵，便不再有新年意味了。显然，正月十五才贴门神，若非愚蠢之极，便是懵懂之人了。正如亡羊补牢，为时已晚也。

---

① 中国风俗词典[M]．上海：上海辞书出版社，1990：150．

关于岁时节俗的歇后语众多,还有如:过了年的桃符——没用处;大年不换门神——依旧;灶王爷吃糖瓜——稳拿;三十晚上杀母猪——供不了神,又害了一条命;拜年的嘴巴——尽说好话;大年夜的爆竹声——此起彼落;八月节放鞭炮——没人当回事;正月初六卖菖蒲——过时货;七月七日的夜——心(星)连心(星);牛郎会织女——喜相逢;八月十五云遮月——不该兔子露脸;五月龙舟逆水去——人人使劲;逆水赛龙舟——力争上游;五月初四包粽子——扎扎实实;端午节的粽子——一串儿;五月端午吃和菜——老习惯了;八月十五的团圆饼——不给外人;正月十五观灯——眼花缭乱;逆水赛龙舟——力争上游;清明节放风筝——玩上了天;重阳节上山——站得高,看得远;正月十五的高跷——半截不是人;大年初一借袍子——不是时候;清明节的竹笋子——节节高;大年三十吃稀粥——没有过年的架势。

上述歇后语中前一部分所反映的节日文化,为汉民族所特有,如若逐词复制成外语,西方读者多有不甚明白之处,故翻译时重点处理歇后语后一部分信息,择其大意即可。

(2)妇女观在歇后语中的体现。从古至今,世界一般被认为是以男性为主导的社会形态。倘若真的曾经有过母系氏族社会,那么妇女在历史上也曾辉煌过。遗憾的是,有学者考证,所谓普遍的母系社会即女权时代纯属子虚乌有。"至少有一点可以肯定,倍倍尔《妇女与社会主义》一书所依据的巴霍芬'母权论'学说已被现代人类学基本否定了:在更广阔的视野中所观察到的大量材料表明,并不存在一种由母权到父权的史前社会普遍模式"。[①]在文明高度发达的当代,在人们高喊男女平等的今天,妇女从事和男子一样的工作,付出与男子同样多的努力,但是却没有获得和男子等同的机会、等同的权利。从古至今总有些优秀的、有智识的男人为女子鸣冤叫屈,为妇女的彻底解放而呼吁奔走,显示出了一个真正的人的大度胸怀。有意思的是,古代的圣贤们似乎格外重视妇女,对女性的美、女性的德、女性的操行等都有具体的要求,什么妇容、妇德、妇行、妇功、妇戒等一应俱全,但是却没有与之相应的专门的男性之美、男性之德、男性之操行的具体规定。在等级的社会中,人们对女子的看法也是不一样的,大量的涉及妇女的歇后语就集中体现了老百姓的妇女观。

封建传统观念以女性柔弱为美。这种美表现在德行上,就是要柔顺谦恭

---

① 叶舒宪. 诗经的文化阐释[M]. 武汉:湖北人民出版社,1994.

守妇德;表现在姿态上,就是婀娜窈窕雅步纤纤。而其中贯穿着一个因素,就是女人对男人的服从,妇德、妇容等等都以此为据。何为妇德?汉代班昭的《女诫》给予了具体阐释:清闲贞静,守节整齐,行已有耻,动静有法。这显然是男人所要求的妇德。体态的婀娜窈窕当然也是供男人欣赏的。出门走路脚步细碎迟缓,则既是守妇德的表现,同时也是男人眼中的一种美。"佼人僚兮,舒窈纠兮",自《诗经》始,女子纤纤作细步,行走姿态舒缓摇曳,就成了历代文人雅士所欣赏所歌咏的对象。但是这并不合乎普通老百姓的审美观念,受自身经济地位的制约,劳动人民的妇女是弱不起的,弱的特权属于富贵人家的小姐;在老百姓的眼里"弱不禁风"实在不是赞美之词;走路时脚步细碎迟缓而身体故意左右扭动的"扭扭捏捏",也仅是富贵人家小姐的专利。这些都是老百姓所难以欣赏的,因此文人雅士眼中的美,在歇后语中却大有贬义,如:

富贵人家的小姐——弱不禁风;

小姐出门——扭扭捏捏。

这两条歇后语准确地表明了老百姓自己的审美观念。

而女人柔弱美的极点,就是裹小脚。裹小脚可算是中国人的一个发明了。文人雅士只管欣赏、把玩,何等细腻!而歇后语所揭示的则是妇女缠足所受到的苦和罪,一针见血:

小脚女人的脚趾头——受窝囊;

裹脚老太婆的脚趾头——窝囊一辈子;

老太太的脚背骨——屈(曲)了一辈子。

而雅士们所欣赏的小脚之徐行雅步,在老百姓的眼里毫无美感而言,例如:

小脚女人赶路——慢慢吞吞;

小脚婆娘过独木桥——摇摇摆摆。

此外,旧时的婚姻制度也反映了当时妇女的社会地位。例如:

新媳妇坐在花轿里——任人摆布。

花轿:旧时婚礼中新娘乘坐的装饰华丽的轿子。指自己的事情不能由自己做主,要听从别人的支配。例如:

后来还是老太婆想起了董桂花,她是妇女主任,又是亲戚,总会知道些情形。她便叫媳妇来问问,看看究竟怎么样,他们也好有个打算。唉,逢到了这种年头,真是新媳妇儿坐在花轿里,左右都是任人摆布呀!(丁玲《太阳照在桑

千河上》》)

这条歇后语涉及中国封建社会的婚姻制度。在中国古代通行婚姻包办制度,所谓"父母之命,媒妁之言"是宗法社会里一条至关重要的准则。《诗经·齐风·南山》中有一句话:"娶妻如之何? 必告父母"。《孟子》讲:"不待父母之命,媒妁之言,钻穴隙相窥,逾墙相从,则父母国人皆贱之"。也就是说,一男一女,没有父母之命而自由结合,是家庭和社会都不允许的。恩格斯也指出:"古代婚姻都是由父母包办,当事人则安心顺从"。按照《礼记·昏义》的说法,它的目的有两个方面。一个方面指外部关系,叫作"合二姓之好",也就是通过婚姻的纽带将两个宗族连接起来,结成一种亲属同盟。另一个方面指内部关系,叫作"上以事宗庙,下以继后世"。也就是祭祀祖先、延续后嗣,说通俗点就是传宗接代,维系宗法血缘关系。总之,不管婚姻关系的缔结还是解除,都是出于家族、家庭利益的需要,而不是为了当事人个人的幸福;婚姻行为实际上是家族行为而不是个人行为。既然是出于亲属集团的利益需要,是家族行为,自然就要由家长做主,而没有什么婚姻自由可言。因此,这种非自由恋爱的婚姻当事人婚前根本互相不认识就不足为奇了。

(3)日常生活在歇后语中的体现。例如:二更打两点——一点儿不差。

旧时夜间每到一更,巡夜的人要打梆子或敲锣报时。指完全对,没有错。表示肯定或赞同。例如:

王志成给养女改名叫寿姑,她聪明伶俐,十分听话,深得志成夫妇两口儿的喜爱。一来二去,日渐长大。人常说,女大十八变,越变越好看,真是二更打两点,一点儿不差。她长得不高不低,不胖不瘦,柳眉凤眼,脸上有红似白,谁见了谁爱。(李德魁《双婿争媳》)

在古代,人们缺少精确的报时手段,晚上的报时就几乎全靠打更的了。其至很多农村城镇仍保留了打更的习俗。那时候大家晚上少有文化娱乐生活,基本上是日出而作,日落而息。人们听到更夫的打更声,便知道了时间,按惯例该做什么,人们都过着一种按部就班的平静生活。新中国成立后,随着人们物质文化生活水平的提高以及钟表的普及,人们对时间的要求远非打更可以满足了。自然而然的,打更这门古老职业也就逐渐消失了。在著名的《红楼梦》就有这样一段描写"晚上吴贵到家,已死在炕上。外面人人因那媳妇儿不妥当,便都说妖怪爬过墙吸精而死。于是老太太着急得了不得,替另派了好些人将宝玉的住房围住,巡逻打更……"

由此可见,不同的文化观念不可避免地会发生局部的交叉、碰撞和冲突,从而给语言的翻译带来种种障碍和困难,正如翻译家尤金·奈达所指出的:"对于真正成功的翻译而言,熟悉两种文化甚至比掌握两种语言更为重要,因为词语只有在其作用的文化背景中才有意义。"

第三章 等值理论视角下的歇后语翻译

何谓"翻译"？朱自清曾把翻译定义为"是把外国文翻译成本国文"；有些翻译教科书把翻译定义为"运用一种语言把另一种语言所表达的思维内容准确而完整地重新表达出来的语言活动"；也有的将其定义为"一种语言的话语材料用另一种语言的等值话语予以替代"。还有的从文化研究的角度对翻译的概念予以界定，如德国功能学派的学者贾斯塔·霍尔兹·曼塔利用"跨文化合作"(intercultural cooperation)来指翻译；德国学者诺德①用"跨文化交际"(intercultural communication)来替代翻译；杨士章则在他的《略论翻译与文化的关系》一文中指出，从跨文化交流的角度看，原作和译作都是文化产物。因此，翻译不仅是双语的互动性转换，更是一种跨文化交流。而从人类语言学角度看，翻译被视为是以现实体验为背景的认知主体将一种语言映射转述成另一种语言的认知活动，即译者在透彻理解源语言语篇所表达出的各类意义的基础上，尽量将其在目标语言中映射转述出来，在译文中应着力勾画出作者所欲描写的现实世界和认知世界。

在一批批国内外学者就何谓"翻译"进行论述的同时，各种翻译理论和翻译标准也层出不穷。从我国严复提出的"信、达、雅"到美国翻译理论家劳伦斯·韦奴蒂于 1995 年在其《译者的隐身》或《译者的不可见性》(*The Translator s Invisibility*)一书中提出的异化法和归化法以及美国著名的翻译理论家尤金·奈达(Eugene A. Nida)的功能等值翻译理论(The Theory of Functional Equivalence in Translation)等，对翻译从艺术向科学的发展起到了有效的推进作用。

---

① CHRISTIANE N. Text Analysis in Translation [M]. GA：Amsterdam Atlanta，1991.

第一节　当代西方翻译等值理论回顾

翻译的等值(equivalence,有人翻译成对等)作为翻译活动的重要标准,是现代翻译学的核心概念之一。在西方,从18世纪英国文艺理论家泰特勒在其著作《翻译原理简论》中提出"等值原则",到费道罗夫再次关注该理论并于1953年在《翻译理论概要》中提出"作用相符、语言与文本相符"的等值理论,等值理论逐渐受到西方翻译理论家的重视。各理论家也纷纷提出自己对等值的看法,如雅各布森的差异值理论、奈达的动态等值理论等,都大大地发展了等值理论并进而推动了翻译理论的发展。

一、语言学派等值理论代表

语言学派中对等值理论的探讨较有影响的主要是雅各布森和卡特福德。

(一)雅各布森的等值理论

(1)提出"在语际翻译的层面上,一般在符号单元之间没有完全对等"。此处的符号单元实质上就是单词或词组。即在不同的语言之间,字与字、词与词是不可能完全对等的。如英语中"cup"一词在汉语中的对应词是"杯子",但事实上根据《朗文当代高级英语辞典》中的解释,"cup"指"a small round container with a handle, that you use to drink tea, coffee etc."而汉语中的"杯子"一词显然不止包含 cup,还应包含 glass、vessel 等容器。因此,即使是最常用的词也不可能达到完全的对等。但这并不是说这些语言是不可译的,"种种信息可以对外来的符号单元或信息做出充分解释。"即可以用目的语的完整信息来解释源语的信息,以达到意义上的等值。

(2)根据雅各布森的观点,还提出"差异等值"的理论。"意义和对等的问题主要在于语言结构和语言用语中的差异,而不在于强调一种语言能否表述以另一种口头语写成的信息……即跨语言的差异主要集中在一定的语法和词汇形式。"这段话表明,雅各布森承认语言的可译性的同时,还跳出了直译和意译的束缚,提出了差异等值。但是雅氏仅将语言方面的差异集中在一定的语法和词汇形式上,显然是片面的。

(二)卡特福德的等值理论

(1)提出了翻译等值关系的概念。即"当原语文本或文本中的单位与译语文本或文本中的单位对该语境相同(或至少部分相同)的特征相关时,就发生翻译等值关系。"并提出翻译等值关系的两个限度。即:"媒介之间的翻译是不可能的。无论是媒介层次（音位学或字形学）之间还是语法和词汇层次之间的翻译都是不可能的（即不能把原语音位译成译语语法，或把原语词汇译成译语字形等等）"。

（2）对形式对等和文本等值做了重要区分。形式对等是指"任何目的语范畴（单位、类别、结构成分等）在目的语机体中占有的地位，应尽可能与原语范畴在原语中占有的地位相同"。文本等值是指"特定语境中的任何目的语文本或部分文本……成为原文本或部分文本的等值成分。"从中可以看出，形式对应趋向于从宏观的角度去研究原语与目的语的对应关系，而文本等值似乎更注重特定的具体的原语与目的语的等值关系。

由此可以看出，卡氏的理论比雅各布森的理论又深入了一层，他的主要贡献在于翻译转换理论。该理论似乎可以看作是对差异等值的解释和发展。但他仍然只是从语言学的角度去探讨等值，而没有考虑影响语言或翻译的其他因素。

二、交际学派等值理论代表

交际学派也提出等值理论，有三位代表人物：奈达、卡德和科勒。

（一）奈达的等值理论

交际学派提出等值理论的最有影响力的人物是奈达。他提出了回项理论。

（1）上下文等同优先于词汇等同，因为在翻译过程中选择恰当的词汇来翻译原文，主要考虑的是原文上下文之间的关系，其次才是词汇的等同。

（2）动态等值优先于形式等值，因为形式等值关注的是原文所体现的信息与译文所体现的信息本身的形式和内容的对应关系。译者更关注"诗与诗、句与句、概念与概念之间的对应"。但采取形式等值得到的译文仍可能扭曲接受语的语法与文体模式，进而曲解原文信息。于是奈达又提出了动态等值。所谓动态对等是指"译文接收者对译文的反应要基本等同于原文的接收者对原文的反应"。奈达非常重视译文的接收者对译文的反应，认为要评判译文质量的优劣，不仅要看原文与译文在语言形式上是否对等，还要看译文接收者对译文的反应如何，是否与原文接收者对原文的反应基本一致。动态等值的策略对于许多文学文本的翻译产生了深远的影响。然而，正如著名翻译理论家纽马克所指出的那样，语言不仅仅具有交际性，还具有很多其他的功能，因此仅仅强调其交际性显然是片面的。

（3）语言的口头形式优先于书面形式，是因为译文如果能被听懂就肯定能被看懂,因此翻译时要尽量避免使用含义模糊的词、发音容易引起误解的词、书面形式不一定粗俗但发音粗俗的词以及双关语等。

（4）听众及读者通用、接受的形式优先于传统的享有威望的形式。这样可以使读者易于理解和接受。

（二）科勒关于等值的论述

科勒关于等值和对等也做过深入的研究,尤其是在其著作《翻译科学介绍》和《翻译科学研究》中详尽地探讨了等值的概念。

（1）将等值（equivalence）和对等（correspondence）这两个术语做了区分。科勒认为对等属于对比语言学的范畴,而将等值归为翻译科学的范畴,对等的研究范围也显然不如等值的研究范围那么宏观。此外,掌握对等体现的是外语能力,而掌握等值体现的则是翻译的能力。

（2）划分了五种不同类型的等值。外延等值,指的是与一个语篇的语言外部内容等值;内涵等值,指词汇选择,尤其是近义词之间的选择;语篇规约等值,与语篇类型有关;语用等值或交际等值,相当于奈达的动态对等;形式等值,与语篇的形式和美感有关,包括原语文本中的文字游戏和文体特色。科勒划分的这五种等值大大拓宽了等值的范围,并且考虑到了语言外的等值,这对于以前的等值理论来说是一个很大的进步。

三、苏俄翻译的等值理论

（一）费道罗夫的等值理论

"翻译的等值意味着充分传达原文的意思内容并在功能修辞方面与原文完全一致",通过再现原文的形式特点或创造这些特点的功能对应物,来传达原文特有的内容与形式的关系。也就是说,在再现原文形式无法表达原文的内容或内涵时,可以通过改变原文的语言形式来求得整体效果的等值。

费氏认为"牺牲"原文里的一些语言形式或较次要的东西来达到整体的等值,不是一种例外,而是一种规律。等值要求传达原文的内容与形式,并尽可能地在语言手段所及的范围内再现原文形式的特点。然而,一篇译文并非原文的各个部分的机械等值,而是建立在整体的系统的效果等值基础之上的。而被牺牲的东西相比较来说,总是次要的。虽然被牺牲掉了,但并不影响整体翻译的确切性,并且这种牺牲可以使原文中更加重要的东西传达出来。因此,费道罗夫的等值理论也不是局限于形式上的等值,而是一种功能作用上的等值。

(二)拉特舍夫的等值思想

拉特舍夫从哲学角度分析等值关系时指出,世界万物中没有绝对等同的两个事物。无论在生活中,还是理论上,不同的事物却常常被人们当作等同的事物来对待。[①] 事物的个体差异与等值原则并不矛盾,因为当我们说两个事物等值时,并不是指它们本体论上的绝对等同,而是指认识论上的等值,即事物对我们来说,在实践中,在认识它们的过程中是等值的。

(三)巴尔胡达罗夫的等值层次

巴尔胡达罗夫从语义角度把翻译单位划分六个层次:音位层、词素层、词层、词组层、句子层和话语层,他把等值层次同语言的等级层次和翻译单位联系在了一起[②],并且赋予了等值概念具体的内容,认为只有必要和足够层次的翻译才是等值翻译。所谓必要和足够是就传达不变内容并遵循译语规范而言的。他强调了语言对比分析对翻译研究的重要性,对指导翻译实践有深远的影响。在等值的分类方面,尽管他区分了一些翻译等值单位,但是却没有提出具体的手段来防止译者在追求较高层次的意译过程中有可能滑向另一个极端,其结果会过犹不及。此外,巴尔胡达罗夫的等值观是立足于语形,局限于语义,没有对语言功能给予应有的关注。

(四)科米萨罗夫的等值理论

科米萨罗夫区分了释译与翻译的不同。他认为,翻译着重于准确地再现原文,而释译要从译者的主观方面对原文作出解释,从而降低了原文相对于译文的客观性。当译者在译语里找不到对应的词语或无法表达出原语的深层含义时,就要使用释译的策略。因此,从另一层面来说,释译虽然无法实现形式上的等值,却是为了实现整体意义上的、真正的等值。

科米萨罗夫提出了翻译的五项个标准:等值性、文体风格、语言的地道使用、实用功能和惯例。其中,等值一词是从纯语言意义上来考虑的,指的是对应语言单位的含义一致,从语言单位这一层面追求最大程度的等值。这里所提到的等值,不仅包含形式意义上的等值,还包括文体风格、美感、情感等其他功能的等值。但科米萨罗夫接着又指出,等值是有一定限度的,即不能妨碍其他规范性要求的使用。科米萨罗夫的等值理论也已经摆脱了语言学的束缚,扩展到了更为广阔的语言交际的层面上。

科米萨罗夫根据原文与译文意思相同的程度不同把等值划分为五个层

---

① 华莉. 对翻译等值理论的再思考[J]. 四川外语学院学报,2000(10):77.

② 蔡毅,段京华. 苏联翻译理论[M].武汉:湖北教育出版社,2000.

次：①交际目的等值；②情景等值；③情景描述方法等值；④句法结构意义等值；⑤文字符号等值。他强调，交际目的等值是等值关系成立的必要条件，在这五个层次中，等值范围从①到⑤，一层大于一层，即后者的等值关系既包括又大于前者的等值关系。如后者不包括前者或不完全包括前者，后者的等值关系就不成立。科氏把等值理论看成一个单向的立体结构，这是等值理论中的一大突破，也是现代等值理论研究中较为理想的模式。

综上所述，不同的译学家，在不同时期对翻译性质进行的全面研究，从不同角度阐述了对等值的观点和看法，每一种译论都大大丰富发展了等值理论并推动了翻译理论的发展，对翻译实践有较好的指导作用。通过对比研究，笔者更为推崇什维策尔的翻译等值模式，现试分析其等值模式与其他等值理论的异同及其意义和影响。

第二节 什维策尔的翻译等值模式

一、什维策尔翻译等值模式的精髓

苏联翻译理论中等值思想发展成熟时期的一位代表人物是什维策尔，他在 1988 年出版的《翻译理论：地位、问题、面面观》中，从符号学的角度，通过分析不变量问题，建立起等值的模式，并严格区分了"等值"与"对等"两个概念。什维策尔的等值模式可通过表 3-1 来表示（其中"＋"表示保留，"－"表示不保留）：①

表 3-1 什维策尔的等值模式表

等值层面		不变量的类型			
句法等值		句法	语义	所指	语用
		＋	＋	＋	＋
语义等值	成分等值	－	＋	＋	＋
	所指等值	－	－	＋	＋
语用等值		－	－	－	＋

表 3-1 说明，作者借鉴符号学研究的三方面：句法（符号与符号的关系）、

---

① 杨仕章. 苏俄翻译理论中等值思想的演变[J]. 中国俄语教学，2001(2)：50.

语义(符号与所指的关系)和语用(符号与人的关系),将等值划作三个层面:句法等值,语义等值和语用等值。

句法层面的等值是形式的替代,是言内的等值。该层面上的翻译是用一种符号(语言单位)替代另一种符号并保持句法关系不变。

语义层面的等值是指意义的等值,它包含两个层面:成分等值和所指等值。成分层次保留原文中的语义成分义素,采用不同的形式结构手段,主要是使用语法转化法。所指层次指的是保留原文话语的所指意,即使用与原文不同的语义符号组成语义等值的话语,这里要进行复杂的词汇语法转换,既涉及语法方面,也涉及词汇语义方面。

语用等值是最高层次,该层次包含一些重要的交际因素,如交际意图,交际效果,收信人的接受能力,并制约其他所有层次,居于其他各等值层面之上。[①]

在论述不同层面的等值的基础上,什维策尔阐明了"等值"与"对等"的关系。"等值"指原文与译文之间的关系,是针对翻译的结果而言;"对等"针对的则是翻译的过程。这两个范畴都具有标准评判的性质。然而,"等值"要回答的问题是:译文是与原文相符;而"对等"要回答的问题是:翻译作为一个过程是否符合一定的交际情景。"等值"的概念与"不变量"的概念紧密相关。完全等值是指完全表达原文的"交际功能不变量",这是对翻译的最高要求。"对等"对翻译的要求是如何翻译才最为合适,翻译对等的标准是:偏离等值的做法是客观必需的,而不是译者的个人意愿。完全等值的翻译并非一定就是对等的翻译,反过来,对等的翻译也并非总是建立在原文和译文完全等值的基础上。"对等"是一个相对的概念,某一翻译流派认为是对等的翻译,在别的流派看来也许就不是对等的。[②]

二、什维策尔的翻译等值模式与其他翻译理论家等值思想的比较

什维策尔的等值模式不仅包含语形和语义等值,还强调了语用等值。在这三类等值层面中,每一类较低层面的等值以较高层面的等值为前提,如句法等值的前提是语义等值和语用等值,成分等值以所指等值和语用等值为前提,而所指等值的前提是语用等值。何自然[③]曾列举了一个流行的标语:"高高兴

①　蔡毅,段京华.苏联翻译理论[M].武汉:湖北教育出版社,2000:30-33.

②　杨仕章.苏俄翻译理论中等值思想的演变[J].中国俄语教学,2001(2):51.

③　何自然.语用学与英语学习[M].上海:上海外语教育出版社,1997:87.

兴上班去,平平安安回家来"。如果我们遵照巴尔胡达罗夫划分的翻译单位进行必要和足够层次的翻译,得到的翻译应是,"Go to work happily and come back safely",可是如果这样翻译的话,是无法向译语读者传达其恰当的交际意图的。而什维策尔的语用等值是研究语言同使用者之间的关系,是如何理解语言在实际话语中的意义。如果这块标语贴在汽车上,则是提醒司机一路小心驾驶,平安回家,一句 Drive carefully! 或 Safety first in driving,甚至 Good luck! 都可以表达其中的意图和愿望。这个标语如果挂在建筑工地上,则是要求建筑工人安全操作:Safety first in working。如果这个标语贴在工厂、企业及其他事业单位,则是希望职工们工作时积极乐观,休息时轻松愉快,即:Go to work happily and return home safely 或 Be enthusiastic in working and enjoy yourself after working,等等。同样的词和句,由于语言使用场合不同,交际的对象不同,所表达的意义不同,使用的翻译方法不同,取得的语用效果也不同。

可见,什维策尔将"等值"看作是一个规范性的概念,选择何种层面的等值,由具体情景的语言因素与非语言因素的组成特点决定。违反上述等值层面的等级关系会破坏翻译标准,导致"死译"和"乱译"。什维策尔不仅重视语用等值,还为我们提出了规范性手段防止"死译"与"乱译"。应该说,是巴尔胡达罗夫等值层次的一大补充和完善。

奈达为了突破仅仅从语义角度看待等值问题的局限性,提出了同"形式等值"相对立的"功能等值"概念。[①] 他把功能等值定义为:"翻译质量,即用接受语传达原文思想内容,使译文接受者的反应与原文接受者的反应基本相同。"然而,由于难以制定衡量、对比两种反应的客观标准,所以译者操作的依据往往是根据自己的主观预测,这就使翻译评价难免流于主观性和经验性。

与此相比,什维策尔的等值模式则具有较强的可操作性。虽然奈达承认翻译只能达到"实际上的交际等值",并提出不同层次的翻译对等,但是他并没有划分具体的等值层次,使我们在实践中缺乏规范性的操作依据。现以萨克雷《名利场》中一段话的翻译为例说明这个问题:

"The girls were up at four this morning, packing her trunks, sister," replied Miss Jemina, "We have made her a *bow-pot*."

"Say bouquet, sister Jemina, tis more genteel."

---

① NIDA E A. From One Language to Another:Functional Equivalence in Bible Translating [M]. Chicago:Thomas Nelson Publishers, 1986:36.

"Well，a booky as big almost as a hay-stack，…"

如果译文以奈达的功能等值为标准，译者脑子里想着原文读者的反应是什么，该怎么翻译才能使译文读者产生相同的反应，这是一个很难把握的问题。对此，奈达并未给我们一个可操作的依据。

而什维策尔认为等值是个规范性概念，也就是从译者角度出发，翻译应该和如何达到预定目标。等值不是描写性概念，不能采取过于宽容的态度。他划分的等值层次的类型就反映了对翻译的规范性要求，为我们提供了一个可操作的模式。

这句话里 bow-pot，bouquet 和 booky 的指称意义都是指一束花，其言内意义是词汇上的变化，而语用意义十分丰富，讽刺了两个说话人通过话语表现出的个性特征：Jemina 文化程度的低下、粗鄙，她姐姐的咬文嚼字、自命不凡。杨必的译文是这样的：

"女孩子们清晨四点钟就起来帮她理箱子了，姐姐。我们还给她扎了一捆花儿。"

"妹妹，用字文雅点儿，说一束花。"

"好的。这一簇花儿大得像个草堆儿，……"

"捆""束""簇"三个相应的汉语表达形式无论从指称（语义等值）、言内（句法等值）还是语用意义（语用等值）来看，都恰当地表达了原语的意义。因此，堪称什维策尔的等值翻译。

科米萨罗夫与什维策尔从不同的角度研究等值的问题，但其结果大体是一致的。科氏的交际目的等值和什氏的语用等值，科氏的情景等值、情景描述方法等值和什氏的语义所指等值、语义成分等值，科氏的句法结构意义等值、文字符号等值和什氏的句法等值，它们的基本内容具有很大的相似性。但科氏划分的句法结构意义等值和文字符号等值在语言结构差异大的双语转换中是难以达到的，例如汉语与印欧语间的对译就是如此。

什维策尔利用符号学中的三种符号意义，来划分意义的等值层面，它们强调的是三者关系的转换，对原语和译语进行语际和语用的调整，力争两者最大限度地达到交际功能等值。下面举例说明：

韩老六立刻嬉皮笑脸地说道："有十来多个。"（周立波《暴风骤雨》）

句中"嬉皮笑脸"，从句法等值来看，即言内意义上是汉语成语，含有贬义，语用意义上体现了韩老六的嘴脸。译成英语是："More than a dozen."answered the landlord with a snigger."译文中对于言内意义即它是个成语做了个舍弃，也就是不保留句法层面等值，而是较好地传达了指称和语用意义，感情色彩正确,也就是保留语义层面等值和语用层面等值。

通过什维策尔和其他翻译理论家等值思想的比较,不难看出,什维策尔的等值思想比较成熟,无论是等值术语的界定,等值类型的分化程度,还是等值层面的等级次序,其都有较深入的研究,并且这些研究成果具有较强的可操作性,对翻译实践与译作评价都有着理论指导与实用意义。

第三节 等值翻译理论的制约因素

一、语境因素

在等值翻译中语境是制约其有效与否的重要因素。波兰籍人类语言学者马斯诺夫斯基①提出了"语境"(context)这个术语,并把语境分为文化语境(context of culture)和情境语境(context of situation)。按照马斯诺夫斯基的看法,基本的语义单位不是单词或单句,而是处在一些语言表达式的上下文中的句子,句子的意义体现为它在一个更大的意义整体中的功能。20世纪90年代以来,奈达博士又从词语的多义性入手,考察了语境限制与语义选择的关系,强调了根据上下文的信息提示获得正确的语义解读。当然,从语义学的角度看,一个词在语境中的语义是该形式对整体意义最少的部分,因为任何一种符号系统都把语境的作用看得最大,把个别项目的作用看得最少。② 由此可见,语境直接影响着译者对句子、篇章的解读,而译者对译文的正确解读是达到等值翻译的关键。譬如,从许渊冲③所翻译的唐代诗人柳宗元《江雪》一诗的英译作中就能看出译者对于语境的理解在等值翻译中所起到的重要作用。

From hill to hill no bird in flight. (千山鸟飞绝)

From path to path no man in sight. (万径人踪灭)

A lonely fisherman afloat. (孤舟蓑笠翁)

Is fishing snow in lonely boat. (独钓寒江雪)—— Fishing in Snow(江雪)

Liu Zongyuan(柳宗元)

译文的前两句采用了动词的静化处理,即通过介词短语"in flight"和"in

---

① 杜诗春,宁春岩.语言学方法论[M] 北京:外语教学与研究出版社,1997.

② 杨永林.社会语言学研究[M] 北京:高等教育出版社,2004.

③ 许渊冲.中国古诗精品三百首[M] 北京:北京大学出版社,2004

sight"达到了静中有动。原诗中一般化的动态"山上的鸟飞"和"路上的人踪"通过"灭"和"绝"一下子变成了极端的寂静、绝对的沉默，形成了一种空旷和幽僻的意境。此处译者通过这种静化处理达到了与原诗所产生的同样的效果。在处理"千山"和"万径"两个词语时采用了介词短语"from... to..."的形式使诗的背景更加寥廓，几乎到了浩瀚无边的程度。同时选择了具有相同韵脚的"flight"和"sight"，体现了诗的风格。诗的后两句译者采用了现在进行时"is fishing"突出了静中有动的生气，这与原作者的本意不谋而合。同样，译者在两句的句尾选用韵脚相同的"afloat"和"boat"，使译文与原文保持了形式上的对等和一致，传神达意。由于译者把握了原诗的精髓，正确解读了原诗的具体情境语境，把诗中作者那种摆脱世俗、超然物外的清高孤傲的思想感情淋漓尽致地表达出来，达到了形式、意义和风格上的对等，使译入语读者对译文的反应与原文读者对原文的反应基本一致，感受收到同样的效果。再如，尤金·奈达对《桃花源记》的英译作中个别部分进行了修改，其目的是追求译作和原作在情境语境上的一致。原文中"芳草鲜美，落英缤纷"被翻译成"The sweet-smelling dass was fresh and beautiful, and the fallen blossoms scattered in confusion"，奈达在评议这句翻译时把后半句改成"and the fallen blossoms blanketing（carpeting）the ground"，真切地传达了原文中桃花繁多，散落满地的美妙图景。而"scattered in confusion"给读者留下的是一种桃花凋零散落在地的凄楚感觉，不能表达文中的美好意境。

可见，译者对语境的正确解读是使译文与原文在意义、形式和风格上保持一致的关键。

二、思维差异

不同社会文化背景下的人会有不同的思维方式和习惯，在寻求英汉文化翻译等值时，必定会涉及两种文化迥异的思维模式，且思维模式的差异是文化深层次的差异。这种差异在英汉翻译过程中会成为译者的阻碍，使其不能准确而简洁地表达源语言的真正含义。西方人的思维是直线式的，继承的是柏拉图-亚里士多德顺序。在遣词造句谋篇上遵循从一般（general）到具体（specific），从概括（summarize）到举例（exemplify），从整体（whole）到个体（respective）的演绎推理原则。而中国人侧重于直观及意象思维，对事物进行归纳推理，这种思维方式的不同直接体现在英汉语言表达上。例如：

Soccer is a difficult sport. A player must be able to run steadily without rest. Sometimes a player must hit the ball with his or her head. Players must be willing to bang into and be banged into by others. They must put up with aching feet and sore muscles.

这则短文的主题句是第一句,即先概括。后面四句是用来说明主题句的,即举例说明。因此在翻译成汉语时,为了达到等值翻译,使译语读者听起来或读起来达到与源语同等的效果,译文就应该先分后总,先说原因后说结果。

译文如下:

足球运动员必须能不停地奔跑,有时得用头顶球,撞别人或被别人撞,必须忍受双脚和肌肉的疼痛。所以说足球运动是一项难度大的运动。

通常,中西方的思维角度和习惯的不同直接体现在一些词组的表达方式上。如"spy film"为"谍战片",而不是"间谍影片";"wet paint"为"油漆未干",而不是"湿油漆";"life sentence"为"无期徒刑",而不是"活期徒刑";"stop watch"为"跑表",而不是"停表"等。因此,在翻译类似词组或句子时就要求译者排除源语言思维差异的干扰,唯有如此才能取得翻译中的最大等值。

三、英(俄)汉文化差异

语言是文化的载体,具有明显的文化特征。同时语言又是人们表达思想、交流感情的工具,所以世界各族人民所使用的语言之间的共性是广泛存在的,这是两种语言相互间进行翻译的基础。然而,由于英汉语言生长的环境包括在地理、宗教信仰、生活方式、历史传统,以及审美价值等方面的差异,反映在语言表达方式上往往呈现出较大的文化差异性。因此,在英(俄)汉互译过程中,译者应该正确理解原文的文化内涵,分析源语和译语的文化差异,并在翻译过程中采用各种手段,将文化因素带来的各种信息准确有效地加以传递,尽可能做到翻译的等值。通常,两种语言文化之间的差异越大,其等值转换就越难,等值程度就越受到影响。正如纽马克①所说:"一个文本的文化色彩(地方色彩)越浓,时空距离越远,等效就越不可思议。"因此,文化差异是影响等值翻译程度的又一重要因素。例如,中西方宗教信仰上的差异导致其在语言运用中有着各自的特点。西方文化里,特别是英国和其他英语国家,人们信奉基督教,《圣经》是其神论观念经典。因此,在英语中,经常出现"God""hell""devil""heaven"等字样。如 God helps those who help themselves. (自助者,天助也。)在翻译中,译者既要了解西方文化的内涵,又要对译入语文化有深刻的理

---

① NEWMARK P. A Textbook of Translation [M]. 上海:上海外语出版社,2001.

解。把"God"不翻译成"上帝"，而是翻译成"天"或"老天"，符合中国人的思维习惯。再如，汉语俗语"谋事在人，成事在天"（Man proposes，God/heaven disposes.）当翻译成英语时"成事在天"的"天"便还原为"God"或"Heaven"，这样使译入语读者产生了更为贴切的联想，达到了读者感受和客观效果上的对等与一致。

镇上的居民们习惯了他之后，倒是觉得他"长了副凶神相，有一颗菩萨心。"（古华《芙蓉镇》）

Когда сельчане узнали его получше, они поняли, что у него лицо демона, но сердце бодисатвы, который добровольно возвращается из нирваны в этот мир, чтобыспасать других людей.（перевод В. Семанова《 В долине лотосов》）

由于俄罗斯人不懂何为"菩萨"，故译者处理成"涅槃来到尘世的菩萨"。又如，在英（俄）汉两种文化中，由于词的内涵不同，其比喻与联想意义也各不相同，把"as stubborn as mule"，"упрям，как осел"译成"倔得像头牛"是等值翻译，若译成"倔得像头骡子"就会造成文化误读现象，不能传达原文的喻义，达不到语用等值标准，其原因是英汉不同文化造成词义的差异，制约着等值翻译。

四、译者本身

与任何一种语言行为一样，翻译也离不开人类活动，其作品翻译的好坏在很大程度上取决于译者。可以说，译者是原文和译文之间的桥梁。每个译者都是独立的个体，他的自身兴趣、爱好、优势、语言能力和语言外经历都影响着其翻译结果。译者除了至少要通晓两种语言之外，还必须熟谙两种文化，这样才能意会"弦外之音"，才能够领会源语文本中有意含蓄的内容，并把它们恰如其分地在译文中表达出来。因此，译者自身水平的高低，包括译者的双语掌握程度、对两种文化的认识深度和敏感度、对各种领域知识的通晓程度，以及写作能力等都会影响翻译的等值效果。通常，译者解决问题的能力越强、综合素质越高，获得等值的可能性就越大，等值程度也就越高。"须知译本的优劣，关键在于译者，在于译者的译才，在于译者的译才是否得到充分施展。重在传神，则要求译者能入乎其内，出乎其外，神明英发，达意尽蕴……大凡一部成功的译作,往往是翻译家翻译才能得到辉煌发挥的结果"。①

综上所述,译者的综合素质和能力是实现原文与译文等值的关键。译者只有不断提高自身各方面的综合素质,充分拓展自己的潜能,才能在翻译中做到游刃有余,尽显原文的风采。

第四节　翻译质量评估

翻译实践中存在各式各样的翻译。这里有好的翻译,有基本上过得去的翻译,也有糟糕的翻译,这就涉及译文的质量问题。如何评判一篇译文的质量?显然,用前人提出的抽象翻译标准是无法进行译文质量评估的,如清末学者马建忠关于"善译"的标准——译成之文适如其所译而止,英国学者泰特勒的翻译三原则等等,都太过抽象,不宜作为评判标准。翻译质量评估必须建立自己的评判标准和模式。翻译质量评估的核心是翻译观和翻译质量观。翻译本质的认识和翻译质量标准的厘定决定翻译质量评估的结果。

翻译批评及翻译质量评估研究对于翻译学的发展具有重大的理论和实践意义,在国际翻译批评界两位女学者莱斯和豪斯的研究成果极具价值和影响力。翻译质量评估领域的研究核心是如何对译文质量进行科学而客观地评估,学界探索译文评估标准和模式建构的努力皆源于此。此外翻译批评与翻译质量评估的概念区分、定量与定性研究相结合等也是值得学界讨论的地方。

一、当代西方翻译质量评估模式的进展

西方主观化的翻译批评模式向客观化的翻译质量评估模式的转型发生在20世纪70年代。威尔斯②认为,转型的主要推动者包括:瑞斯,克莱格勒,波波维,豪斯,柯勒。现在看一看二十年来西方翻译质量评估模式的进展。关于西方翻译质量评估模式的流派,克莱格勒曾将其分为四大流派:①心灵主义流派;②反应主义流派,又分为行为主义流派和功能主义流派;③语篇主义流派,又分为描述翻译学流派、后现代和解构主义流派、语言学流派;④功能-语用主义流派。笔者认为,豪斯的这种分法并没有考虑到翻译批评和翻译质量评估

---

① 罗新璋. 翻译新论中外翻译观似与等[M] 武汉:湖北教育出版社,1996.

② WILSS W. The Science of Translation:Problems and Methods[M]. Shanghai:Shanghai Foreign Language Education Press:217.

的差别。威拉姆斯认为,所有的翻译质量评估模型,无论是已被应用的还是未被应用的,都有一个共同特征,即它们的核心理念都是错误分类。这种分类的理念又有两个标准:一是它们是否采用量化的方法;二是它们是标准参照模式(standard-referenced)还是准则参照模式(criterion-referenced)。在此基础上,威拉姆斯将所有的翻译质量评估模式分为了两大类:量化模式与非量化模式。总体上来讲,Williams的分类方式更符合翻译质量评估模式的应用性特征,因而更合理,但完全依量化与否来分类,似过度突出了翻译质量评估中量化的作用,因此不如按第二个标准,即依据其参照模式进行划分。此外,威拉姆斯将非常相近的两个概念"标准(standard)"和"准则(criterion)"相对应,易产生混淆,不如改为"原则"和"参数",这也比较接近翻译质量评估模式中的常用术语。按这样的分法,下文认为西方当代真正意义上的翻译质量评估模式主要有两大类:原则参照模式与参数参照模式。

(一)原则参照模式

这类翻译质量评估模式的特点是:只在翻译质量评估的宏观层面上制定纲领性的原则作为译文评价的标准,没有具体的评估指标。在一定意义上来说,这种原则参照模式以定性研究为主要特点。当代西方的翻译质量评估原则参照模式又可分为:反应原则参照模式、语篇类型原则参照模式和功能原则参照模式。

妮达提出了最佳译文的三项原则:交际过程的整体效率、意图的理解和反应的对等。心理学家卡罗尔提出了更广泛意义上的翻译质量评估原则:可读性和信息性。对于上述反应原则参照模式,豪斯①认为其有三个缺点:①忽视了人脑的认知过程;②犯了归结主义的错误;③没能提供具体的行为判断所依赖的规范。此后,瑞斯在Btihler的三种语言功能划分的基础上提出了语篇类型原则。而 Hans G. Honig 认为瑞斯迈出的这一步,虽然很小,但意义重大,这表明瑞斯跳出了对比分析中的词汇和句法层,进入了语篇层。瑞斯认为翻译中最重要的不变量是语篇类型。瑞斯将语篇类型分为:重内容的文本、重形式的文本和重感染力的文本。瑞斯的语篇类型是建立在支配或等级概念基础上的,例如广告文本可能既有形式手段又有感染手段,此时就看谁占据支配地位。在此意义上,翻译质量评估就是语篇类型的对应评估,也就是语篇类型原

---

① HOUSE J. Quality of translation[C]//Baker. M. Routledge Encyclopedia of Translation Studies[M]. Shanghai：Shanghai Foreign Language Education Press,1998.

则参照模式。反应原则参照模式与语篇类型原则参照模式之后,翻译质量评估可以说进入了功能原则参照模式的时代,这一模式由豪斯,妮达,Honig 和 Brunette 等进行了充分发展。豪斯在 Halliday 的系统——功能语言学基础上提出了功能原则参照模式。1997 年,豪斯又依据言语行为理论、语篇分析和语用学的知识对自己的模式进行了修订。新的模式认为,翻译质量评估应在三个层次上进行:语言/语篇;语域;体裁。豪斯评估的核心概念是功能对等。豪斯[①]认为,描述原文与译文间最合适的对等类型就是功能——语用对等。妮达认为,根据译文的功能和翻译发起人的指示,译者可以决定是保留原文所有的语义和形式特征还是对原文进行大面积的改动,所以评估人必须以译文的目的作为翻译质量评估的出发点。诺德还认为,错误分析是不够的,整个语篇的功能和效果才是翻译质量评估中最关键的因素。功能原则参照模式的另一位重要代表人物是 Hans G. Hong。Hans G. Honig 认为在翻译质量评估中不存在共同的标准,翻译质量评估应根据具体的评估情形而定,翻译质量评估分为治疗性(therapeutic)与诊断性(diagnostic)两种模式。治疗性模式关注翻译能力,寻找错误原因,是非功能性的,而诊断性模式则主要关注译文的使用者及使用者的预期反应,是功能性的。Hans G. Honig 共分出了六种翻译评估情形:语言习得;翻译课程;译员测试;质量控制;译文使用者;译文批评者。语言习得情形应用治疗性模式;译员测试与质量控制情形应用诊断性模式;译文使用者与译文批评者既应用治疗性模式也应用诊断性模式,但以诊断性模式为主;翻译课程既应用治疗性模式也应用诊断性模式,但以治疗性模式为主。但随后,安德玛和罗杰斯[②]就批评 Hans G. Honig 的治疗性与诊断性两种模式的分类法令人困惑。在医学上,这两个概念存在时间上的先后关系,必须诊断在前,治疗在后,诊断是治疗的前提,但 Honig 在翻译评估中将它们列为具有不同焦点的两种备选方式,这就歪曲了这两个概念的本意;并且安德玛和罗杰斯从翻译教学的角度指出功能原则参照模式虽适合于职业翻译情形,但不适合译员培训情形。纽马克坚持认为翻译评估应以语言为主,

---

① House J. Translation quality assessment: Linguistic description versus social evaluation[J]. Meta. XLVI,2001:243 - 257.

② ANDERMAN G,MARGARET R. What is that translation for? A functionalist view of translation assessment from a pedagogical perspective: A response to Hans G. Honig[C]//Schaffer:57.

对 Hans G. Honig 进行了尖锐的批评。在此基础上,Brunette(2000)区分了五种翻译评估方法:形成性修正(didactic revision);翻译质量评估(TQA);质量控制;语用修正;二度审视(fresh look)。所有这些概念的提出,有助于建立更为科学、客观的翻译质量评估模式。

(二)参数参照模式

　　参数参照模式就是评估人根据自己的判断预先设计出一组自己认为最相关的参数,赋予各个参数一定的权重,然后以参数为参照将原文与译文进行对比,最后对译文作出评价或定级。翻译质量评估中的定量研究主要体现在参数参照模式中。

　　威尔斯曾提出过一个粗略的参数参照模式(见表3-2)。

表3-2　参数参照模式评估表

项　目	错　误	不恰当	不确定	正　确	恰　当
句法					
语义					
语用					

　　随后,本索桑和罗森豪斯在赛尔,哈利迪,哈桑,威多森和范代克的理论基础上提出了自己的翻译质量评估模式。这种模式将错误分为两大类:一是宏观层面上的误译(框架,图式);二是话语(命题内容,交际功能)和词(词或短语,词性或动词时态,代词一致性,可接受性和语域)微观层面上的误译。2000年,有学者在综合了纽马克,哈特姆和艾姆森,施泰纳和豪斯所提出的参数的基础上,提出了一个折衷模型,包含七个参数:①语篇类型;②形式对应;③主位结构的连贯;④衔接;⑤语篇——语用对等;⑥词汇性质(语域);⑦语法/句法对等。2004年,威拉姆斯以语篇为基础提出了一种全新的翻译质量评估模式——论辩理论模式。威拉姆斯认为文本的论辩图式(Argument Schema)应是 TQA 的最佳准则,翻译质量应主要取决于译文是否准确地反映了原文的论辩图式,如果在论辩图式层面上没有错误,译文文本就满足了最低质量标准。图尔明等指出所有的语篇都有相同的论辩图式。所有语篇这种上位特征正符合了 TQA 要适应各种语篇的普遍性诉求,所以论辩理论是 TQA 理想的理论依据。威拉姆斯的 TQA 评估模式中包括两大类参数:核心参数与实地/具体使用参数如下(见表3-3)。

表3-3　TQA 评估模式表

参　数		翻译质量评估
核心参数	论辩图式	
	组构关系	
	命题功能/连接词/推理指示词	
	论辩类型	
	辞格	
	叙事策略	
实地/具体使用参数		

此 TQA 模型的优点是,它涵盖了整个语篇的所有成分:宏观成分、微观成分及宏观成分与微观成分间的相互关系,充分考虑了评估的各个方面,因此也就达到了 TQA 模型的效度要求。同时,其还考虑到了具体使用因素,即翻译评估的主体性特点。但是,威拉姆斯的论辩理论模式体系比较庞大,参数概念也都比较抽象。

此外,许多机构制订的翻译质量评估模式都是参数参照型的,如加拿大翻译局研发的"加拿大语言质量测评体系",简称 SIAL;加拿大的"翻译协会体系",简称 CTIC;2000 年由美国工程协会研发的"J2450 翻译质量标准"。

二、当代中国翻译质量评估模式的进展

国内在翻译批评理论、翻译批评标准等方面的研究成果丰硕,相关的文章和专著相继发表。翻译质量评估领域的研究,虽然是翻译批评中的重要部分,但研究的深度和广度以及与其他学科的交叉研究都有待进一步深化。

(一)翻译批评与翻译质量评估界定

翻译批评与翻译质量评估通常被学界换用,或被看作是相似的概念,不加区分。也很少有人愿意花力气去弄清楚两者的区别与联系,迄今为止,译界尚未准确界定翻译评估与翻译批评。尽管两者之间的界限确实比较模糊,但为了避免混乱,我们有必要也应该能够把两个概念进行区别。在翻译质量评估研究中,两个概念的区分意义重大。国内的不少学者在这方面做出了努力,如司显柱、杨晓荣、武光军及温秀颖等。

杨晓荣给出的比较完整的翻译批评定义是:"依照一定的翻译标准,采用

某种论证方法,对一部译作进行分析、评论、评价,或通过比较一部作品的不同译本对翻译中的某种现象作出评论。"①纽马克指出:"翻译批评是翻译理论与实践之间联系的必要环节。"②根据他对于翻译批评的详细阐述,翻译质量评估只是翻译批评中的一个部分。

司显柱认为,翻译批评和翻译质量评估两个概念是从属关系,即"翻译批评是'种',翻译评估是'属',换用语言学的说法,翻译批评是上义词……翻译质量评估是下义词。"③对此,武光军持有同样的看法:翻译批评包括文本批评、翻译批评理论和对翻译理论的评述等,翻译质量评估指对译文质量的价值判断,包括从文本本身的角度和文本外的因素出发考察语篇的语言特征和翻译质量。我们可以看出,司教授借用逻辑学关于概念的"属""种"论述明确而清晰地向我们呈现了翻译批评和翻译质量评估这两个看似模糊的概念。

(二)国内翻译质量评估研究

相比西方的研究成果,国内在翻译质量评估领域的研究还很有限。在中国期刊网上搜索到的刊发在核心期刊上以"翻译质量评估"或"译文评介"为主题的论文三十篇左右,可以对这些文章进行以下分类:国外翻译质量评估理论引介;翻译质量评估评估模式建构;译文评介量化研究;口译翻译质量研究等。其中司显柱教授的研究成果最为丰硕,也更具启发意义。国内在该领域的研究评述如下:

(1)译文评价标准的过于抽象化与过于量化。关于译文评价的研究古来有之,中国的学者提出了很多有益的译文评价的标准。影响最深远的要数严复的"信、达、雅",此外还有傅雷和钱钟书倡导的"重神似不重形似""化境"等传统翻译评估标准;李运兴提出多元系统翻译标准,吕俊据哈贝马斯的普遍语用学理论提出后现代文化语境中的翻译标准等。正如王宏印所说,"这些标准评价项目太少或覆盖面不宽,不宜操作更不易量化"。④李晓敏、杨自俭也认为"以上诸标准皆过于抽象概括,具有多解性,可操作性不强……"⑤

---

①　杨晓荣. 翻译批评导论[M]. 北京:中国对外翻译出版公司,2005.:3.

②　PETER N. A Textbook of Translation [M]. Shanghai:Shanghai Foreign Language Education Press,2001:184.

③　司显柱. 论功能语言学视角的翻译质量评估模式研究[J]. 外语教学,2004(4):45－50.

④　王宏印. 参古定法,望今制奇:探寻文学翻译批评的评判标准[J]. 天津外国语学院学报,2002(3):35－38.

⑤　李晓敏,杨自俭. 译文评价标准新探索[J]. 上海科技翻译,2003(3):17－20.

另一类译文评价标准过于量化,如范守义借助模糊数学的隶属度概念对译文质量进行量化分析,对译文质量评估的客观化进行了探索;徐盛桓提出分四个等级的数学模型,以句子为单位进行评价;吴新祥把语言按静态等级和动态层次纵横切分成十五个平面,立体地研究原作与译作的等值关系,通过衡量跟原作相比其等值量的大小来对译文质量的高低进行量化分析;穆雷用模糊数学评价译文的质量。量化标准固然使译文评价具有客观性和科学性,但是正如李晓敏、杨自俭指出的"实际操作起来,工作量太大"。

(2)司显柱翻译质量评估模式述评。目前,译界尝试从新的角度研究翻译质量评估,并建构译文评估模式,司显柱教授独树一帜。正如黄国文教授所言:司显柱"从功能语言学角度研究翻译问题,这是一种有益的尝试;它所带来的启示是很多人原先预想不到的"。

2004 年以来,他已经在《中国翻译》等国内著名期刊上连续发表了十多篇相关的学术论文。司教授于 2004 年开始从功能语言学的视角论述翻译问题,首先论述了言语交际的交际本质、语篇属性与翻译,接着论述了翻译研究的系统功能语言学模式,其研究内容、研究目标和秉持的研究思路与采取的方法。司教授尝试运用功能语言学理论来拓展对翻译研究中的重要分支领域——翻译批评的研究,详细地论述了功能语言学视角的翻译质量评估模式的建构思路和包括的内容。从而建构出一种较具系统性、客观性和较强操作性的翻译质量评估模式。运用该模式进行翻译批评实践能最大程度上避免那种对译文进行的带有主观性、经验式和感悟式的评价,因其"是按评价指标体系并依据其背后的理论而系统、全面地按照上下结合,微观宏观并举,定性和定量共用的程序审视译文……。"①

2007 年他根据博士论文修订了专著《功能语言学与翻译研究——翻译质量评估模式建构》(由北京大学出版社出版)。司教授在对已有翻译批评和翻译质量评估研究现状的成就与不足(重点是豪斯的翻译质量评估模式分析)的基础上,以功能语言学和语篇类型学理论为指导,建构出了一种基于语篇的翻译质量评估模式。

司显柱模式虽基于豪斯修正模式(revised model),却是一种继承和发扬。明确提出应充分利用系统功能语言学关于体现语言元功能的词汇-语法系统作为工具来对原文和译文的概念意义和人际意义进行全面、系统地发掘,这是

---

① 司显柱. 论功能语言学视角的翻译质量评估模式研究[J]. 外语教学,2004(4):45-50.

司显柱研究中的一个创新点,弥补了豪斯修正模式中所缺乏的用于对文本意义/功能进行分析和发掘的参数。司显柱模式中首要也是最重要步骤就在于依据词汇-语法这一系统对原文和译文里的小句进行及物性、语气、情态、评价和主位分析,以揭示和描写它们的概念意义和人际意义,据此较为全面和系统地判断译文对原文是否或哪里发生了偏离。

国内仅有的几篇以司显柱模式为研究对象的论文,限于对其模式的介绍,缺乏批评。司显柱的研究具有系统性、一定的科学性,但也存在可继续进行深入实践和探讨的地方。

第一,司教授提出了可适用于各类文本翻译质量评估的共同标准值得商榷。此标准为"包括语言功能和语篇功能在内的'功能对等'"。[①] 翻译实践是丰富多彩的,以一个统一的模式来验证所有语篇的翻译质量有很大难度。朱志瑜对这一共同标准提出了异议,指出应针对不同类型的文本实施不同的策略和标准,认为"功能对等"过于抽象,对于具体的翻译评估不具有可操作性。

第二,在翻译质量评估模式建构中,文本类型和体裁被看作相同的概念。实际上它们是两种不同形式的语篇分类方式。在系统功能语言学的视角下,体裁是"属于同一文化背景里的人进行的一项有阶段、有目标方向、有目的的社会活动"。[②] 语篇体裁通过纲要式结构和体现样式来体现。据莱斯阐述,文本类型是根据语言的主要交际功能划分的;语篇体裁是按照语言特征或惯例常规分类。[③] 在莱斯看来,每种文本类型都可能包括多种不同的体裁,但一种体裁不一定只涉及一种文本类型,因此也不限于一种交际功能。

第三,司教授的翻译质量评估模式建构缺乏足够的实证研究。司教授虽在其著作的实证研究部分分别运用"信息类""表情类"和"操作类"的三类语篇做个案分析,来论证其模式的可行性和适用性。但对于一个科学、系统的翻译质量评估模式来说,实证案例数量过少,论证就显得不充分,缺乏信服力。司教授本人也意识到了这一不足,吕桂在对系统功能语言学翻译质量评估模式的实证进行研究与反思时也明确了这一点。

第四,司显柱翻译质量评估模式对于广告翻译的适用性没有得到令人信

① 司显柱. 功能语言学视角的翻译标准再论[J]. 外语教学,2006(2):63-67.

② Martin JR. Language, Register and Genre[A]. In F. Christie. (ed.) Children Writing:R eader[C]. Geelong:Deakin University Press,1984:25.

③ NORD C. Translating as a Purposeful Activity: Functionalist Approaches Explained[M]. Shanghai:Shanghai Foreign Language Education Press,2001:37.

服的验证。司显柱研究的创新是在模式中添加了词汇-语法系统作为工具对文本意义功能进行分析和发掘。但是在实证部分涉及几篇广告的译文评估时,这一强有力的工具却并未得到运用。司教授只是在考虑文化语境(即语篇体裁)和其他诸如意识形态之类的文化因素对于译文语言编码的影响下,讨论了汉英广告翻译应该采取的合适的翻译策略。基于此,司教授谈到了在广告翻译质量评估时应该注意的问题和评估的方法。

(三)翻译质量评估发展方向的探索

(1)增加语料库为基础的研究,使译文评估客观、科学。目前,受西方翻译理论和语言学理论研究方法的影响,国内学界评析译文的手段大大丰富了,且定性评价的影响还很深远。译文质量的评估受到很多主观因素的影响,因此我们有必要借助定量和定性分析相结合的方法。如前所述,国内已有的译文质量量化分析模式实际操作起来,但因工作量太大,可操作性不强。

司显柱等学者从理论的角度阐述了评估译文质量的标准,建构了对译文质量进行评估的模式。他们的研究能够规范翻译行为。罗选民等在论述翻译研究时指出,"以往的研究多以定性为主,理论阐释居多,而缺乏数据和量化的支持"。① 司显柱翻译质量评估研究的不足之处也在于此,他虽然尝试以实证研究来验证其模式的适用性,但例证不够充分。这些从理论角度提出的模式要想指导具体的翻译实践,更具说服力,必须要依靠科学的认识论和先进的技术方法——翻译研究语料库进行验证和说明。

翻译语料库为翻译研究提供了新的工具,扩展了翻译的研究范围,也提出了新的研究思路。语料库的研究方法是定量式的"数据驱动"分析,是从具体数据推导出理性结论,因此能十分有效地克服研究中的主观性。翻译语料库是建立在现代计算机技术基础上的,把它与翻译质量评估研究相结合能极大提高译文评价的效度和信度,当然我们应当注意定量与定性研究的结合,这样的研究才是健康的和科学的。

(2)建立译文质量评估的等级标准。翻译质量评估模式的欠缺直接导致了国内长期存在的译文质量评估的"非科学性和表层性,缺乏说服力"。② 对翻译作品的评论是我国翻译研究的传统项目,而汉英语言和文化差异极大。

---

① 罗选民,董娜,黎土旺. 语料库与翻译研究:兼评 Maeve Olohan 的《翻译研究语料库入门》[J]. 外语与外语教学,2005(12):52-56.

② 司显柱. 功能语言学与翻译研究:翻译质量评估模式建构[M]. 北京:北京大学出版社,2007:15.

面对纷繁复杂的翻译文本,仅仅想用好或坏评价一篇译文的质量是不科学的,也是不负责任的,对译文质量的评估"应该更细化、具体,更具科学性"。为实现对译文更具科学性的质量评估,可以将译文的质量依据一定的标准分成不同等级(qualitative rank),而这也是豪斯和司显柱翻译质量评估模式中所缺乏的。对于翻译质量的等级标准来说,维尔斯和王宏印的提法都很有借鉴价值。

早在 1977 年维尔斯就提出了翻译质量的等级标准,"错误,不恰当,不可确定的情况,正确,恰当"。虽然如维尔斯所指出的:其研究只是尝试性的,旨在为翻译批评未来的发展方向提供建议,但不可否认的是这种"尝试性"的研究极具启发意义。王宏印总结出了一个划分文学译作品级的简要条目,他认为可以依据质量对译文进行划分,即"妙译、佳译、拙译"。虽然他的研究是以文学翻译批评为基础的,但他对翻译质量等级的划分仍然很有借鉴价值。

第五节 等值理论在翻译质量评估中的应用

《红楼梦》是中国古典文学的瑰宝,也是世界文学中的一朵奇葩。曹雪芹在《红楼梦》中以"满纸荒唐言,一把辛酸泪"生动地描述了一个封建大家族从兴盛走向衰败的过程,塑造了许多生动形象的人物。同时,他还描绘了一幅幅生动的中国封建社会生活的画卷。它是中国封建社会和文化的缩影,与整个中华民族文化紧密联系在一起。

一、《红楼梦》两个英译本、一个俄译本中歇后语翻译的三个等值层面

随着中外文化交流的日益发展,《红楼梦》已被翻译为十多种文字,迄今为止,《红楼梦》共产生了 9 个英文译本,包括摘译本、节译本及全译本。其中,最有影响的两个全译本是产生于 20 世纪 70 年代,由杨宪益、戴乃迭夫妇合译的 *A Dream of Red Mansions* 和大卫·霍克斯与约翰·闵福德翻译的 *The Story of the Stone*。自 20 世纪 70 年代起,翻译研究出现"文化转向"以来,翻译中的文化视角一直是学者们关注的热点,特别是对于《红楼梦》这样一本中国文化的百科全书来说,它的两个全译本更是得到了令人瞩目的关注。自从两个译本问世后,关于它们的译论译评一直从未间断。当今学者们一致认为杨译本在翻译策略上多采用异化,属于语义翻译;霍译本则倾向于归化,属于交际翻译。可以说对于《红楼梦》译本的研究,对比和评析居多,但深入地探讨

影响译本的因素尤其是影响文化内容翻译的因素,这方面的研究还比较少,其中专门将红楼梦中歇后语的翻译处理拿来比较的更是少之又少。本章节试图将依据程乙本红楼梦的杨宪益译本与霍克斯译本在处理《红楼梦》中歇后语时各自达到的等值层面进行实证分析。

(一)句法等值

(1)黄柏木做磬槌子——外头体面里头苦。

贾珍笑道:"所以他们庄家老实人,外明不知里暗的事。黄柏木作了磬槌子,——外头体面里头苦。"(宁国府除夕祭宗祠,荣国府元宵开夜宴)

Hawkes's version[①]:"These simple country souls see the bright outside but not the dark within, said Cousin Zhen. The situation our Rong-guo cousins are in is like the proverbial chime-hammer made of phellodendron wood: imposing to look at but bitter inside."

(2)锯了嘴子的葫芦——没口齿。

(凤姐:)"自古说,'妻贤夫祸少,表壮不如里壮'。你但凡是个好的,他们怎得闹出这些事来?你又没才干,又没口齿,锯了嘴子的葫芦,就只会一味瞎小心应贤良的名儿。"(苦尤娘赚入大观园,酸凤姐大闹宁国府)

The Yangs's version[②]: As the saying goes, "A good wife keeps her husband out of trouble a sound woman counts for more than a sound man." If you were any good, how could they do such things? You're as stupid and dumb as a gourd with its tip sawn off. All you care about, you fool, is getting a name for goodness.

(3)仓老鼠问老鸹去借粮——守着的没有,飞着的倒有。

柳氏啐道:"发了昏的,今年不比往年,把这些东西都分给众妈妈了。一个个像抓破了脸的,人打树底下一过,两眼就像那鹭鸶似的,还动他的果子!可是你舅母姨娘两三个亲戚都管着,怎不和他们要的,倒和我来要。这可是'仓老鼠问老鸹去借粮——守着的没有,飞着的倒有'。"(鼠忌器宝玉瞒赃,判冤决狱平儿行权)

The Yangs's version:Mrs. Liu spat. "You're crazy!" she scoffed. "This year's not like the old days. Everything here has been put in the care

---

① The Story of the Stone, tr, by David Hawkes, Penguin Books, 1973.

② A Dream of Red Mansions, tr, by Yang Hsien-yi and Gladys Yang, Foreign Language Press, 1978.

of different women, every single one of them spoiling for a fight. Just walk under a tree, and they glare like broody hens. How can you touch their fruit? The other day I was walking under a plum tree when a bee brushed past my face, and just as I flapped it away that aunt of yours spotted me. She was too far away to see what I was doing and thought I was picking plums, so she let out a screech, then started squawking at the top of her voice that this fruit hadn't yet been offered to Buddha, that their Ladyships being away hadn't tasted it yet, and that after the best had been sent to the mistress the rest of us would get our share, carrying on as if I were dying for her plums! I didn't take it too kindly, so gave her tit for tat. But you have several aunts in charge of things here. Why not ask them for what you want? Why apply to me? This is like the rat in the barn who asked a crow for grain, as if a bird on the wing had some while the rat living in the barn had none."

（4）吃了蜜蜂儿屎——轻狂。

凤姐儿笑道：“我们是没有人疼的了。”尤氏笑道：“有我呢，我搂着你。也不怕臊，你这孩子又撒娇了，听见放炮仗，吃了蜜蜂儿屎的，今儿又轻狂起来。”凤姐儿笑道：“等散了，咱们园子里放去。我比小厮们还放的好呢。”（史太君破陈腐旧套，王熙凤效戏彩斑衣）

The Yangs's version："No one cares for poor little me!" Xifeng complained. "I do," chuckled Madam You. "Come and sit on my knee and don't be afraid. You're behaving like a spoilt brat again. The sound of fireworks has sent you off your head, just as if you'd eaten bees' wax." "When this party's over let's go and let off fireworks in the Garden," proposed Xifeng gaily. "I'm better at that than those page boys."

（5）虎头上捉虱——自寻死。

金桂冷笑道：“如今还有什么奶奶太太的，都是你们的世界了。别人是惹不得的，有人庇护着，我也不敢去虎头上捉虱子。你还是我的丫头，问你一句话，你就和我摔脸子，说谎话。你既这么有势力，为什么不把我勒死了，你和秋菱不拘谁做了奶奶，那不清净了么！偏我又不死，碍着你们的道儿。”（史太君失语难瞑目，金鸳鸯守志宁玉碎）

The Yangs's version：Jingui laughed scornfully. "Are you still calling me madam? You two have it all your own way. She's untouchable because she has a protectress，and I dare not catch the lice on a tiger's head，but you are still my maid. Yet when I ask you a question you scowl at me and snap back! If you're so powerful，why not strangle me? Then either you or Qiuling could be the mistress — wouldn't you like that better? It's too bad that I'm not dead yet，blocking your path!"

（6）癞蛤蟆想吃天鹅肉——异想天开。

平儿因问道："这瑞大爷是为什么只管来?"凤姐儿遂将九月里宁府园子里遇见他的光景，并他说的话，都告诉平儿。平儿说道："癞蛤蟆想吃天鹅肉，没人伦的混账东西，起这个念头，叫他不得好死!"凤姐儿道："等他来了，我自有道理。"（庆寿辰宁府排家宴，见熙凤贾瑞起淫心）

Hawkes's veision："What does Mr Rui want?" asked Patience. "Why does he keep coming like this?"In reply Xi-feng gave her a full account of her encounter with him in the garden of the Ning-guo mansion and of the things he had said to her on that occasion，"What a nasty，disgusting man!" said Patience. "A case of the toad on the ground wanting to eat the goose in the sky". He'll come to no good end，getting ideas like that! "Just wait till he comes! "said Xi-feng. "I know how to deal with him. "

（7）没笼头的马——野惯了。

宝玉忙请了安，薛姨妈忙一把拉了他，抱入怀内，笑说："这么冷天，我的儿，难为你想着来，快上炕来坐着罢。"命人倒滚滚的茶来。宝玉因问："哥哥不在家?"薛姨妈叹道："他是没笼头的马，天天逛不了，哪里肯在家一日。"（比通灵金莺微露意，探宝钗黛玉半含酸）

The Yangs's version：He paid his respects to his aunt，who caught him in her arms and hugged him. "How good of you to come，dear boy，on a cold day like this. " She beamed. "But get up here quickly on the warm kang. " She ordered hot tea to be served. "Is Cousin Pan at home?" asked Baoyu. "Ah，he's like a horse without a halter，" she sighed. "He's forever rushing about outside. Not a day does he spend at home. "

Hawkes's version：Her response to his greeting was to draw him towards her and clasp him to her bosom an affectionate embrace. "What a nice，kind boy to think of us on a cold day like this! Come up on the kang and get warm!" She ordered a maid to bring him some boiling hot tea. Bao-yu inquired whether Cousin Pan was at home. Aunt Xue sighed. "Pan is like a riderless horse：always off enjoying himself somewhere or other. He won't spend a single day at home if he can help it."

(8)坐山观虎斗——坐收其利。

(凤姐)你是知道的,咱们家所有的这些管家奶奶们,哪一位是好缠的? 错一点儿,他们就笑话、打趣;偏一点儿,他们就指桑骂槐的抱怨;坐山观虎斗,借剑杀人,引风吹火,站于岸儿,推倒油瓶不扶,都是全挂子的武艺。(贾元春才选凤藻宫,秦鲸卿夭逝黄泉路)

The Yang's version： And you know how difficult our old stewardesses are，laughing at the least mistake and "accusing the elm while pointing at the mulberry tree if one shows the least bias. Talk about sitting on a hill to watch tigers fight，murdering with a borrowed sword，" "borrowing wind to fan the fire，" "watching people drown from a dry bank" and "not troubling to right an oil bottle that's been knocked over" they're all old hands at such tricks.

(二)语义等值

(1) 狗咬吕洞宾——不识好人心。

彩霞咬着牙,向贾环头上戳了一指头,说道:"没良心的! 狗咬吕洞宾,不识好人心。"(魇魔法姊弟逢五鬼,通灵玉姐弟遇双仙)

The Yangs's version： Caixia bit her lips and with one finger rapped him on the forehead. "You ungrateful thing! Like the dog that bit Lü Congbin — you bite the hand that feeds you."

Hawkes's version： Sunset clenched her teeth. She stabbed the air above his head with her finger："You ungrateful thing! You're like the dog that bit Lü Dong-bin：you don't know a friend when you see one."

(2)千里搭长棚——没有不散的筵席。

小红道:"也犯不着气他们。俗语说的,'千里搭长棚,没有个不散的筵席',谁守谁一辈子呢? 不过三年五载,各人干各人的去了。那时,谁还管谁呢?"(蘅芜苑设言传密语,潇湘馆春困发幽情)

The Yangs's version： "It's hardly worth being angry with them," retorted Xiaohong. "The proverb says Even the longest feast must break up at last. Who's going to stay here for life? A few more years and we'll all go our different ways. When that time comes who will worry about anyone else?"

(3)见提着影戏人子上场——好歹别戳破这层纸。

尤三姐听了这话,就跳起来,站在炕上,指贾琏笑道:"你不用和我花马吊嘴的,清水下杂面,你吃我看见。见提着影戏人子上场,好歹别戳破这层纸儿。你别油蒙了心,打量我们不知道你府上的事。这会子花几个臭钱,你们哥儿俩拿着我们姐儿两个权当粉头来取乐儿,你们就打错了算盘了。我也知道你那老太婆太难缠,如今把我姐姐拐了来做二房,偷的锣儿敲不得。(贾二舍偷娶尤二姐,尤三姐思嫁柳二郎)

The Yangs's version:Third Sister jumped on to the kang then and pointed at Jia Lian. "Don't try to get round me with your glib tongue!" She cried. "We'd better keep clear of each other. I've seen plenty of shadow-plays in my time;anyway don't tear the screen to show what's behind the scenes. You must be befuddled if you think we don't know what goes on in your house. Now after spending a bit of your stinking money, you two figure you can amuse yourselves with us as if we were prostitutes! Well, you're out in your calculations. I know your wife's such a termagant that you tricked my sister into coming here to be your second wife;but you can't beat a stolen gong. "

(4)吃了蜜蜂屎的——轻狂。

凤姐儿笑道:"我们是没有人疼的了。"尤氏笑道:"有我呢,我搂着你。也不怕臊,你这孩子又撒娇了,听见放炮仗,吃了蜜蜂儿屎的,今儿又轻狂起来。"凤姐儿笑道:"等散了,咱们园子里放去。我比小厮们还放的好呢。"(史太君破陈腐旧套,王熙凤效戏彩斑衣)

Hawkes's version:"What about me?" said Xi-feng. "Doesn't anyone love me?""I'll hold you," said You-shi, laughing, "though why you should act the shrinking young thing now I can't imagine. Normally when you hear fireworks you get so excited I'd sooner eat a bee's turd than stand by and watch you!""Wait until this is over," said Xi-feng. "We'll go out in the courtyard and let some off ourselves. I'm sure I can do it better than these boys. "

(5)耗子尾巴上长疮——多少脓血儿。

你兄弟又不在家,又没有个人商议,少不得拿钱去垫补,谁知越使钱越叫人拿住了刀把儿,越发来讹。我是耗子尾上长疮——多少脓血儿!所以又急又气,少不得来找嫂子。(尤娘赚入大观园,酸凤姐大闹宁国府)

The Yangs's version: Besides, with my husband away, I had no one to consult; I could only try to patch things up with money. Yet the more I gave him, the more I was at his mercy and the more he blackmailed me. But how much can he squeeze out of me? No more than from a pimple on a rat's tail. That's why I panicked and flew into such a rage that I came looking for you.

Hawkes's version: What could I do? Lian was away. There was no one at hand to advise me. All I could think of was to try and buy him off. But the trouble is, the more you give to people like that, the more they twist the knife in you and think up more and more pretexts for getting money out of you. And I am like a boil on a mouse's tail: there's a limit to what can be squeezed out of me. It was because I was feeling so desperate that I.

（6）黑母鸡——一窝儿。

估着有好事,他就不等别人去说,他先抓尖儿;或有了不好事,或他自己错了,他便一缩头推到别人身上来,他还在旁边拨火儿。如今连他正经婆婆都嫌他,说他"雀儿拣着旺处飞,黑母鸡一窝儿,自家的事不管,倒替人家去瞎张罗"。（贾二舍偷娶尤二姨,尤三姐思嫁柳二郎）

The Yangs's version: If anything good happens, she rushes to take the credit before anyone else can report it. If anything bad happens, or if she herself makes some mistake, she ducks and shifts the blame on to other people, stirring up more trouble too on the side. Now even her own mother-in-law, the Elder Mistress, can't stand her, calling her a fair-weather sparrow, or a black hen that neglects her own nest but keeps butting in everywhere else.

（7）黄鹰抓住鹞子的脚——扣了环了。

到了贾母跟前,凤姐笑道:"我说他们不用人费心,自己就会好的。老祖宗不信,一定叫我去说合。我及至那里要说合,谁知两个人倒在一处对赔不是了。对笑对诉,倒像'黄鹰抓住了鹞子的脚,两个都扣了环了,'那里还要人去说合。"说的满屋里都笑起来。（宝钗借扇机带双敲,龄官划蔷痴及局外）

The Yangs's version: "I said don't worry, they'll make it up themselves," announced Xifeng cheerfully. "Our Old Ancestress didn't believe me, and insisted I go along as peacemaker. I found they'd already asked each other's forgiveness, and were clinging together like an eagle sinking its talons into a hawk. They didn't need any help. "

（8）癞蛤蟆想吃天鹅肉——异想天开。

平儿因问道：“这瑞大爷是为什么只管来？”凤姐儿遂将九月里宁府园子里遇见他的光景，并他说的话，都告诉平儿。平儿说道：“癞蛤蟆想吃天鹅肉，没人伦的混账东西，起这个念头，叫他不得好死!”凤姐儿道：“等他来了，我自有道理。”（庆寿辰宁府排家宴，见熙凤贾瑞起淫心）

The Yangs's version："Why does he keep calling?" Xifeng described their meeting and all he had said to her in the Ning Mansion garden during the ninth month. "A toad hankering for a taste of swan," scoffed Pinger. "The beast hasn't a shred of common decency. He deserves a bad end for dreaming of such a thing. "Let him come," said Xifeng. "I know how to deal with him. "

（9）懒狗——扶不上墙。

这张华也深知利害，不敢造次。旺儿回了凤姐，凤姐气得骂道：“真是他娘的话! 怨不得俗语说的,'懒狗扶不上墙'的! 你细细地说给他,'就告我们家谋反也没要紧',不过是借他一闹,大家没脸;若闹大了,我这里自然能够平服的”（苦尤娘赚入大观园,酸凤姐大闹宁国府）

The Yangs's version：Zhang Hua, however, only too well aware of the danger involved，dared not bring such a charge. When Lai Wang reported this to Xifeng she fumed："Damn him for a mangy cur that won't let itself be hepler over a wall! Go and explain to him that it doesn't matter even if he accuses our family of high treason. I just want him to make a row so that everyone loses face. If big trouble comes of it，I can always smooth things over. "

Hawkes's version：A strong instinct of self-preservation at first prompted Zhang Hua to refuse. When Rrigntie told Xi-feng this she was furious. A young idiot，she called him；a lame dog who wouldn't allow one to help him over the stile. "You will have to explain it to him very carefully. Tell him he can charge this family with high treason for all I care；all I want is a pretext for making it hot for them. But tell him that if things show any sign of getting too hot, I am perfectly well able to cool them down again. "

（10）聋子放炮仗——散了。

众人听说，复又笑将起来。凤姐儿笑道：“外头已经四更，依我说，老祖宗

也乏了,咱们也该'聋子放炮仗——散了'罢。"(史太君破陈腐旧套,王熙凤效戏彩斑衣)

The Yangs's version：At this they laughed again. "The fourth watch has sounded outside," announced Xifeng. "I think our Old Ancestress is tired, and it's time for us to whizz off too like that deaf man's fire-cracker."

Hawkes's veision：This brought another burst of laughter. "That's two o'clock sounding outside," said Xi-feng. "I'm sure Grannie must be tired. If you ask me, I think we all ought to be like the deaf man's firework and trickle away."

(11)跑解马的打扮儿——伶伶俐俐。

麝月道:"你就这么'跑解马'似的打扮得伶伶俐俐的出去了不成?"宝玉笑道:"可不就这么去了。"麝月道:"你死不拣好日子! 你出去站一站,把皮不冻破了你的。"(薛小妹新编怀古诗,胡庸医乱用虎狼药)

The Yangs's version："Surely you didn't slip out like that, in that tight-fitting horse-thief's out fit?" asked Shanyue. "Oh yes, she did', said Baoyu. 'You deserve to catch your death!' exclaimed Shanyue. 'What a day to choose! Why, just standing outside for a minute would chap your skin."

Hawkes's version："Is that all you were wearing when you went outside, that circus rider's outfit you've got on now ?" "That's all she was wearing," said Bao-yu. "You'll die before your time!" said Musk. "What, standing around with only that on? It's enough to freeze the skin off you!"

(12)兔死狐悲——物伤其类。

宝钗见问,不好隐瞒他两个,遂将方才之事都告诉了他二人。黛玉听了,"兔死狐悲,物伤其类",不免也感叹起来。湘云听了,却动了气,说:"等我问着二姐姐去! 我骂那起老婆子丫头一顿,给你们出气如何?"说着,便要走。(慧紫鹃情辞试忙玉,慈姨妈爱语慰痴颦)

Hawkes's version：Bao-chai saw that Xiu-yan's circumstances could no longer be concealed and explained to them both what had happened. Dai-yu, feeling "the fox's sympathy for the hunted hare", was much distressed, but Xiang-yun's reaction was one of anger. "I'm going straight over to see Ying-chun about this," she said. "You'll feel better, both of you, when I've given those beastly servants a piece of my mind." She would have gone, too, had not Bao-chai restrained her. "Are you out of your mind? Sit down and stay where you are."

(13)羊群里跑出骆驼来了——就只你大。

贾母道:"我不信,不然就也是你闹了鬼了。如今你还了得,'羊群里跑出骆驼来了,就只你大。'你又会做文章了。"宝玉笑道:"实在是他作的。师父还夸他明儿一定有出息呢。老太太不信,就打发人叫了他来亲自试试,老太太就知道了。"(博庭欢宝玉赞孤儿,正家法贾珍鞭悍仆)

The Yangs's version:"I don't believe you. You must have been up to more monkey busıness. You're getting above yourself nowadays — a camel in a flock of sheep — being the eldest and the one who can write!" "He really wrote them himself," insisted Baoyu, smiling. "And our teacher praised him, saying he'll go far in future. If you don't believe me, madam, you can send for him and test him yourself; then you'll know."

Hawkes's version:"I don't believe you!" said Grandmother Jia. "It was you at your tricks again, I'll be bound. Hark at you! A camel among sheep! Just because you're so grown-up now, and so good at your compositions..." Bao-yu smiled. "No, seriously, Lan managed perfectly well on his own. The Preceptor was very pleased and said he had a brilliant future ahead of him. If you don't believe me, Grannie, send for him and test him yourself."

(14)银样镴枪头——中看不中用。

说的林黛玉嗤的一声笑了,揉着眼睛,一面笑道:"一般也唬的这么个样儿,还只管胡说。'呸,原来是个银样镴枪头。'"宝玉听了,笑道:"你这个呢?我也告诉去。"林黛玉笑道:"你说你会过目成诵,难道我就不能一目十行么?"(西厢记妙词通戏语,牡丹亭艳曲警芳心)

The Yangs's version:Daiyu burst out laughing at this and wiped her eyes. "You're so easy to scare, yet still you indulge in talking such nonsense," she teased. "Why, you're nothing but a flowerless sprout, 'a lead spearhead that looks like silver.'" It was Baoyu's turn to laugh. "Now listen to you! I'll tell on you too." "You boast that you can 'memorize a passage with one reading.' Why can't I 'learn ten lines at a glance'?"

Hawkes's version:His ridiculous declamation provoked a sudden explosion of mirth. She laughed and simultaneously wiped the tears away with her knuckles："Look at you - the same as ever! Scared as anything，but you still have to go on talking nonsense. Well，I know you now for what you are：Of silver spear the leaden counterfeit!" "Well! You can talk! said Bao-yu laughing. Listen to you! Now I'm going off to tell on you!" "You needn't imagine you're the only one with a good memory，" said Dai-yu haughtily. "I suppose I'm allowed to remember lines too if I like. "

(15)坐山观虎斗——坐收其利。

(凤姐)你是知道的,咱们家所有的这些管家奶奶们,哪一位是好缠的？错一点儿,他们就笑话、打趣,偏一点儿,他们就指桑骂槐的抱怨；坐山观虎斗,借剑杀人,引风吹火,站干岸儿,推倒油瓶不扶,都是全挂子的武艺。(贾元春才选凤藻宫,秦鲸卿天逝黄泉路)

Hawkes's version：And you know what a difficult lot those old stewardesses are. The tiniest mistake and they are all laughing at you and making fun；the tiniest hint of favoritism and they are grumbling and complaining. You know their way of "cursing the oak-tree when they mean the ash". Those old women know just how to sit on the mountain-top and watch the tigers fight；how to murder with a borrowed knife，or help the wind to fan the fire. They will look on safely from the bank while you are drowning in the river. And the fallen oil-bottle can drain away：they are not going to pick it up.

(三)语用等值

(1)千里搭长棚——没有不散的筵席。

小红道："也犯不着气他们。俗语说得好,'千里搭长棚,没有个不散的筵席',谁守谁一辈子呢？不过三年五载,各人干各人的去了。那时谁还管谁呢？"(蘅芜苑设言传密语,潇湘馆春困发幽情)

Hawkes's version："I don't see much point in getting angry," said Crimson. "You know what they said about the mile-wide marquee：Even the longest party must have an end？Well，none of us is here for ever，you know. Another four or five years from now when we've each gone our different ways it won't matter any longer what all the rest of us are doing. "

(2)宋徽宗的鹰,赵子昂的马——都是好画儿。

鸳鸯听说,立起身来,照他嫂子脸上下死劲啐了一口,指着他骂道:你快夹着屁嘴离了这里,好多着呢! 什么"好话"! 宋徽宗的鹰,赵子昂的马,都是好

画儿。什么"喜事"! 状元痘儿灌的浆儿又满是喜事。(尴尬人难免尴尬事,鸳鸯女誓绝鸳鸯侣)

The Yangs's version: Yuanyang sprang up and spat hard in her face. Pointing an accusing finger at her she swore. "Shut your foul mouth and clear off, if you know what's good for you. What's all this talk of good news and good fortune?"

Hawkes's version: Faithful stood up and spat hard and deliberately in her sister-in-law's face. "Why don't you take your bloody trap out of here?" she shouted, pointing at her angrily. "Wonderful news" indeed!

(3)黄柏木作磬槌子——外头体面里头苦。

贾珍笑道:"所以他们庄家老实人,外明不知里暗的事。黄柏木作了磬槌子——外头体面里头苦。"(宁国府除夕祭宗祠,荣国府元宵开夜宴)

The Yangs's version: "These simple country folk don't realize that not all is gold that glitters," chuckled Jia Zhen. "Wormwood carved into a drumstick may look imposing, but it's bitter inside!"

(4) 锯了嘴子的葫芦——没口齿。

(凤姐)自古说,'妻贤夫祸少,表壮不如里壮'。你但凡是个好的,他们怎得闹出这些事来? 你又没才干,又没口齿,锯了嘴子的葫芦,就只会一味瞎小心应贤良的名儿。"(苦尤娘赚入大观园,酸凤姐大闹宁国府)

Hawkes's version: There's a very old saying: "A good lining gives a garment strength and a husband with a good wife has few calamities." If you'd been a good wife to Zhen, he and the others would never have got up to this mischief. You haven't the wit to k anything useful; and as for saying for all the good sense that ever comes out of your mouth you might as well be a bottle! You seem to think that you have only got to sit tight and do nothing and people will praise you for your virtue!'

(5)仓老鼠问老鸹去借粮——守着的没有,飞着的倒有。

柳氏啐道:"发了昏的,今年不比往年,把这些东西都分给众妈妈了。一个个像抓破了脸的,人打树底下一过,两眼就像那鹥鸡似的,还动他的果子! 可是你舅母姨娘两三个亲戚都管着,怎不和他们要的,倒和我来要。这可是'仓老鼠问老鸹去借粮——守着的没有,飞着的倒有'。"(投鼠忌器宝玉瞒脏,判冤决狱平儿行权)

Hawkes's version: "You must be mad!" said the cook. "We can't do that sort of thing any more now. Nowadays it's all divided up among the garden-women; and there isn't one of them, either, that wouldn't just as soon scratch your eyes out as look at you. You only have to walk under one of the fruit-trees and they're watching you like hawks. Fat chance I should have of picking any of the fruit for you I only yesterday I was walking underneath a plum-tree and raised my hand to drive a bee away that was buzzing in front of my face. One of your old aunties happened to see me, but as she was quite a long way off, she couldn't quite make out what I was doing. She thought I was picking the plums. Oh, you should have heard her shout! Don't take them! We haven't offered the first-fruits yet. No one must have any of those plums until Their Ladyships have got back and made the offerings. You'll get your share in time. I suppose she thought I had a craving and couldn't wait! I'm afraid I wasn't very polite. I gave her a piece of my mind. You ask one of your old aunties if you want some fruit, my boy, it's no good asking me. You asking me for fruit is like the granary rat asking the crow for corn: Have asking Have-not!"

(6)黑母鸡———一窝儿。

估着有好事,他就不等别人去说,他先抓尖儿;或有了不好事,或他自己错了,他便一缩头推到别人身上来,他还在旁边拨火儿。如今连他正经婆婆都嫌他,说他'雀儿拣着旺处飞,黑母鸡一窝儿,自家的事不管,倒替人家去瞎张罗'。(贾二舍偷娶尤二姨,尤三姐思嫁柳二郎)

Hawkes's version：Whenever anything good happens, you can be sure that she'll get in with the news first, before anyone else does, so that she can reap the benefit. But when things go wrong or she's made a slip herself, she'll very quickly step aside and fasten the blame for it on someone else. She'll even fan the flames up and make it hotter for that other person once she's safely out of it herself. Even her mother-in-law can't stand her. "The magpie looking for a bigger nest who set up house with the crow." she calls her. She says she's no business meddling with the affairs of our household when she ought to be looking after her own.

(7)虎头上捉虱———自寻死。

金桂冷笑道:"如今还有什么奶奶太太的,都是你们的世界了。别人是惹不得的,有人庇护着,我也不敢去虎头上捉虱子。你还是我的丫头,问你一句话,你就和我摔脸子,说撒话。你既这么有势力,为什么不把我勒死了,你和秋菱不拘谁做了奶奶,那不清净了么!偏我又不死,碍着你们的道儿。"(史太君失语难瞑目 金鸳鸯守志宁玉碎)

Hawkes's version:"Spare me the Mrs, will you!" said Jin-gui with a malicious smile. "You and that Lily think you run the place, don't you? I can't get near that little Miss Unmolestable, with all her friends in high places to take care of her — all right! I won't stick my neck out in that direction! But you're still my maid, I don't have to take cheek from you! If you're so sure of yourself, why not get on with it and strangle me? Then you and Lily can have the field to yourselves. I'm just in your way — go on, say it!"

(8)黄鹰抓住鹞子的脚——扣了环了。

到了贾母跟前,凤姐笑道:"我说他们不用人费心,自己就会好的。老祖宗不信,一定叫我去说合。我及至那里要说合,谁知两个人倒在一处对赔不是了。对笑对诉,倒像'黄鹰抓住了鹞子的脚,两个都扣了环了',那里还要人去说合。"说的满屋里都笑起来。(宝钗借扇机带双敲,春龄画蔷痴及局外)

Hawkes's version:They went out of the Garden and through into Grandmother Jia's apartment. "I told you they could be left to themselves to make it up and that there was no need for you to worry," said Xi-feng to Grandmother Jia. when they were all in the old lady's presence;"but you wouldn't believe me, would you? You insisted on my going there to act the peacemaker. Well, I went there; and what did I find? I found the two of them together apologizing to each other. It was like the kite and the kestrel holding hands; they were positively locked in a clinch! No need of a peacemaker that I could see."

(9)可着头做帽子——一点儿富余也不能。

贾母因见尤氏吃的仍是白粳米饭,因问道:"怎么不盛我的饭?"丫头道:"老太太的饭吃完了。今日添了一位姑娘,所以短了些。"鸳鸯道:"如今都是可着头做帽子了,要一点儿富余也不能的。"王夫人忙回道:"这一二年早涝不定,田上的米都不能按数交的。这几样细米更艰难,所以都可着吃的做。"(开夜宴异兆发悲音,赏中秋新词得佳谶)

The Yangs's version:The Lady Dowager, her hands behind her as she looked on with amusement, noticed one of the maids offer Madam You a bowl of the ordinary white rice for the servants. "Are you out of your mind，serving your mistress that rice?" she demanded. "Your rice is finished，madam，" said the maid. "And as there's an extra young lady today，we're short." "We have to cut our coat according to our cloth，" Yuanyang put in. "Nowadays there's no margin at all." Lady Wang explained，"The last couple of years，what with floods and drought，our farms haven't been able to produce their quota，especially of the rice of the finer kind. So we only issue as much as we think will be needed，for fear of running out."

Hawkes's version： It suddenly struck her that the rice being served was the plain white rice normally eaten by the servants and that You-shi，too，was eating it. "Why are you giving Mrs Zhen this stuff?" she asked them. "There isn't any of Your Old Ladyship's rice left，" said the maids. "You had an extra young lady eating with you today，don't forget." "Meals are made to measure nowadays，" said Faithful. "We can't afford to be extravagant the way we used to be." "There have been so many floods and droughts during the past few years，" said Lady Wang. "Our farms haven't been able to make up their quotas. These special kinds of rice are particularly hard to' come by."

(10)兔死狐悲——物伤其类。

宝钗见问，不好隐瞒他两个，遂将方才之事都告诉了他二人。黛玉听了，"兔死狐悲，物伤其类"，不免也感叹起来。湘云听了，却动了气，说："等我问着二姐姐去！我骂那起老婆子丫头一顿，给你们出气如何？"说着，便要走。（慧紫鹃情辞试忙玉，慈姨妈爱语慰痴颦）

The Yangs's version： Realizing that she could no longer hide the truth from them，Baochai explained what had happened. Daiyu exclaimed in distress and sympathy，but Xiangyun grew most indignant. "Wait till I go and take this up with Yingchun，" she fumed. "I shall give those matrons and maids a piece of my mind. Won't that help us to get our own back?" Baochai caught hold of her as she was starting off. "Are you out of your mind again?' she cried. 'Sit down."

(11)掩耳盗铃——哄人。

贾政也撑不住笑了。因说道："哪怕再念三十本《诗经》，也都是掩耳盗铃，哄人而已。"（训劣子李贵承申饬，嗔顽童茗烟闹书房）

The Yangs's version：Even Jia Zheng himself could not help smiling. "Even if he studied another thirty volumes，it would just be fooling people. " he retorted.

Hawkes's version：Even Jia Zheng could not restrain a smile，"If he read thirty books of the Poetry Classic，" said Jia Zheng，"it would still be tomfoolery. No doubt he hopes to deceive others with this sort of thing，but he does not deceive me. "

（12）燥屎——干撅（搁）着。

（赵嬷嬷）我还再四的求了你几遍，你答应的倒好，到如今还是燥屎。（贾元春才选凤藻宫，秦鲸卿天逝黄泉路）

The Yang's version：yet I've begged you again and again and you've always agreed，but to this very day not a thing have you done.

Hawkes's version：I've asked you again and again to help them，and you always says yes；yet to this very day nothing has ever come of it.

（13）没嘴的葫芦——没口齿。

贾母笑道："原来这样，如此更好了。袭人本来从小儿不言不语，我只说他是没嘴的葫芦。既是你深知，岂有大错误的。"（老学士闲征姽婳词，痴公子杜撰芙蓉诔）

The Yang's version：If that's the case，so much the better. Hsi-jen's always been so quiet I felt she was rather stupid；but as you know her so well you can't be wrong.

Hawkes's version："I see，" said Grandmother Jia，smiling. "Oh well，that's all right then. Even better. Aroma never had much to say for herself，in my recollecting. I always thought her rather a dull little stick. However，you obviously know her much better than I do. I'm sure you can't be wrong. "

以上从句法、语义和语用等值三个层面对《红楼梦》两个英译本中的歇后语翻译进行了研究。

《红楼梦》歇后语俄语译文等值层面见表3-4。

表 3-4 《红楼梦》歇后语俄语译文等值层面一览表①

等值层面		歇后语原文	译 文
句法等值		虎头上捉虱子	Ловить Вшей у тигра
		癞蛤蟆想吃天鹅肉	Паршивая лягушка захотела полокомиться мясом небесного лебедя
		没笼头的马	Конь без узды
		骑上老虎背	Села верхом на тигра, а сойти не могу
		掩耳盗铃,哄人	《заткнув уши, красть колокол》, _ толку никакого, один обман
语义等指	成分等值及所指等值	狗咬吕洞宾,不识好人心	Как собака, которая кусала Люй Дунбиня, не ведая, что творит
		懒狗扶不上墙	Паршивой собаке не перепрыгнуть через стену
		羊群里跑出骆驼来了,就只你大	Ведь ты старший и должен среди них выделяться, как верблюд в стаде баранов.
		丈八的台灯——照见人家,照不见自家	Как фонарь на длинном шесте, на других светит, а сам в темноте.
		千里搭长棚,没有个不散的宴席	Даже под навесом в тысячу ли пир кончается
		仓老鼠问老鸹去借粮——守着的没有,飞着的倒有	Просила крыса зерна у журавля! Крыса в амбаре живет, где хранится зерно, а журавль в небе летает! Где ему взять
		耗子尾上长疮,——多少浓血儿	Из крысиного хвоста, много не выжмешь
		金簪子掉在井里头,有你的只是有你的	Упавшая в колодец золотая шпилька все равно принадлежит тому, кто ее уронил
		聋子放炮仗——散了	Как тем глухим, пускавшим ракету, пора расходиться
		美人灯儿,风吹吹就坏了	Как фонарцк, подует ветер_угаснет.
		锯透了嘴子的葫芦	У тебя вместо головы тыква, нужное слово с языка не слетит

① 《红楼梦》俄译本由苏联汉学家 B. A. 帕那苏克翻译,1958 年在莫斯科国家文学出版社出版。

续 表

等值层面		歇后语原文	译 文
语义等指	成分等值及所指等值	黑母鸡——一窝儿	Подобно воробью, летит туда, где можно поживиться, и, словно крот, прячется в землю от неприятностей
		黄鹰抓住了鹞子的脚,两个都扣了环了	Держатся за руки, да так крепко, как держит голубя ястреб, невозможно оторвать друг от друга.
交际作用等值		宋徽宗的画,赵子昂的马,都是好画儿	Хорошая новость, нечего сказать
		梅香拜把子,都是奴才	Пусть я рабыня, пусть все мои братья и сестры рабы, но вы с какой стати меня оскорбляете.
		见提着影戏人子上场,好歹别戳破这层纸儿	Смотри не подавись! А меня лучше не задевай
		可着头做帽子了,要一点儿富余也不能	Сколько едоков, столько и еды
		"跑解马"似的打扮得伶伶俐俐	Ты бегала на улицу в одной кофте
		偷的锣儿敲不得	Как говорится, в краденый барабан бить нельзя
		兔死狐悲,物伤其类	Недаром говорят: 《Когда гибнет заяц, и лисица плачет》
		黄柏木作了磬槌子——外头体面里头苦	Посмотришь на кипарис — он будто бы крепкий, а внутрьдзаглянешь_весь сгнил
		吃了蜜蜂儿屎的,今儿又轻狂起来	Капризничаешь, словно ребенок. Медом тебя не корми_дай посмотреть, как пускают ракеты

二、《西游记》英、俄译本中歇后语翻译的三个等值层面

《西游记》作为我国古代最为伟大的神魔小说,与《三国演义》《水浒传》和《红楼梦》并称为我国古代四大名著。其书以唐僧到天竺取经、游学这一历史事实为依据,讲述了唐朝玄奘法师及其徒弟一行四人西天取经的故事,表现了惩恶扬善的古老主题。它是我国古代长篇浪漫主义小说的高峰,在世界文学史上也是一部浪漫主义杰作。

《西游记》为读者创造了一个神奇、幻化的世界,将神话人物、神话环境和各种神奇的魔法和谐地统一。《西游记》融合了中国传统文化中的佛、道、儒三家的思想和内容,构造出四个世界:地上以皇帝唐太宗李世民为首的人间世界;地府以阎罗为首的幽冥界;天上以玉帝为首的神仙世界;以及西方以如来佛祖为首的极乐世界。在这样的构想下,《西游记》中的众多人物粉墨登场,演绎出一个脍炙人口的唐僧取经的故事。

《西游记》自成书以来已有四百余年的历史,其间曾多次被译成外国文字,有很多不同的翻译版本,书中的神魔故事不仅吸引着中国的读者,而且也吸引着众多的外国读者。在众多的《西游记》译本中,有两个影响较大的英语译本,一个是英国汉学家詹纳尔翻译的、由外文出版社出版的英汉对照全译本 *A Journey to the West*(简称詹译本),另一个为节译本 *Pilgrim-age to the West*,出自杨宪益、戴乃迭夫妇所译的《三部古典小说节选》。杨氏夫妇选取其中比较有趣味的三回,即围绕孙悟空三借芭蕉扇的59~61回进行了翻译,由《中国文学》杂志社出版,中国国际书店发行,于1981年发行第一版(简称杨译本)。目前英文全译本中影响最大的要数詹译本,这也是最接近原著的英译本。下面以詹纳尔的译本作为范例,讨论《西游记》中歇后语翻译实现的等值层面。

(一)句法等值

(1) 猫咬尿泡——空欢喜。

娘娘叫:"安排酒来与大王解劳。"妖王笑道:"正是正是,快将酒来,我与娘娘压惊。"假春娇即同众怪铺排了果品,整顿些腥肉,调开桌椅。那娘娘擎杯,这妖王也以一杯奉上,二人穿换了酒杯。假春娇在旁执着酒壶道:"大王与娘娘今夜才递交杯盏,请各饮干,穿个双喜杯儿。"真个又斟上,又饮干了。假春娇又道:"大王娘娘喜会,众侍婢会唱的供唱,善舞的起舞来耶。"说未毕,只听得一派歌声,齐调音律,唱的唱,舞的舞。他两个又饮了许多。娘娘叫住了歌舞。众侍婢分班,出屏风外摆列,唯有假春娇执壶,上下奉酒。娘娘与那妖王专说得是夫妻之话。你看那娘娘一片云情雨意,哄得那妖王骨软筋麻,只是没福,不得沾身。可怜!真是猫咬尿胞空欢喜!(行者假名降怪,狐观音现象伏妖王)

"Bring wine for His Majesty," the queen said. "He's exhausted." "Indeed I am," said the demon king with a smile, "indeed I am. Fetch some at once. It'll calm our nerves." The imitation Spring Beauty and the other servants then laid out fruit and high meat and set a table and chairs. The queen raised a cup and the demon king did likewise; each gave the other a drink from their own. The imitation Spring Beauty, who was standing beside them, said as she held the jug, "As tonight is the first time Your Majesties have given each other a drink from your own cups I hope that you will each drain them dry for double happiness." They did indeed both refill their cups and drain them again. "As this is so happy an occasion for Your Majesties why don't we slave girls sing and dance for you?" the imitation Spring Beauty suggested. Before the words were all out of her mouth melodious voices could be heard as the singing and dancing began. The two of them drank a lot more before the queen called for the singing and dancing to end. The slave girls divided themselves into their groups and went to line up outside the screen, leaving only the imitation Spring Beauty to hold the jug and serve them wine. The queen and the demon king spoke to each other like husband and wife, and the queen was so full of sensuality that the demon king's bones turned soft and his sinews went numb. The only trouble was that the poor demon was not lucky enough to enjoy her favours. Indeed, it was a case of "happiness over nothing, like a cat biting a piss bubble."[①]

(2)三钱银子买个老驴——自夸骑得。

沙僧上前,把他脸上一抹道:"不羞,不羞! 好个嘴巴骨子! 三钱银子买了老驴,自夸骑得! 要是一绣球打着你,就连夜烧退送纸也还道迟了,敢惹你这晦气进门!"八戒道:"你这黑子不知趣! 丑自丑,还有些风味。自古道,皮肉粗糙,骨骼坚强,各有一得可取。"行者道:"呆子莫胡谈! 且收拾行李。但恐师父着了急,来叫我们,却好进朝保护他。"八戒道:"哥哥又说差了。师父做了驸马,到宫中与皇帝的女儿交欢,又不是爬山蹍路,遇怪逢魔,要你保护他怎的! 他那样一把子年纪,岂不知被窝里之事,要你去扶揸?"行者一把揪住耳朵,轮拳骂道:"你这个淫心不断的夯货! 说那甚胡话!"(给孤园问古谈因,天竺国朝王遇偶)

Friar Sand went up to Pig, rubbed his face and said, "Shameless, you're shameless! That's a handsome mug, I must say. You're like the man

---

① Journey to the West, tr. by W. J. F Jenner[M], Beijing: Foreign Language Press, 1993.

who bought an old donkey for three-tenths of an ounce of silver and boasted that he'd be able to ride it. If she'd hit you first time she wouldn't have wanted to wait till tonight before burning spells to get rid of you. Do you think she'd have let trouble like you into the palace?" "You're being very disagreeable, you blacky," Pig replied. "Ugly I may be, but I've got class. As the old saying goes, 'When skin and flesh are coarse, the bones may yet be strong: everyone is good at something.'" "Stop talking nonsense, idiot," Monkey retorted, "and pack the baggage. I expect the master will get anxious and send for us, so we must be ready to go to protect him at court." "You're wrong again, brother," said Pig. "If the master's become the king's son-in-law and gone to take his pleasure with the king's daughter, he won't be climbing any more mountains, or tramping along the road, or running into demons and monsters. So what'll he want you to protect him from? He's old enough to know what happens under the bedcovers. He won't need you to hold him up." Monkey grabbed Pig by the ear, swung his fist, and said abusively, "You're as dirty-minded as ever, you cretin! How dare you talk such nonsense!"

(3)雪狮子向火——不觉化去。

那呆子看到好处,忍不住口嘴流涎,心头撞鹿,一时间骨软筋麻,好便似雪狮子向火,不觉得都化去也。只见那女王走近前来,一把扯住三藏,悄语娇声,叫道:"御弟哥哥,请上龙车,和我同上金銮宝殿,匹配夫妇去来。"这长老战战兢兢立站不住,似醉如痴。行者在侧教道:"师父不必太谦,请共师娘上辇,快快倒换关文,等我们取经去吧。"长老不敢回言,把行者抹了两抹,止不住落下泪来,行者道:"师父切莫烦恼,这般富贵,不受用还待怎么哩?"三藏没及奈何,只得依从,揩了眼泪,强整欢容,移步近前,与女主同携素手,共坐龙车。(法性西来逢女国,心猿定计脱烟花)

Seeing how beautiful she was the idiot could not help drooling. His heart pounded and his limbs went weak; he melted like a snow lion next to a bonfire. When the queen came closer to Sanzang she took hold of him and said in a most beguiling voice, "Dear emperor's brother, won't you come into my dragon coach, ride back with me to the throne hall and marry me?" The venerable elder trembled, feeling unsteady on his feet. It was as if he were drunk or stupefied. "Don't be so shy and modest, Master," urged monkey，who was standing beside him. "Please get into the carriage with your future wife. Have our passport returned to us as soon as possible so that we can continue on our journey to fetch the scriptures." Sanzang could not bring himself to reply as he put his hand on Monkey，unable to hold back his tears. "Don't be so upset，Master," Monkey said. "Here's your chance to enjoy wealth and honour，so make the most of it." Sanzang had no choice but to do as Monkey bade him. Wiping his tears away he forced himself to smile as he stepped forward to Hold the queen's white hand Sitting in the dragon carriage.

(二)语义等值

（1）八仙过海——各显神通。

我也曾花果山伏虎降龙，我也曾上天堂大闹天宫，饥时把老君的丹，略略咬了两三颗；渴时把玉帝的酒，轻轻鲛了六七钟。睁着一双不白不黑的金睛眼，天惨淡，月朦胧；拿着一条不短不长的金箍棒，来无影，去无踪。说什么大精小怪，哪怕他愈愒罢农！一赶赶上去，跑的跑，颤的颤，躲的躲，慌的慌；一捉捉将来，铧的铧，烧的烧，磨的磨，舂的舂。正是八仙同过海，独自显神通！众和尚，我拿这妖精与你看看，你才认得我老孙！（镇海寺心猿知怪，黑松林三众寻师）

"I used to subdue tigers and dragons on the Mountain of Flowers and Fruit；I once went up to Heaven and made great havoc in its palace. When I was hungry I nibbled just two or three of Lord Lao Zi's elixir tablets；When I was thirsty I sipped six or seven cups of the Jade Emperor's own wine. When I glare with my golden eyes that are neither black nor white，The sky turns deathly pale while the moon is hidden in cloud. When I wield my gold-banded cudgel that's the right length，It strikes unseen and leaves no trace behind. What do I care about big or little monsters，however rough or vicious they may be? Once I go for them They may run away，nimble about，hide or panic. Whenever I grab one they'll be filed down，cooked，ground to bits or pulverized in a mortar. I'm like one of the eight immortals crossing the sea，each of whom gives a unique display of his magical powers. Lamas，I'll catch that evil spirit and show it to you：Then you'll know what sort of person this Monkey is."

（2）贩古董的——识货。

小妖道:"猪八戒与沙和尚倒哄过了,孙行者却是个贩古董的——识货,识货!他就认得是个假人头。如今得个真人头与他,或者他就去了。"老怪道:"怎么得个真人头——我们那剥皮亭内有吃不了的人头选一个来。"众妖即至亭内拣了个新鲜的头,教啃净头皮,滑塔塔的,还使盘儿拿出,叫:"大圣爷爷,先前委是个假头。这个真正是唐老爷的头,我大王留了镇宅子的,今特献出来也。"扑通的把个人头又从门窟里抛出,血滴滴的乱滚。(木母助威征怪物,金公施法灭妖邪)

"Zhu Bajie and Friar Sand were taken in, but Monkey's like an antique dealer — he really knows his stuff," the junior demon replied. "He could tell it was an imitation head. If only we could give him a real human head he might go away." "But how are we to get one?" the senior demon wondered, then continued, "Fetch a human head we haven't eaten yet from the flaying shed." The devils then went to the shed and choose a fresh head, after which they gnawed all the skin off it till it was quite smooth and carried it out on a tray. "My lord Great Sage," the messenger said, "I am afraid it was a fake head last time. But this really is Lord Tang's head. Our king had kept it so as to bring good fortune to our cave, but now he's making a special offering of it." He then threw the head out through the hole in the gates, it landed with a thud and rolled on the ground, gory with blood. Seeing that this human head was a real one Monkey could not help starting to wail, in which he was joined by Pig and Friar Sand.

(3)棺材座子——专一害人。

落下云头叫道:"师父!"沙僧听见,报怨八戒道:"你是个棺材座子,专一害人!师兄不曾死,你却说他死了,在这里干这个勾当!那里不叫将来了?"八戒道:"我分明看见他被妖精一口吞了。想是日辰不好,那猴子来显魂哩。"行者到跟前,一把挝住八戒脸,一个巴掌打了个跟跄,道:"夯货!我显什么魂?"呆子捂着脸道:"哥哥,你实是那怪吃了,你、你怎么又活了?"(心神居舍魔归性,木母同降怪体真)

Bringing his cloud down, Monkey shouted, "Master!" As soon as Friar Sand heard this he started complaining to Pig. "All you want is to see people dead, just like a coffin stand," he said. "Our elder brother wasn't killed but you said he was and started this business here. Of course he's bound to kick up a row." "But I saw him with my own eyes being eaten up by the evil spirit in one mouthful," Pig replied. "I'm sure we're just seeing that ape's spirit because it's an unlucky day." Monkey then went up to Pig and hit him in the face with a slap that sent him staggering. "Cretin!" he said. "Is this my spirit you can see?" Rubbing his face, the idiot replied, "But the monster really did eat you up, brother. How can you — how can you have come back to life?"

(4)滚汤泼老鼠——一窝都是死。

那女子都跳下水去,一个个跃浪翻波,负水玩耍。行者道:"我若打他啊,只消把这棍子往池中一搅,就叫作滚汤泼老鼠,一窝儿都是死。可怜,可怜!打便打死他,只是低了老孙的名头。常言道,男不与女斗,我这般一个汉子,打杀这几个丫头,着实不济。不要打他,只送他一个绝后计,教他动不得身,出不得水,多少是好。"好大圣,捏着诀,念个咒,摇身一变,变作一个饿老鹰。(盘丝洞七情迷本,濯垢泉八戒忘形)

The women all jumped into the water and enjoyed themselves as they frolicked in the waves. "If I wanted to hit them," Monkey thought, "I'd only need to stir the water with my cudgel. It would be like pouring boiling water on a nest of mice: I could kill the lot of them. What a pity. If I hit them I'd kill them, but it wouldn't do my reputation any good. As they say, a real man doesn't fight women. It'd be hopeless if a man like me killed these girls. If I'm not going to hit them I'll have to make things difficult for them so that they can't move." The splendid Great Sage made a spell with his hands, said the words of it, shook himself and turned into a hungry eagle.

(5)和尚误了做,老婆误了娶——两下里耽搁。

老高又道:"师父们既不受金银,望将这粗衣笑纳,聊表寸心。"三藏又道:"我出家人,若受了一丝之贿,千劫难修。只是把席上吃不了的饼果,带些去做干粮足矣。"八戒在旁边道:"师父、师兄,你们不要便罢,我与他家做了这几年女婿,就是挂脚粮也该三石哩。丈人啊,我的直裰,昨晚被师兄扯破了,与我一件青锦袈裟;鞋子绽了,与我一双好新鞋子。"高老闻言,不敢不与,随买一双新鞋,将一领褊衫,换下旧时衣物。那八戒摇摇摆摆,对高老唱个喏道:"上复丈母、大姨、二姨并姨夫、姑舅诸亲,我今日去做和尚了,不及面辞,休怪。丈人啊,你还好生看待我浑家,只怕我们取不成经时,好来还俗,照旧与你做女婿过活。"行者喝道:"夯货,却莫胡说!"八戒道:"哥呵,不是胡说,只恐一时间有些

儿差池,却不是和尚误了做,老婆误了娶,两下里都耽搁了?"(云栈洞悟空收八戒,浮屠山玄奘受心经)

"If you won't take gold or silver," Squire Gao said, "please be good enough to accept these rough clothes as a mark of our gratitude." "If we monks accepted a single thread, we would have to atone for it for a thousand ages," replied Sanzang. "It will suffice if we take the pancakes and fruit that we haven't eaten with us as provisions for the journey." "Master, elder brother," said Pig, who was standing beside them, "it's all right for you two to refuse them, but I was a son-in-law in this family for several years, and I deserves three bushels of grain to take with me. On yes, father-in-law, my tunic was torn by elder brother yesterday and my shoes have split, so please give me a black brocade cassock and a good pair of new shoes." Old Squire Gao, who could scarcely refuse this request, gave him the new shoes and a tunic in exchange for his old ones. Pig swaggered over to Old Gao, chanted a "na-a-aw" of respect, and said, "Please inform my mother-in-law, my sisters-in-law, my brothers-in-law, and my uncles that I have become a monk today, and ask them to excuse me for not saying good-bye to them in person. Father-in-law, look after my wife well. If we don't get the scriptures, I'll go back to lay life and work for you as a son-in-law again." "Moron," shouted Monkey, "stop talking nonsense." "I'm doing nothing of the sort," Pig replied, "I am thinking that if things go wrong I'd be wasting my time as a monk, and my wife's marriage would have been ruined, both for nothing."

(6)黄梅不落青梅落——老天偏害没儿人。

八戒道:"好贵名!怎么叫作一秤金?"老者道:"我因儿女艰难,修桥补路,建寺立塔,布施斋僧,有一本账目,那里使三两,那里使五两,到生女之年,却好用过有三十斤黄金。三十斤为一秤,所以唤做一秤金。"行者道:"那个的儿子么?"老者道:"舍弟有个儿子,也是偏出,今年七岁了,取名唤做陈关保。"行者问:"何取此名?"老者道:"家下供养关圣爷爷,因在关爷之位下求得这个儿子,故名关保,我兄弟二人,年岁百二,止得这两个人种,不期轮次到我家祭赛,所以不敢不献。故此父子之情,难割难舍,先与孩儿做个超生道场,故曰预修亡斋者,此也。"三藏闻言,止不住腮边泪下道:"这正是古人云,黄梅不落青梅落,老天偏害没儿人。"(圣僧夜阻通天水,金木垂慈救小童)

"That's a very grand name," said Pig. "But why Pan of Gold?" "Because we were childless we built bridges, repaired roads, contributed to putting up monasteries and pagodas, gave donations and fed monks. We kept an account of all this, and what with three ounces spent here and five spent there it added up to thirty pounds of gold by the time the girl was born. Thirty pounds is a pan of gold, and hence the name." "What about sons?" Monkey asked. "My brother has a son who was also by a concubine. He is six this year, and we call him Chen Guan—given." "Why did you call him that?" Monkey asked. "In our family we worship Lord Guan Yu, and we called him Guan—given as it was from the statue of Lord Guan that we begged and obtained this son. My brother and I are 120 between us if you add our ages together, and these are our only two offspring. We never imagined that it would fall to us to provide the sacrificial offerings this year, and this is a duty we cannot escape. It is because as fathers we cannot bear to part from our children that we held this service to bring about rebirth, this maigre—feast to prepare for death." This brought the tears pouring down Sanzang's cheeks as he replied, "This is what the ancients mean when they said, Long before the ripe ones the green plums always fall; The harshness of heaven hits the childless worst of all."

(7)烂板凳——高谈阔论。

却说行者取了辟火罩,一筋斗送上南天门,交与广目天王道:"谢借,谢借!"天王收了道:"大圣至诚了。我正愁你不还我的宝贝,无处寻讨,且喜就送来也。"行者道:"老孙可是那当面骗物之人?这叫做好借好还,再借不难。"天王道:"许久不面,请到宫少坐一时何如?"行者道:"老孙比在前不同,烂板凳高谈阔论了。如今保唐僧,不得身闲。容叙,容叙!"急辞别坠云,又见那太阳星上,径来到禅堂前,摇身一变,变做个蜜蜂儿,飞将进去,现了本象,看时那师父还沉睡哩。(观音院僧谋宝贝,黑风山怪窃袈裟)

Brother Monkey grabbed the Anti-fire Cover, took it back to the Southern Gate of Heaven with a single somersault, and returned it to the Broad-visioned Heavenly King with thanks. "Great Sage," said the Heavenly King as he accepted it. "You are as good as your word. I was so worried that if you didn't give me back my treasure, I'd never be able to find you and get it off you. Thank goodness you've returned it." "Am I the sort of bloke who'd cheat someone to his face?" asked Monkey. "After all, 'If you return a thing properly when you borrow it, it'll be easier to borrow it next time.'" "As we haven't met for so long, why don't you come into the palace for a while?" said the Heavenly King. "I'm no longer the man to sit on the bench till it rots, talking about the universe,'" Monkey replied. "I'm too busy now that I have to look after the Tang Monk. Please excuse me." Leaving with all speed, he went down on his cloud, and saw that the sun was rising as he went straight to the meditation hall, where he shook himself, turned into a bee, and flew in. On reverting to his true form he saw that his master was still sound asleep.

(8)磨砖砌的喉咙——又光又溜。

那和尚与老者,一问一答的讲话,众人方才不怕。却将上面排了一张桌,请唐僧上坐;两边摆了三张桌,请他三位坐;前面一张桌,坐了二位老者。先排上素果品菜蔬,然后是面饭、米饭、闲食、粉汤,排得齐齐整整。唐长老举起箸来,先念一卷《启斋经》。那呆子一则有些急吞,二来有些饿了,那里等唐僧经完,拿过红漆木碗来,把一碗白米饭,扑地丢下口去,就了了。旁边小的道:"这位老爷忒没算计,不笾馒头,怎的把饭笾了,却不污了衣服?"八戒笑道:"不曾笾,吃了。"小的道:"你不曾举口,怎么就吃了?"八戒道:"儿子们便说谎!分明吃了。不信,再吃与你看。"那小的们,又端了碗,盛一碗递与八戒。呆子晃一晃,又丢下口去就了了。众僮仆见了道:"爷爷呀!你是磨砖砌的喉咙,着实又光又溜!"(圣僧夜阻通天水,金木垂慈救小童)

As the monks talked to the old man the servants lost their fear and set a table in front of the Tang Priest, inviting him to take the place of honour. They then put three more tables on both sides of him, at which they asked the three disciples to sit, and another in front of these for the two old men. On the tables were neatly arranged some fruit, vegetables, pasta, rice, refreshments and pea-noodle soup. Sanzang raised his chopsticks and started to say a grace over the food, but the idiot, who was impatient and hungry to boot, did not wait for him to finish before grabbing a red lacquered wooden bowl of white rice that he scooped up and gulped down in a single mouthful. "Sir," said the servant standing beside him, "you didn't think very carefully. If you are going to keep food in your sleeves shouldn't you take steamed bread instead of rice that will get your clothes duty?" "I didn't put it in my sleeve," chuckled Pig, "I ate it. " "But you didn't even open your mouth," they said, "so how could you have eaten it?" "Who is lying then?" said Pig. "I definitely ate it. If you don't believe me I'll eat another to show you. " The servants carried the rice over, filled a bowlful, and passed it to Pig, who had it down his throat in a flash. "Sir," said the astonished servants, "you must have a throat built of whetstones, it's so smooth and slippery. "

(9)皮笊篱——一捞个罄尽。

老君喝道:"去,去,去!"这大圣拽转步,往前就走。老君忽的寻思道:"这猴子愈懒哩,说去就去,只怕溜进来就偷。"即命仙童叫回来道:"你这猴子,手脚不稳,我把这还魂丹送你一九罢。"行者道:"老官儿,既然晓得老孙的手段,快把金丹拿出来,与我四六分分,还是你的造化哩。不然,就送你个皮笊篱,一捞个罄尽。"那老祖取过葫芦来,倒吊过底子,倾出一粒金丹,递与行者道:"止有此了,拿去,拿去!送你这一粒,医活那皇帝,只算你的功果罢。"行者接了道:"且休忙,等我尝尝看,只怕是假的,莫被他哄了。"扑的往口里一丢,慌得那老祖上前扯住,一把揪着顶瓜皮,擅着拳头骂道:"这泼猴若要咽下去,就直打杀了!"行者笑道:"嘴脸!小家子样!那个吃你的哩!能值几个钱?虚多实少的,在这里不是?"原来那猴子颔下有嗉袋儿,他把那金丹噙在嗉袋里,被老祖捻着道:"去吧,去吧!再休来此缠绕!"这大圣才谢了老祖,出离了兜率天宫。
(一粒金丹天上得,三年故主世间生)

"Get out! Get out! Get out!" roared Lord Lao Zi, at which Monkey turned away and went. It then suddenly occurred to Lord Lao Zi that Monkey was so wicked that even after he had announced his departure and gone, he might slip back and steal some. So he sent some immortal boys to call Monkey back. "You're so light-fingered, you monkey," he said, "that I'd better give you a Soul-returning Pill. " "Since you know my powers, old man," said Brother Monkey, "bring out all your golden elixir and split it forty-sixty with me. You can consider yourself lucky. I might have taken the lot of them, like scooping up water in a leather sieve. " The patriarch produced the gourd and turned it upside-down. A solitary golden pill fell out. "It's the only one I have," said Lord Lao Zi, handing it to Monkey. "Take it. I'm giving it to you to revive the king with and you can take the credit for it. " "Just a moment," thought Monkey as he accepted it. "Let me taste it. He might be trying to fool me with a fake." He popped it into his mouth, to the consternation of the patriarch, who grabbed him by the skullcap with one hand and seized his fist with the other. "Damned ape," roared Lord Lao Zi, "if you've swallowed that I'll have had you killed." "What a face," laughed Monkey. "How petty you look. I wouldn't want to eat your pill. It's not worth tuppence, and it's nothing like it's cracked up to be. Here it is." Monkey had a pouch under his chin in which he had been keeping the pill. Lord Lao Zi felt it, then said, "Clear off, and never come back here to pester me again." The Great Sage then thanked the patriarch and left the Tushita Palace.

（10）蛇头上的苍蝇——自来的衣食。

那长老看见他这般模样,唬得打了一个倒退,遍体酥麻,两腿酸软,急忙地抽身便走。刚刚转了一个身,那妖魔,他的灵性着实是强大。撑开着一双金睛鬼眼,叫声:"小的们,你看门外是什么人!"一个小妖就伸头望门外一看,看见是个光头的长老,连忙跑将进去,报道:"大王,外面是个和尚哩,团头大面,两耳垂肩,嫩刮刮的一身肉,细娇娇的一张皮,且是好个和尚!"那妖闻言,呵声笑道:"这叫作个蛇头上苍蝇,自来的衣食。你众小的们,急忙赶上去,与我拿将来,我这里重重有赏!"那些小妖,就是一窝蜂,齐齐拥上。三藏见了,虽则是一心忙似箭,两脚走如飞,终是心惊胆战,腿软脚麻,况且是山路崎岖,林深日暮,步儿那里移得动?被那些小妖,平抬将去。(花果山群妖聚义,黑松林三藏逢魔)

Sanzang was so terrified at the sight of him that he shrank back, his whole body numb with terror. No sooner had he turned to go than the monster, whose powers really were tremendous, opened a fiendish eye with a golden pupil and shouted, Who is that outside the door, little ones? "A junior devil poked his head out to look, saw a shaven—headed priest, and ran in to report, "A monk, Your Majesty. He has a large face and a round head, and his ears hang down to his shoulders. His flesh looks most tender and his skin extremely delicate. He's a very promising monk. The monster cackled and said, "This is what they call 'a fly landing on a snake's head, or food and clothing presenting themselves to you'. Go and catch him for me, lads, and bring him back here. I'll reward you well." The junior demons rushed out after Sanzang like a swarm of bees; and Sanzang, in his alarm, started to run so fast he seemed to fly. But he was so terrified that his legs were soon like numb jelly, and on top of this the path was very uneven and it was twilight in the deep forest. He could not move fast enough, and the junior demons picked him up and carried him back.

（11）铁刷帚刷铜锅——家家挺硬。

且不言唐长老困苦，却说那三个魔头齐心竭力，与大圣兄弟三人，在城东半山内努力争持。这一场，正是那铁刷帚刷铜锅，家家挺硬。好杀—— 六般体相六般兵，六样形骸六样情。六恶六根缘六欲，六门六道赌输赢。三十六宫春自在，六六形色很有名。这一个金箍棒，千般解数；那一个方天戟，百样峥嵘。八戒钉耙凶更猛，二怪长枪俊又能。小沙僧宝杖非凡，有心打死；老魔头钢刀快利，举手无情。这三个是护卫真僧无敌将，那三个是乱法欺君泼野精。起初犹可，向后弥凶。六枚都使升空法，云端里面各翻腾。一时间吐雾喷云天地暗，哮哮吼吼只闻声。（群魔欺本性，一体拜真如）

We will tell now not of the sufferings of the venerable Tang Elder but of the three demon chiefs in strenuous combat with the Great Sage and his two brother disciples in the low hills to the East outside the city. It was indeed a good hard battle, like an iron brush against a copper pan: Six types of body, six types of weapon, Six physical forms, six feelings. The six evils arise from the six sense organs and the six desires; The six gates to nirvana and the six ways of rebirth are struggling for victory. In the thirty-six divine palaces spring comes of itself; The six times six forms do not want to be named. This one holding a gold-banded cudgel Performs a thousand movements; That one wielding a heaven-square halberd Is exceptional in every way. Pig is even more ferocious with his rake; The second demon's spear—play is superb and effective. There is nothing commonplace about young Friar Sand's staff As he tries to inflict a blow that is fatal; Sharp is the senior demon's saber Which he raises without mercy. These three are the true priest's invincible escorts; The other three are evil and rebellious spirits. At first the fight is not so bad, But later it becomes more murderous. All six weapons rise up by magic To twist and turn in the clouds above. They belch out in an instant clouds that darken the sky, And the only sounds to be heard are roars and bellows.

（12）鱼水盆内捻苍蝇——有何难。

　　小妖道："如今把洞口大小群妖,点将起来,千中选百,百中选十,十中只选三个,须是有能干,会变化的,都变做大王的模样,顶大王之盔,贯大王之甲,执大王之杵,三处埋伏。先着一个战猪八戒,再着一个战孙行者,再着一个战沙和尚。舍着三个小妖,调开他弟兄三个,大王却在半空伸下拿云手去捉这唐僧,就如探囊取物,就如鱼水盆内捻苍蝇,有何难哉!"老妖闻言,满心欢喜,道:"此计绝妙,绝妙! 这一去,拿不得唐僧便罢,若是拿了唐僧,决不轻你,就封你做个前部先锋。"小妖叩头谢恩,叫点妖怪。即将洞中大小妖精点起,果然选出三个有能的小妖,俱变做老妖,各执铁杵,埋伏等待唐僧不提。(心猿妒木母,魔主计吞禅)

　　"Call the roll of all the devils in the cave," the junior devil replied. "Choose the best hundred from all thousand of them, then the best ten out of that hundred, and finally the best three out of the ten. They must be capable and good at transformations. Have them all turn into Your Majesty's doubles, wear Your Majesty's helmet and armor, carry Your Majesty's mace, and lie in wait in three different places. First send one out to fight Zhu Bajie, then one to fight Sun the Novice and finally one to fight Friar Sand. This way you'll only have to spare three junior devils to draw the three disciples away. Then Your Majesty will be able to stretch down from mid-air with your cloud-grabbing hand to catch the Tang Priest. He'll be in the bag. It'll be as easy as catching flies in a dish of fish juice. Nothing to it." This suggestion delighted the demon king, who said, "What a brilliant plan, brilliant! If I don't catch the Tang Priest this way, that'll be that. But if I do I can assure you you'll be richly rewarded. I'll make you commander of the vanguard." The junior devil kowtowed to thank him for his grace and went off to call the roll of the devils. After all the monsters in the cave had been carefully checked through, three capable junior devils were selected. They turned into the senior devil's doubles and went to lie in wait for the Tang Priest with their iron maces.

　　(13)糟鼻子不吃酒——枉担其名。

　　菩萨道："也不曾害人,自他到后,这三年间,风调雨顺,国泰民安,何害人之有?"行者道:"固然如此,但只三宫娘娘,与他同眠同起,玷污了他的身体,坏了多少纲常伦理,还叫作不曾害人?"菩萨道:"点污他不得,他是个骗了的狮子。"八戒闻言,走近前,就摸了一把,笑道:"这妖精真个是糟鼻子不吃酒——

枉担其名了!"行者道:"既如此,收了去吧。若不是菩萨亲来,决不饶他性命。"那菩萨却念个咒,喝道:"畜生,还不皈正,更待何时!"那魔王才现了原身。菩萨放莲花罩定妖魔,坐在背上,踏祥光辞了行者。咦!径转五台山上去,宝莲座下听谈经。毕竟不知那唐僧师徒怎的出城,且听下回分解。(一粒金丹天上得,三年故主世间生)

"He never killed anyone," the Bodhisattva replied. "In the three years since his arrival the winds and rains have come at the right time, the state has been strong and the people have known peace. He did nobody any harm." "Even if all that is granted," said Monkey, "he's been sleeping with the queen and the consorts in the harem. Surely this has sullied them and been an affront to morality." "He has not sullied them at all," the Bodhisattva replied. "He's a gelded lion." Hearing this Pig went up to the creature and had a feel. "This evil spirit's got a bad reputation he doesn't deserve," he chuckled, "like a teetotaler with a red nose." "In that case," said Monkey, "take him with you. If you hadn't come, Bodhisattva, I'd never have spared his life." The Bodhisattva then said a spell and shouted, "Return to the Truth, beast. What are you waiting for?" Only then did the fiend—king return to his original form, Manjusri placed a lotus—blossom over the monster to tame him, sat on his back, and left Monkey amid golden light. Ah! Manjusri returned to Wutai Mountain To hear the scriptures taught beneath the lotus throne. If you don't know how the Tang Priest and his disciples left the city, listen to the explanation in the next installment.

(14)大海里翻了豆腐船,汤里来,水里去。

行者道:"别你后,顷刻就到这座山上,见一个女子问讯,原来就是他爱妾玉面公主。被我使铁棒唬他一唬,他就跑进洞,叫出那牛王来。与老孙暧言暧语,嚷了一会,又与他交手,斗了有一个时辰。正打处,有人请他赴宴去了。是我跟他到那乱石山碧波潭底,变作一个螃蟹,探了消息,偷了他辟水金晴兽,假变牛王模样,复至翠云山芭蕉洞,骗了罗刹女,哄得他扇子。出门试演试演方法,把扇子弄长了,只是不会收小。正揣了走处,被他假变做你的嘴脸,返骗了去,故此耽搁两三个时辰也。"八戒道:"这正是俗语云,大海里翻了豆腐船,汤里来,水里去。如今难得他扇子,如何保得师父过山?且回去,转路走他娘罢!"(猪八戒助力败魔王,孙行者三调芭蕉扇)

"I reached this mountain soon after I left you," Monkey replied, "and saw a woman. When I questioned her she turned out to be his favorite concubine Princess Jade. I gave her a bit of a fright with my cudgel, so she fled into the cave and sent her Bull Demon King out. He and I swapped a few insults then started fighting. We'd been at it for a couple of hours when someone came to invite him to a banquet. I tailed him to the bottom of the Green Wave Pool on Ragged Rock Mountain and turned into a crab to do a little spying. Then I stole his water-averting golden-eyed beast and changed myself into the Bull Demon King's double to go back to the Plantain Cave on Mount Turquoise Cloud, where I conned Raksasi into giving me the fan. I went outside to try the magic spell out on the fan and made it grow, but I didn't know how to make it shrink again. As I was walking along with it on my shoulder he turned himself into your spitting image and tricked it back off me again. That's how I wasted six hours." "As the saying goes," Pig replied, "it's just like a boatful of beancurd sinking: it came out of the wet and it disappeared into the wet. Easy come, easy go, But how are we going to take our master across the mountains if we're having so hard a time getting the fan? We'll just have to go back and make a bloody detour."

(15)苍蝇包网儿,好大面皮。

天王道:"那壁厢敢是不该下雨哩。我向时闻得说:那郡侯撒泼,冒犯天地,上帝见罪,立有米山、面山、黄金大锁,直等此三事倒断,才该下雨。"行者不知此意是何,要见玉帝。天王不敢拦阻,让他进去。径至通明殿外,又见四大天师迎道:"大圣到此何干?"行者道:"因保唐僧,路至天竺国界,凤仙郡无雨,郡侯召师祈雨。老孙呼得龙王,意命降雨,他说未奉玉帝旨意,不敢擅行,特来求旨,以苏民困。"四大天师道:"那方不该下雨。"行者笑道:"该与不该,烦为引奏引奏,看老孙的人情何如。"葛仙翁道:"俗语云:苍蝇包网儿,好大面皮!"许旌阳道:"不要乱谈,且只带他进去。"(凤仙郡冒天止雨,孙大圣劝善施霖)

"I don't think it's supposed to rain there," the heavenly king said. "I heard just now that the marquis of Fengxian had behaved disgracefully and offended both Heaven and Earth. His Majesty took it badly and immediately had a rice mountain, a flour mountain and a huge gold lock set up. It won't rain till all three have been knocked over or snapped." Not understanding what all this was about, Monkey demanded to see the Jade Emperor, and, not daring to stop him, the heavenly king let him in. Going straight to the

Hall of Universal Brightness, Brother Monkey was met by the four heavenly teachers, who asked, "What are you here for, Great Sage?" "On my journey escorting the Tang Priest I've reached Fengxian Prefecture on the frontiers of India, where there is a drought," Monkey replied. "The marquis there has been asking for magicians to pray for rain. I sent for the dragon king to order him to make rain, but he said that he could not do so on his own authority without an edict from the Jade Emperor. I have now come to request an edict in order to relieve the people's suffering." "But it's not supposed to rain there," said the four heavenly teachers. "As to whether it's supposed to rain or not," said Monkey with a smile, "could I trouble you to take me in to submit a memorial so that I can find out whether I can still get a favour done?" To this the heavenly teacher Ge Xianweng replied, "As the saying goes, 'a fly that needs a net for a veil — what a nerve!'" "Don't talk nonsense," said Xu of Jingyang. "Just take him in."

(三)语用等值

(1)吃了磨刀水的——秀气在内。

那老者满心欢喜,即命家僮请几个左邻右舍,表弟姨兄,亲家朋友,共有八九位老者,都来相见。会了唐僧,言及拿妖一事,无不欣然。众老问:"是那一位高徒去拿?"行者叉手道:"是我小和尚。"众老悚然道:"不济,不济! 那妖精神通广大,身体狼犺。你这个长老,瘦瘦小小,还不彀他填牙齿缝哩!"行者笑道:"老官儿,你估不出人来。我小自小,结实,都是吃了磨刀水的,秀气在内哩!"众老见说只得依从道:"长老,拿住妖精,你要多少谢礼?"行者道:"何必说要什么谢礼! 俗语云,说金子晃眼,说银子傻白,说铜钱腥气! 我等乃积德的和尚,决不要钱。"(拯救驼罗禅性稳,脱离秽污道心清)

The old man was delighted. He sent his slaves to invite seven or eight old men from among his next-door neighbors, his cousins, his wife's family and his friends. They all came to meet the strangers, and when they had greeted the Tang Priest they cheerfully discussed the capture of the demon. "Which of your distinguished disciples will do it?" they asked. "I will," said Monkey, putting his hands together in front of his chest. "You'll never do, never," said the old man with horror. "The evil spirit's magic powers are enormous, and it's huge too. Venerable sir, you're so tiny and skinny you'd slip through one of the gaps between its teeth." "Old man," said

Monkey with a smile, "You're no judge of people. Small I may be, but I'm solid. There's a lot more to me than meets the eye." When the elders heard this they had to take him at his word. "Venerable sir," they said, "how big a reward will you want for capturing the demon?" "Why do you have to talk about a reward?" Monkey asked. "As the saying goes, 'Gold dazzles, silver is white and stupid, and copper coins stink.' We're virtuous monks and we definitely won't take money."

（2）和尚拖木头——做出了寺。

行者寻着唐僧,和那龙马,和那行李。那老怪寻思无路,看着哪吒太子,只是磕头求命。太子道:"这是玉旨来拿你,不当小可。我父子只为受了一炷香。险些儿和尚拖木头,做出了寺!"幸声:"天兵,取下缚妖索,把那些妖精都捆了!"老怪也少不得吃场苦楚。返云光,一齐出洞。行者口里嘻嘻嘎嘎。天王掣开洞口,迎着行者道:"今番却见你师父也。"行者道:"多谢了! 多谢了!"就引三藏拜谢天王,次及太子。沙僧八戒只是要碎剐那老精,天王道:"他是奉御旨拿的,轻易不得。我们还要去回旨哩。"(心猿识得丹头,姹女还归本性)

Monkey found the Tang Priest, the dragon horse and the baggage. The senior demon was at her wit's end. All she could do was to kowtow to Prince Nezha, begging him to spare her life. "We are here to arrest you at the Jade Emperor's command," Prince Nezha replied, "which is not something to be treated lightly. My father and I were nearly in terrible trouble because of you." He then shouted at the top of his voice, "Heavenly soldiers, fetch demon—binding rope. Tie all those evil spirits up." The senior demon too had to suffer for a while. They all went back out of the cave together by cloud. Monkey was chuckling with delight when the heavenly king withdrew his guard from the mouth of the cave and greeted Monkey with the words, "Now I can meet your master." "Many thanks," said Monkey, "many thanks," and he led Sanzang to bow in gratitude to the heavenly king and the prince. Friar Sand and Pig were all for chopping the senior devil into tiny pieces, but the heavenly king said, "She was arrested at the Jade Emperor's command, and must not be mistreated. We must go to report back on our mission."

（3）尖担担柴——两头脱。

长老道:"你去不得。那猢狲原与你不和,你又说话粗鲁,或一言两句之间,有些差池,他就要打你。着悟净去吧。"沙僧应承道:"我去,我去。"长老又吩咐沙僧道:"你到那里,须看个头势。他若肯与你包袱,你就假谢谢拿来;若不肯,切莫与他争竞,径至南海菩萨处,将此情告诉,请菩萨去问他要。"沙僧——听从,向八戒道:"我今寻他去,你千万莫参飙,好生供养师父。这人家亦不可撒泼,恐他不肯供饭,我去就回。"八戒点头道:"我理会得。但你去,讨得讨不得,次早回来,不要弄做尖担担柴两头脱也。"沙僧遂捻了诀,驾起云光,直奔东胜神洲而去。(真行者落伽山诉苦,假猴王水帘洞誊文)

"No," said Sanzang, "not you. You have never got on with that macaque, and besides you're very rough—spoken. If you say anything wrong he'll hit you. Let Wujing go." Friar Sand agreed at once, and Sanzang gave him these instructions: "When you get there you must keep a close watch on the situation. If he is willing to give you back the bundles then pretend to be very grateful when you accept them. If he won't you must on no account quarrel with him. Go straight to the Bodhisattva in the Southern Sea, tell her what has happened, and ask her to demand them from him." Friar Sand accepted his instructions and said to Pig, "I'm off to find Monkey now. Whatever you do, don't complain. Look after the master properly. You mustn't have a row with these people or they might not feed you. I'll soon be back." "I understand," Pig replied with a nod. "Off you go, and come back soon whether you recover the luggage or not. Otherwise we'll have lost both ways," Friar Sand then made a hand spell and headed off by cloud for the Eastern Continent of Superior Body.

(4)乍入芦圩——不知深浅。

行者闻言,把功曹叱退,切切在心,按云头,径来山上。只见长老与八戒、沙僧,簇拥前进,他却暗想:"我若把功曹的言语实实告送师父,师父他不济事,必就哭了;假若不与他实说,梦着头,带着他走,常言道乍入芦圩,不知深浅。倘或被妖魔捞去,却不又要老孙费心?且等我照顾八戒一照顾,先着他出头与那怪打一仗看。若是打得过他,就算他一功;若是没手段,被怪拿去,等老孙再去救他不迟,却好显我本事出名。"正自家计较,以心问心道:"只恐八戒躲懒便不肯出头,师父又有些护短,等老孙羁勒他羁勒。"(平顶山功曹传信,莲花洞木母逢灾)

Monkey dismissed the Duty God. He was feeling worried as he landed his cloud and went up the mountainside until he found Sanzang, Pig and

Friar Sand pressing ahead. "If I tell the master straight what the Duty God said," he thought, "the master won't be able to face up to it and will start crying. But if I don't tell him and keep him in the dark he won't know how things stand, and it'll be a great nuisance for me if he gets captured by monsters. I'd better go and see Pig. I can send him ahead to fight the monster. If he wins, that will be something to his credit. If he can't do it and gets captured by the monster, I can go and rescue him, which will give me a chance to show what I can do and make myself famous." As he made these calculations he wondered whether Pig would try to slip out of it and be protected by Sanzang. He decided he would have to force him into doing it.

以上句法、语义和语用三个等值层面探讨了《西游记》英译本中歇后语的翻译问题。

《西游记》歇后语俄语译文等值层面见表 3-5。

表 3-5 《西游记》歇后语俄语译文等值层面一览表①

等值层面		歇后语原文	译 文
句法等值		黄梅不落青梅落,老天偏害没儿人	Слива Хуан-мэй не опадает, а опадает слива Цин-мэй. Небо наказывает тех, у кого нет детей.
		三钱银子买了毛驴,自夸骑得	Купил себестарого осла за три гроша и хвалится
语义等值	成分等值及所指等值	乍入芦圩,不知深浅	Когда неожиданно попадешь в омут, то поздно раздумывать, глубокий он или мелкий
		雪狮子向火,不觉得都化去	Словно снежный лев у жаркого костра
		滚汤泼老鼠,一窝儿都是死	Кипяток, кипяток! Свари поганых мышей. Пусть весь выводок сразу подохнет
		狗咬尿泡空欢喜	Впустую кот радуется, грызя мочевой пузырь

① 《西游记》俄译本由苏联汉学家 А. Л. 罗卡契夫翻译,1959 年在莫斯科国家文学出版社出版。

续 表

等值层面		歇后语原文	译 文
语义等值	成分等值及所指等值	磨砖砌的喉咙,着实又光又滑	Да что у тебя горло полированным кирпичом, что ли, выложено, что пища проходит, как по маслу, без малейшей задержки
		蛇头上苍蝇,自来的衣食	Когда мухи садятся змее на голову, это все равно, что пища сама лезет в рот.
		贩古董的——识货	Этот старьевщик, который распознает всякий хлам с первого взгляда
		铁刷帚刷铜锅,家家挺硬	Нашла коса на камень
		鱼水盆内捻苍蝇,有何难	Причем с такой же легкостью, как 《достают вещи из сумы》 или 《муху из воды》
交际语用等值		棺材座子,专一害人	Катафалк добра не сулит
		吃了磨刀水的,秀气在内	Вспоили меня водой от точильного камня, лучший из всех пяти жизненных духов играет во мне
		和尚误了做,老婆误了娶,两下里都耽搁	Это, конечно, не значит, что я буду выполнять свой долг недобросовестно. Но если ничего не выйдет, я вдвойне проиграю
		尖胆担柴两头脱	Да будь осторожен, не то сам пропадешь
		烂板凳高谈阔论	Свободно ходить по гостям и вести разговоры
		皮笊篱,一捞个罄尽	Ведь я мог пустить в ход волшебство, и все пилюли мигом очутились бы у меня
		糟鼻子不吃酒——枉担其名	Не даром говорится: 《кто с красным носом, _ не пьют вина》.
		大海里翻了豆腐船,汤里来,水里去	Откуда пришло_туда и ушло.
		八仙同过海,独自显神通	Восьмерых я бессмертных могуществом превосхожу. Тех, что ездили за море. Бросьте сомнения и страхи!

　　结合《红楼梦》和《西游记》中歇后语的翻译实例,不难看出,语义和语用层面的等值普遍要比句法层面的等值来得多。由于汉语语言文化的特殊性及文化空缺的存在,翻译家在对作品中的歇后语进行处理时,往往不能单从字面意义去理解和翻译,或保留形象直译,或转换形象意译,有时舍弃形象意译,以求更准确地传达汉语歇后语所包含的民族和文化特色。

第四章 歇后语的翻译方法

第一节 翻译策略

韦努蒂认为,翻译策略涉及对原文本的选择和翻译原文本时所采取的翻译方法的选择。[①] 本节所探讨的翻译策略仅限于后者。对于翻译策略范畴的划分,不同的学者、不同的学派尽管所用术语各不相同,却有惊人的相似。但对于制约翻译策略选择的因素,他们往往只从自己的视角出发,突出各自不同的影响因素,对其他的因素予以排斥或避而不谈。然而,综合各家理论,我们不难看出,译者选择某种翻译策略是基于各种翻译"间接"的对话交流。

各家翻译理论用于研究翻译策略的术语不尽相同,却基本上可归于两大范畴:归化策略和异化策略。

自奈达把文化概念引入翻译中以来,翻译理论家和实践者就如何处理语言外因素提出各种疑问。和原来翻译界争执不休的"直译"和"意译"不同,他们更关注文化因素在翻译中的得失,因为语言是文化的载体,两种语言的不同不只是语言文字、遣词造句等语言形式的不同,它们蕴含的两种文化的不同之处也会在文章的字里行间传递出来。在翻译中,对于如何处理原文特有的文化信息,翻译家们持两种意见:有些翻译家建议删除原文特有的、译文读者不熟悉的那些文化差异,或者将这些差异转化为译文读者熟悉、和原文对等的译入语中的文化现象;另一些翻译家提倡保留原文语言和非语言的特性,以便译文读者能欣赏原文的异域美,拓展知识。由此产生了两个翻译概念:归化和异化。这一对概念一经提出,围绕它们的争论就无休无止。

1995 年,韦努蒂在 *The Translator's Invisibility* 一书中,将第一种方法称作"异化法",另一种称作"归化法"。韦努蒂从文化和政治的角度,将翻译途

---

① BAKER. Mona Routledge Encyclopedia of Translation Studies[M]. Shanghai: Shanghai Foreign Language Education Press,2004:240 - 244.

径分为归化和异化。前者指翻译"遵循目的语文化的主流价值、对异域文本进行同化";后者指翻译"采用边缘价值、复兴本二经典所排斥的异域文本、培植新文本和新方法(如新的文化形式)来抵制或旨在改变主流价值"。韦努蒂认为,为使异域文本能被本土文化中的特定群体易于理解,翻译是一个不可避免的归化过程,但有时采用归化和异化是有意而为之。①

翻译理论家施莱尔马赫在《论翻译的方法》中提出,翻译的途径只有两种:一种是尽可能让作者安居不动,而引导读者去接近作者;另一种是尽可能让读者安居不动,而引导作者去接近读者。

诺德(Nord)从翻译的目的和文本功能的角度总结出翻译的两大基本策略:"纪实性翻译"(documentary translation)和"工具性翻译"(instrumental translation)。②

多元系统论的代表人物之一图里认为,译者在选择翻译起始规范(initial norm)时有两种选择,偏向于"充分性"(adequacy)或偏向于"可接受性"(acceptability)。

关联翻译理论代表人物 Gutt 提出了"直接翻译"(direct translation)和"间接翻译"(indirect translation)这两种翻译策略。当译文保留原文中所有的交际线索(communicative clue),以求保留原文的风格时,就是"直接翻译"。反之,当译文只求保留原文的认知效果,保留原文的基本意义,对原文的表现形式作较大的改动时,这种翻译就是"间接翻译"。

操纵学派的代表人物勒菲弗尔认为译者可分为"忠实型"或"保守型"译者(faithful or conservative translator)和"灵活型译者"(spirited translator)。③

上述所列举的西方各学派所用的成对术语各不相同,但其实质乃为异化和归化的对立。

而中国译论从支谦的"文""质"之分、玄奘的"求真"与"喻俗"、马建忠的"善译"、严复的"信雅达"、鲁迅的"宁信不顺"、赵景深的"宁顺不信"、傅雷的"神似"、钱钟书的"化境",到当代许渊冲的"语言竞赛论"等,也可归结为异化

① VENUTI L. The Translator's Invisibility: A History of Translation [M]. Shanghai: Shanghai Foreign Language Education Press,2004:99-100.
② NORD C. Translation as a Purposeful Activity Functionalist Approaches Explained[M]. Shanghai: Shanghai Foreign Language Education Press,2001:47-52.
③ LEFEVERE A. Translation, Rewriting and the Manipulation of Literary Fame [M]. Shanghai: Shanghai Foreign Language Education Press,2004:49-51.

和归化之争。在中国，早在 1935 年，鲁迅在《且界亭杂文二集"题未定"草》中就提出"动笔之前，就得先解决一个问题，竭力使它归化还是尽量保存洋气呢?"之后，中国许多翻译理论家如钱钟书、刘应凯、叶子南、许建平、张荣曦等，就归化和异化提出了个人见解。许建平、张荣曦如此定义归化和异化:"所谓异化、归化是就翻译中所涉及的文化转化而言，前者以源文化为归宿(source language culture oriented，i. e. culture-oriented)，后者以目的语文化为归宿(target language culture oriented，i. e. culture-oriented)。即异化提倡译文应当尽量去适应、照顾源语的文化及原作者的遣词用字习惯。而归化则恰恰相反，主张译文应尽量适应、照顾目的语的文化习惯，为读者着想，替读者扫除语言文化障碍。"①

　　实质上，异化和归化之争源于两方面的混淆。一是异化与归化实际上只是程度上的差异，其界限是模糊的，从极端归化到极端异化构成一个连续体。正如韦努蒂认为，翻译是一个不可避免的归化过程，那么异化与归化只是一个度的区别。也就是说，异化策略范畴和归化策略范畴各自包含有一系列的次范畴，它们的边缘次范畴是相互重叠的。此外，异化与归化的程度变化以时间为转移。随着时间的推移与社会的发展，在某一时期被认为是异化策略范畴下的非边缘次范畴有可能变成了归化策略范畴下的非边缘次范畴。二是异化与归化存在于两个层面，即语言层面和文化层面。许多归化异化之争是把两个层面混为一谈。语言层面的异化考虑如何在保持源语形式的同时，不让其意义失真;归化则认为语言有不同的文化内涵和表达形式，当形式成为翻译的障碍时，就要采取归化。而文化层面的异化与归化不考虑是否在翻译中恪守原文句法序列中的个别词语的意义，只关心不同文化之间的差异是否被掩盖，目的语主流文化价值观是否取代了源语的文化价值观。

　　因此，归化和异化是用来解决两者语言及其文化差异所带来的翻译问题的两种策略。归化偏重译入语，放弃译入语中不存在的、源语的文化形象或者语言形式，寻找译入语中对应的或者近似的文化形象或语言形式;异化偏重源语，保留源语中特有而译入语没有的文化形象或者语言形式，而不是用译入语中的文化形象或者表达形式来代替。

一、归化翻译

　　《辞海》对汉语的"归化"作了如下解释:"第一种是，旧称归服于教化。《论

---

　① 许建平，张荣曦. 跨文化翻译中的异化与归化问题[J]. 中国翻译.2002,9(5):36.

衡·程材》：'故习善儒路，归化慕义，志操则励，变从高明。'引申谓归顺。《三国志·魏志·邓艾传》：'作舟船，豫顺流之事，然后发使，告以利害，吴必归化，可不征而定也'。另一解释为'入籍'的旧称。"运用到翻译中，应与"归顺"和"入籍"的意思有密切的关系。

据《辞海》的解释，"异化"的一个意思是语音上的异化，另一意思是德文 entfremdung 的意译，是外来词，汉语中的归化与异化在英文中有两对术语与之对应：第一对是"assimilation, alienation"，第二对是"domestication, foreignization"。在翻译上，"归化"与"异化"跟 assimilation 和 alienation 相同的是，都探讨语言与文化的差异问题，都是以不同语言与文化的平等为基础的。汉语的"归化"也是侧重讲从不同到相似与相同的过程，但 domestication 中的"驯化"之意，"归化"中没有；而汉语的"异化"同样是保持"异己"成分，保留差异，没有文化不平等，作为对文化殖民的斗争与反抗手段的这层意思。"归化"与"异化"跟 assimilation 和 alienation 在含义上更接近一些。

刘英凯对归化概念的解读是：所谓"归化"，按《辞海》的解释，"即'入籍'的旧称"。翻译的"归化"则喻指翻译过程中，把客"籍"的出发语言极力纳入归宿语言之"籍"：英译汉就不遗余力地汉化，汉译英则千方百计地英化……余则类推。译坛上素有"宁顺而不信"论者，而"归化"的译文让人听了耳熟，看了眼熟，毫无不顺感、阻拒感……韦努蒂对归化翻译的定义是：遵守目标语言文化当前的主流价值观，公然对原文采用保守的同化手段，使其迎合本土的典律（canon），出版潮流和政治需求的 *Dictionary of Translation Studies* 根据韦努蒂的解构主义见解，将归化定义为：在翻译中采用透明、流畅的风格，最大限度地淡化原文陌生感（strangeness）的翻译策略。韦努蒂对异化的定义概括起来就是：偏离本土主流价值观，保留原文的语言和文化差异。

归化翻译指的是一种以目的语为导向的翻译，即采用目的语文化所能接受的表达方式，使译文流畅、通顺，更适合目的语读者的口味。归化翻译有影响力的一个代表是尤金·奈达博士，他提倡"动态对等"，把它定义为，"译者应力求的是译文读者对译文信息的反应，与原文读者对原文信息的反应趋于一致"。译文要达到"动态对等"，不仅译文的表达形式要纳入目的语的规范，而且在文化方面也要纳入目的语文化规范。例如，他认为应该把"holy kiss"改译为"hearty handshake"；而把"it is as significant as a game of cricket"和"to grow like mushrooms"译为"这事如同吃饭一样重要"和"雨后春笋"都是成功的翻译。

二、异化翻译

Dictionary of Translation Studies 根据韦努蒂的见解，将异化定义为：在一定程度上保留原文的异域性（foreignness），故意打破目标语言常规的翻译。

异化翻译是以源语文化为导向的翻译，即努力做到尽可能地保持原作的风味，使源语文化的异国情调得以存续。异化论的著名代表是劳伦斯·韦努蒂。他是一位解构主义翻译思想的积极倡导者，而解构主义的翻译思想是要"存异"而不是"求同"。韦努蒂认为翻译的目的不是在翻译中消除语言和文化的差异，而是要表达这种差异。在《译者的隐身》一书中，他指出，"译文应力求透明，以致看起来不像译文"，"译文应该永远不会引起读者感到他们是在读译作"，也就是译文越透明，就越看不见译者的存在，原文作者和意义就被认为越可见。异化翻译成功的例子也很多，如将"Time is money"译成"时间就是金钱"，要比"一寸光阴一寸金"更贴切；将 sour grapes 译成"酸葡萄"，honeymoon 译成"蜜月"也非常生动达意。

第二节　归化和异化在跨文化交际中的作用

翻译作为不同文化间交流的桥梁，本质上是一种跨文化活动。然而，由于物质、风俗、宗教、思想、历史背景、生存环境、语言系统等客观因素的影响，造成了跨文化交际的困难。只有采用恰当的翻译策略，译者才能尽可能地减少文化冲突。那么归化和异化这两种翻译策略在跨文化交际中分别担当着怎样不同的角色呢？

一、归化翻译在跨文化交际中的作用

由于中西方的文化差异，在一种文化中被认为是很有效的交流方式在另一种文化中却不一定如此。如果译者过于严格地追求贴近原文的形式，译文的意义可能会与原文意义大相径庭，这就会造成交流上的障碍。归化的支持者认为，如果不理解原文中的隐含意义，人们就不能有效地进行文化交流。对他们来说，翻译是一个对新观点解释与重组的过程，而不是单纯的词汇转换过程。原文的内容和意义是首要的，而语言形式是次要的。为了避免误解，必须重新构建形式以保留内容的隐含意义。基于人们最容易理解和接受在自己期望范围以内的信息，归化论者提倡采用归化翻译，即通过使用目的语中自然的语法和词汇来重组原文。这样一来,容易混淆的文化概念被与它对等的文化概念所替代,从而消除了理解上的障碍。

然而,归化法也有它们的不足之处。采用归化法,读者的确能够理解原文的含义,同时体会文化间的相似之处,但这些都是以牺牲了大量与源语文化相关的信息为代价的。如果译者总是采用归化法,即用目的语读者所熟悉的东西来替代文化差异的话,目的语读者会越来越远离源语文化。此外,读者阅读归化翻译作品,只不过是重温自己的本族文化,其本身失去了跨文化交际的意义。

可见,文化上的等同只是相对而言的,有时,即便译者在目的语文化中找到等同的文化概念,它的文化内涵并不一定如原作信息中所暗含的那样准确。例如,有人把英语中的"to spring like mushroom"用归化法译为"雨后春笋",看似相似,却不很准确。前者指的是那些产生迅速,消亡也迅速的事物,而后者指的是具有强壮生命力,茁壮成长的事物。如果译者用"雨后春笋"来翻译"to spring like mushroom",读者会错误地认为这两种表达方式具有同样的含义。

总体看来,归化翻译就好比是一个与世隔绝的小国家,它自以为能够自给自足,而阻断了从外来文化中吸收新鲜营养的需要,结果会造成目的语读者与源语文化的疏远,最终阻碍跨文化交际。

二、异化翻译在跨文化交际中的作用

异化论的支持者认为只有当人们同其他的文化接触时才能达到跨文化交际的目的。译者应该给读者提供更多接近源语文化的机会。如果通过异化翻译把国外的文化要素,诸如历史、宗教和风俗等尽可能准确地引进到目的语文章中,读者就能接触更多原始的外来信息。通过对各种文化间差异的比较,他们便能加深对其他文化的理解和接纳,从而迅速达到跨文化交际的目的。

比如说,在每种语言中都有很多有关植物和动物的表达,由于它们各自特殊的外表、颜色、习惯及特性,人们赋予它们特殊的情感。但是由于文化的差异,同样的含义可能被不同的动植物所表达。例如,在西方,狮子因为威猛的外形和勇气而被称作"兽中之王",它是权力、尊严、凶残的象征;而在中国,被称作"兽中之王"的却是老虎。当描述某人处于危险的处境时,英语国家的人会说"to throw to the lions",而中国人会说"深入虎穴"。在阅读异化翻译作品时,读者会很自然地联系本国的表达方式。通过比较,进一步理解两者的不同,从而丰富自己对外国文化的习得和掌握。

当然，要想理解那些异国的文化模式和表达方法需要一定的时间。起初，目的语读者会认为它们很古怪或奇异，而拒绝接受。但是随着时间的推移，人们逐渐开始适应并愿意接纳那些有新意的、最初的表达方式。例如一些来源于西方文化的新词术语："鳄鱼的眼泪""橄榄枝""酸葡萄""白色污染""绿色食品""快餐""超市"等已经成为汉语词汇的有机组成部分，不仅丰富了现代汉语的词汇，还直接影响到人们观念的更新和生活方式的改变。

尽管异化翻译有助于促进跨文化交际，但有时也会妨碍人们去理解别国文化。一般来讲，在异化翻译中，译者要应对的是源语的表层结构，因此异化翻译会导致歪曲原意的、晦涩难懂的表达。如下例：

Consequently, Mr. Micawber was soon so overcome, that he mingled his tears with hers and mine. (C. Dickens; David Copperfield)

译文：结果密考伯先生不久就伤感得把他的眼泪同她的和我的混合起来了。

这里把 mingle 直接译成"混合"，确实让读者感到困惑，因为谁也搞不清这几个人的眼泪是如何混合的。其实，"mingle their tears"在这句话里不过是"一起哭"的意思。尽管译文保持了原文的形式，但是却扭曲了其本意，那么读者又怎能理解和接受这样的译文呢？

有时，由于译者不能提供有关文化内涵的解释，而读者又缺乏这方面的相关知识，就会用自己固有的知识体系和文化标准去理解文章的内容，而背离原文的本意。因此，异化论的支持者建议采用注释作为异化翻译的补充，这样就不需直接改变内容而使得翻译容易被接受。例如，在《红楼梦》中有这样一句话：

宝玉心中想到："难道这也是个痴丫头，又像颦儿来葬花不成？"回又自笑道："若真也葬花，可谓'东施效颦'了。"

起初，杨宪益夫妇使用异化法把这句话译成："Can this be another absurd maid come to bury flowers like Tai — yu?" he wondered in some amusement, "if so, she's 'Tung Shih imitating His Shih'." 然后，他们加了一个脚注来解释这个成语的历史典故：His Shih was a famous beauty in the ancient kingdom of Yieh. Tung Shih was an ugly girl who tried to imitate her ways. 这样一来，"东施效颦"这个具有一定文化内涵的成语便通过注释而得以理解。

当然，异化的使用也是有限的。由于文化的差异，在原文中所表达的东西可能是其文化中独一无二的东西，在目的语中不能找到相应的表达。在这种情况下,必须舍异化而取归化。例如以下:将道人肩上的褡裢抢了过来背着。(曹雪芹《红楼梦》)"褡裢"是中国古代使用的一种背包,现代已不复存在,更别说在英语国家根本没有这种方式。在这种情况下,杨宪益夫妇采用归化法译为"sack",而霍克斯也用归化法译为"satchel",而"sack"与"satchel"都是英语国家人所熟悉的事物。

总体来看,异化法能够表现外来文化的异国情调,给读者提供更多接触它们的机会,在某种程度上可以加速跨文化交际。然而,由于它有时只照顾到表面形式,会对那些缺乏相关文化背景知识的读者造成阅读的困难和理解的含糊不清。

总之,归化法和异化法在跨文化交流中各有自己的优势和不足。不论采取归化翻译还是异化翻译,译者的目的都是为了促进跨文化交际,只要这两种翻译策略能为此做出贡献,就有必要在翻译过程中采用。译文要充分传达原作的"原貌",就不能不走异化的途径;要像原作一样通顺,也不能完全舍弃归化的译法。正是通过这种方式,归化法和异化法在促进跨文化交际中相辅相成、相得益彰。

第三节　翻译策略的选择

翻译策略问题一直被认为是翻译研究的核心问题,因为翻译本身就是实践性很强的学科,基本理论研究和应用理论研究难以分开。传统的翻译研究大多只是以是否忠实于原文为标准,遵照从原文到译文的单一模式,试图找到一种绝对正确、"无限真值"(infinite truth)的翻译策略。但何为"正确"的翻译策略? 什么是"忠实"的译文? 大家对此至今仍然众说纷纭。当代翻译学的研究表明,原文不是译文面貌的唯一决定因素,而译文面貌也不是唯一值得探讨的翻译问题。翻译就是译者不断做出决定和选择取舍的过程。① 从翻译标准的制定和翻译策略的选择,到译文在目标文化中的地位和功能,都取决于译者的判断和选择;②而译者的选择又离不开目标文化之内和之外其他一系列因素的影响和制约。

一、译者与翻译策略的选择

著名翻译理论家吉里·列维在《翻译是个做决定的过程》一文中指出,翻

---

① 李照国. 中医翻译导论[M]. 西安:西北大学出版社,1993:151-154.
② 李永安. 如何处理中医翻译中的文化因素[D]. 西安:西安交通大学,2000.

译活动包括一系列的步骤,每个步骤都会涉及一次选择,翻译的过程就是译者不断进行选择的过程。① 随着对翻译主体性等问题研究的逐步深入,译者已被看作处在翻译活动最中心的位置,是翻译活动中最能动的因素。法国的安托瓦纳·贝尔曼指出,译者的翻译动机、翻译目的、翻译立场、翻译方案以及翻译方法使译者成为翻译中最积极的因素,他/她的态度、方法和立场一旦确立,译者也就为自己定了位置。② 在阐释学的理论基础上,袁莉提出,翻译的实质不是对原作意义的追索或还原,而是译者能动地理解和阐释原作的过程,是译者主体自身存在方式的呈现。③

从翻译活动的整个过程来看,译者的翻译目的、思维模式、价值观念、文化态度、审美取向等决定了翻译标准的确定和翻译策略的取舍与选择。

目的论告诉我们,翻译是人类的一种有目的的行为活动,任何时代、任何背景下的翻译都是因特定目的而产生,并为之服务的。译者可以根据不同的翻译目的选择不同的翻译标准,从而确定相应的翻译策略。比如,鲁迅曾经主张"硬译"的翻译策略,在很大程度上是为了实现其翻译目的服务的。综合起来,不同类型的社会文化需求、文本功能需求以及读者需求构成了总的翻译目的。以社会文化需求为翻译目的,就意味着译者对两种不同文化的对比与选择。如果译者的目的是保持民族传统,巩固目的语文化规范,那么,他就会采用某些变通和补偿的手段,尽可能淡化两种语言和文化的差异;如果译者的目的是引进外来文化模式,促进不同文化和语言间的交流和渗透,他就会采取常规的翻译策略,尽量保持原文的异域风格。以读者需求为翻译目的,译者可以通过研究原文的写作背景、内容信息、语言风格等,预测原作和译作的读者群,从而确定翻译标准和翻译策略。翻译目的和翻译策略应该体现不同类型的文本功能。对于信息交流目的较强、文化意蕴较少的文本(如新闻报道、广告宣传资料、通俗读物等非文学作品),译者可以不拘一格,对原文进行重组,使译文充分展示原文信息表达的效果;对于元描述性(meta—narrative)的文本和意蕴及某种文化基本信仰的中心文本(central text),或是重要的审美性文本(如纯文学、哲学、宗教、政论等文本),译者应该谨慎从事,全面分析,尽量采用

---

① COUSLAND P B. Medical Nomenclature in China[J]. The China Medical Missionary Journal,1905,1(3):115 - 121.

② 许钧."创造性叛逆"和翻译主体性的确立.中国翻译[J],2003,24(1):6 - 11.

③ 袁莉.关于翻译主体研究的构想.[C]//张柏然,许钧.面向 21 世纪的译学研究[C].北京:商务印书馆,2002.

恰当的手段保持原文的风格和特色。①

在任何翻译中,译者都需要经历阅读理解文本和表达文本的阶段,因为译者角色是读者和再作者的结合。作为读者(尤其在文学翻译中),译者需要调动自己的情感、意志、审美、想象等能力,与文本对话,分析作品的文学价值和社会意义,与作品达到视野融合,实现文本意义的完整构建。在文本表达阶段,作为再作者,译者的创造性发挥到极致,不仅要传达原作的基本信息,还要传达其文化意蕴。作为两种文化的中介,译者的文化身份和文化取向不可避免地体现在其翻译选择、翻译策略等方面。越是审美信息、文化意蕴丰富的作品,越是能够体现译者的思维模式、价值观、文化态度、审美取向等个性特征。翻译主体意识的研究表明,译者的主体性是客观存在,贯穿在整个翻译过程中,不应抹杀,也不要刻意“自隐”。② 在翻译材料和翻译策略的选择方面,译者的文化价值取向既可以是对目的语主流文化的认同(如中国 20 世纪 50—60 年代对苏联社会主义现实主义文学的翻译),也可以是对现存文化的否定,通过翻译来达到变革的目的(如梁启超的政治小说)。③

二、影响译者选择翻译策略的其他因素

译者对翻译策略的选择和取舍的过程,实际上也就是从宏观和微观两个方面研究文化与翻译关系的过程。在此过程中,需要考察有哪些文化因素影响和制约了翻译,译者不仅要克服语言的障碍,更要克服文化的障碍,进而达到文化交流的目的。笔者认为,这些因素应主要包括与作者、原作、读者和译本接受环境等相互关联的、相互制约的因素。

(一)作者

作者是译者理解原作、阐释文本、再创造译本活动所需参考、借助的研究对象。翻译就是译者根据自身的时代文化语境和目的与原作者进行交流和对话。要对翻译负责就必须对作者负责,这就意味着把翻译和研究结合起来。译一部作品,译者首先需要研究作者的生平、创作经历、文学成就、文学特色、性格气质、写作目的等,深入体验作者的创作情绪,尽量与作者的心灵和精神契合。这有助于译者(同时作为读者)更深入地理解和体味作品的意蕴,直接

---

① 赵宁. 论充分翻译[J]. 外语教学,2003,24(5):43-46.

② 许钧. 文学翻译的理论与实践:翻译对话录[M]. 南京:译林出版社,2001:29.

③ 查明建,田雨. 论译者主体性:从译者文化地位的边缘化谈起[J]. 中国翻译,2003,24(1):10-15.

影响他的文化价值取向和翻译策略的选择。值得注意的是,对于作者的研究并不等同于对原作的研究,这是因为文学作品一旦完成,便成了独立于作者之外的新的生命,其文学价值和社会意义就不再仅仅局限于作者个人。正如谢天振所言:"一部作品,即使不超越它的语言文化环境,也不能把它的作者意图完整无误地传达给读者,因为每个接受者都是从自身的经验出发,去理解、接受作品的"。① 此外,作者的创作也是在变化的,其不同时期作品的风格也会有所变化。比如,青年华兹华斯和老年华兹华斯不一样,写《满二十三周岁》时的弥尔顿和写《梦亡妻》时的弥尔顿也不一样。译者应该对此掌握好分寸。

(二)原作

翻译活动的第一步是理解原作。要达到对原作的理解,首先就必须对原作进行深入研究。通过研究原作的体裁、意图、风格、内容、时代背景、成书原因等,把握原文的精神实质和语篇功能,以便在内容构思、结构安排、形象塑造和语言运用等方面,尽力尊重和再现原作。然而,对原作的理解过程,不是一蹴而就的。由于译者作为阐释主体的局限性,他所达到的对文本的理解,不一定与原作的本意相吻合。因此,译者需要不断学习和领悟,不断深化其理解。由于文化环境、思维方式、表达习惯上的差异,原语与译语的语篇功能在很多情况下难以一致。译者需要优先考虑译文所期望达到哪种功能,在不违背原作意图的情况下,选择相应的翻译策略,采用灵活得当的手法对原作语篇进行处理,决定在特定语境中哪些原文语篇信息可以保留,哪些必须根据需要进行调整。这一原则跳过了文化差异带来的翻译中的障碍,从宏观策略上为译者确定了方向。②

值得一提的是,对于同一个文本,可能存在许多不同的解读。作为一个读者,译者的解读也只是其中之一。文本的意义会因读者的不同而具有不确定性,成为一个具有无限可能性的开放系统。这也是翻译作为再创造活动的一个方面。由于对原作的把握存在差异性,在此基础上选择的翻译策略也会有所差异。这也是一部作品可以同时拥有多个译本,或在不同时代会不断出现新译本的原因。

(三)读者

从翻译活动的特性来看(原作不等同于译作),这里的读者应该包括两个方面,一个是原作者对其作品所设想的读者,另一个是译者所关注的译文的潜

---

① 谢天振. 译介学[M]. 上海:上海外语教育出版社,1999:141.
② 李运兴. 语篇翻译引论[M]. 北京:中国对外翻译出版公司,2001:251.

在读者。一般而言,作者在从事文学创作时,心目中总有其特定的对象,而且自信其作品能被他的特定对象所理解。读者和译者一样,都是处在一定的时间和空间中,他们的审美需求、认识需求、接受心理无不受到时代的限制,还要受到社会、政治、意识形态等因素的影响。由于原文的读者和译文的读者所处社会、历史环境完全不同,而且读者的世界观、文学观、个人阅历往往会影响其接受文学作品的方式,这两个读者的概念不是完全等同的。译者应该通过阅读有关资料,充分了解作者对原作读者的定位和原文读者的反应共核,尽量做到有的放矢。

译文的潜在读者是译者翻译实践的目的对象。译者为了充分实现其翻译目的和价值,就必须关注目标读者的文化背景和期待视野,从而决定相应的翻译策略。因为读者的阅读活动是翻译活动的最后环节,也是翻译目的最终能否实现的关键。这里,关注目标读者所期待的视野可分为两种截然不同的情况。一种是译者为顺应多数读者的意识形态和阅读趣味而采取相应的翻译策略,以减少或者最小化原文与译文之间的文化差异(如严复、林纾的翻译);另一种是译者试图通过翻译来达到输入异国文化的目的,从而采取不同的翻译策略,这时,他的译作可能与多数读者的期待视野相差甚远(如鲁迅所倡导的"硬译")。不容忽视的是,读者的接受力具有动态性。随着其经验视野的不断变化,独特的文化现象就会不断被译语读者理解和接受,因而有些变通或补偿的翻译策略便可由常规手段来代替。例如,当代外汉翻译中,不少汉语言文化中缺省的词都直接采用了音译,无须多加变通,读者便很容易就接受了。

(四)译本接受环境

原作跨越不同时代、不同民族和语言体系进入一个完全不同的环境,必然受到译入语语言文化规范的制约。"规范"的概念由"描述翻译学派"的代表人物图里提出,指的是社会文化对翻译的约束力。图里认为,"规范"是个程度不同的连续体,有些更具个人特性,有些属于绝对规则。① 译文能否被接受主要在于它能否在译入语体系固有的规范中得到足够的认可,而制定相应的变通策略则是一种必要的灵活手段。比如佛经在译介之初,为了适应处于强势的主体文化范式,就不得不同儒家伦理观念相调和、妥协,形成与儒学相适应的佛教伦理观念。② 另外,根据图里的观点,完全被目的语文化接受和完全表现

---

① GIDEON I. Descriptive Translation Studies and Beyond[M]. Shanghai:Shanghai Foreign Language Education Press,2001:54.

② 屠国元,朱献珑. 译者主体性:阐释学的阐释[J]. 中国翻译,2003(6):8-14.

原文是两个极端,而翻译却在这两者之间:既不可能完全被接受,因为它总带来一些新信息和陌生的形式;又不可能完全适应原文,因为文化规范必然会造成某些转移。① 因此,翻译不能只顾迎合规范,对不合规范的异质文化因素一概排斥;译者要鉴别、衡量采取何种变通和补偿手段,以尽量消除或者减少文化差异带来的隔阂。②

赞助人的权威(包括出版机构)也是一个不容忽视的因素。赞助人通常是翻译活动的发起者,他们可以决定文本的选择和制定特定的译文规范(比如,现在很多外文书的翻译版权由出版社购买,在和译者签订的翻译合同上往往附有他们的翻译规范),甚至确定翻译的目的。一般而言,译者得到赞助人的授权承担翻译活动,赞助人的翻译目的就成了译者的翻译目的,其特定的翻译规范也就成了译者的翻译规范,那么,译者翻译策略的选择必然受到影响和制约。

把翻译研究置于更为广阔的文化研究语境之下,仅仅解决翻译过程中一些操作技巧问题是远远不够的。任何一个译者都不是独立于特定的文化背景而存在的,在每一个译者的头脑中都深深地打着文化的烙印,而译者在翻译过程中不可避免地要受到文化因素的制约或影响。研究影响和制约译者在翻译过程中所做出的各种选择的文化因素,对于揭示翻译活动的规律和丰富翻译理论的研究有着重要意义。

影响和制约译者的翻译策略的文化因素,主要表现在:文化的历史状况、译者对原文文化背景的理解程度、译者的文化立场及翻译意图、译入语的文化及源文文本的目的及类型等方面。

(五)历史文化因素

历史文化因素对翻译的影响是客观存在的。其理论依据可在 Evanzohar 的多元系统论中找到。多元系统论将翻译与民族文化的状况,具体说来是与民族文化的国际地位联系起来,并从中总结出译者在选择某种特定的翻译策略的必然性。Evanzohar 站在历史的高度指出:"在一定的历史时期,由于不同民族文化国际地位的不平等,在这种基础上的文化交流也必然不能平

---

① 潘文国. 当代西方的翻译学研究——兼谈"翻译学"的学科性问题[J]. 中国翻译,2002(3):15-19.

② 孙艺风. 翻译规范与主体意识[J]. 中国翻译,2003,24(3):28-34.

等。"①强势文化由于比较自信,轻视其他文化,所以也就不可能接受外语文本中有别于自己文化价值观的任何成分,因而更多地就会采取归化策略,而抵制异化策略。韦努蒂就认为,英语的翻译自从17世纪以来就以"流畅翻译",即归化翻译为主流,其主导地位一直持续到今天。韦努蒂称这种归化式的翻译称为"文化帝国主义"。②

历史是向前发展的,文化的兴衰变化是自然规律。在文化的制约下,翻译活动中归化与异化两种策略被交替使用,甚至在同一时期并存也是自然的事。

(六)译者的文化立场及其翻译的意图

如果说民族文化及翻译文化的地位是客观的环境因素,那么译者的文化立场及翻译意图就是主观能动的因素,并且后者在翻译策略的选择上起着决定性的作用。虽然文化地位是客观存在的,但是目的语与源语文化相比,谁强谁弱,在很大程度上是译者主观决定的。在目的语文化与源语文化之间,译者一旦决定了自己的文化立场,就会采用自己认为合适的翻译策略。这种选择有可能遵循多元系统理论,也有可能反其道而行之。

五四运动时期,中国处于半殖民地半封建地位,几千年的传统文化也受到严重的打击,面临严峻的挑战。按照文化多元系统理论,中国当时的情形属于文化地位产生危机、翻译文化在多元系统内处于主要地位的情况。按理,此时的翻译应以异化为主导。以鲁迅先生为代表的左翼进步力量就是采用异化式翻译的先驱。他们敢于直面文化落后的现实,向封建文化发出挑战,勇敢地用高度异化的方式介绍西方文化。翻译家们希望用西洋文学"改造国民劣根性","重铸国民灵魂"。林琴南对西洋文学的翻译在今天译界看来可能有很多"误译""乱译"的绝妙例证,但从译者的文化立场及翻译意图来考查,其意义却非同小可。③

然而,泱泱大国、文化之邦的意识在另一部分人的思想中根深蒂固,他们心理上不太愿意承认文化地位的差距。因此,在他们的心目中翻译文化仍处于次要地位,他们仍旧维护封建落后的传统文化,并因此在翻译过程中倾向于归化的方式。所以在同一历史时期,一样的文化背景下出现了两种不同的

---

① 李建忠. 文化差异与翻译[C]//语言文学与文化[M].北京:知识产权出版社,2001:91-93.

② 袁晓宁. 关于翻译中归化和异化的哲学思考[J]. 外语与外语教学,2003(1):45-47.

③ 韩子满. 文化失衡与文学翻译仁[J]. 中国翻译,2000(2):32-35.

选择。

译者翻译一部作品的意图在译者的翻译取舍过程中也起着至关重要的作用。每一位译者在翻译一部作品的时候都受到一定目的和动机的驱使,都在有意识或无意识地去趋向读者的期待视野。比如奈达就曾经指出,《圣经》应有不同的译本,以满足不同阶层、不同年龄、不同教育和文化背景的不同读者群。另外,对于一部作品,如果译者旨在把源语文化介绍给目的语文化的读者,使读者对源语文化的内涵有更多的了解,那么他将遵循异化的方法,在处理文化因素时尽可能地保留源语文化的特征。然而,如果译者只是为了取悦目的语文化的一般读者,以满足他们休闲消遣的心理,那么源语文化中异质的文化因素将不会受到重视,将会被译者归化为目的语文化的语言表达形式。如傅东华先生翻译的《飘》中,人名和地名听上去很像是中国的人名和地名,完全是归化的译法。还有一些译者只是为了自娱才进行翻译,以原作的模子为依据,借以发挥自己的创作欲望。林琴南的翻译就是一个典型的例子。目的不同、采用的手段也就不同,所起到的效果也不尽相同。

(七)译者对源文文化背景的理解程度

这包括两个方面,一是对原作语言含义的掌握,二是对原作文字以外文化背景的理解。作为翻译活动的主体,译者对源语文化背景的理解对整个翻译过程产生着不可忽视的影响。然而正如英国语言学家里昂所说:"特定社会的语言是这个社会文化的组成部分,每一种语言在词语上的差异都会反映使用这种语言的社会的事物、习俗以及各种活动在文化方面的重要特征。"[①]一般来说,译者在翻译一部文学作品之前,需要读通所译作者的主要作品并研究其特点以及该作家的传记等。由于文学作品中的内容涵盖面极广,涉及社会、文化的方方面面,涉及哲学、美学等众多学科,因此,一个合格的译者还应该尽可能多地掌握丰富的历史、地理、社会文化史、风俗习惯乃至音乐、美术等方面的知识,具有深厚的文化修养,具有广博的文化知识,否则在翻译活动中就可能出现败笔。英国牛津大学教授大卫·霍克恩,翻译中国古典名著《红楼梦》秦可卿向凤姐托梦的一句话:

如今我们家赫赫扬扬,已将百载,一日倘或乐极生悲,若应了那句树倒猢狲散的俗话,岂不虚称了一世诗书旧族了?

霍克思的英译如下:

Our house has now enjoyed nearly a century of dazzling success.

① 沈育英.论译者作为文化操作者[J].外语教学,2003(1):40-43.

Suppose one day joy at its height engenders sorrows. And suppose that, in the words of another proverbs, "when the tree falls, the monkeys scatter." Will not our reputation as one of the great, cultured households of the age then turn into a hollow mockery?

　　宋淇称赞说:"读起来十分舒畅,简直不像翻译,尤其把'诗书旧族'译为 great,cultural households;'虚称'译为 a hollow mockery,实在异常妥帖。"这说明了文化对翻译的重要性,事实上缺乏文化元素的译文等于缺乏了灵魂的翻译。因此,"翻译者必须是一个真正意义上的文化人"。①

(八)源文文本的目的和类型

　　一些以介绍源语文化为目的的历史、哲学著作、政论文以至民间故事等等,其本身目的就是为了传播源语文化,故而应重视并保留其中的文化内涵,一般遵循异化的原则。对诸如科普文章、通俗文学、广告、新闻等大众读物则不需太强调文化色彩,原则上应以通俗易懂为主,遵循以目的语文化为归宿的原则。

　　试想如果这句广告词"长城电扇电扇长城"被直接译为"The Great Wall Fan,The Fan of the Great wall"的话,有多少读者能明白其中的含义呢? 在中国的文化里,长城是强大、势不可挡的象征,但是英语读者的思维中却没有相应的联想。所以此处不宜强硬地保留汉语文化,应该把其中的喻意译出来,传达出"长城牌电扇是电扇中的佼佼者"这一基本信息。将其改译为:"A fan is no comparison to the Great Wall, but the Great Wall Fan will show you that it is just as cool."这样,译文才达到既通顺,又传神的效果。

(九)译入语文化

　　迥然不同的两种文化在发生接触的过程中,不能排除两者在价值观念方面有许多契合的情况,这是由人类共通性决定的。比如,世界上有很多民族都倡导舍己救人、忠诚可靠、重视朋友等价值观念,但是价值观念的差异还是存在的,不同民族之间在价值观念的倾向性方面也是有所不同的。当译者、译文读者的价值观念与原作者的价值观念发生冲突或是不太契合时,译者该何去何从呢? 这是一个比较与选择的过程,从中不难看出译入语文化对译者的影响和制约作用。

　　赫胥黎在他的《天演论》中曾经提及哈姆雷特,他是莎士比亚剧中的人物,在英国家喻户晓。但在当时西方文化尚未传入中国的情况下,翻译家严复害

---

　　① 王佐良. 翻译:思考与试笔[M]. 北京:外语教学与研究出版社,1989:89.

怕国人看不明白,采用了增译的手法,处理为:"罕木勒特,孝子也。乃以父仇之故,不得不杀其继父,辱其亲母。"这里严复将哈姆雷特描述为"孝子",不能不说是受到中国传统礼教影响的结果。现在读来,让人感觉不伦不类,因为中国人心目中的"孝子"与西方人心目中的 A child who loves one's parent 是大相径庭的。因而也就不难理解林纾翻译哈葛得的小说 *Montezuma's Daughter*(《蒙特祖马的女儿》)时,为何刻意将小说的名字译为《英孝子火山报仇记》,而在翻译狄更斯的小说 *The Old Curiosity shop*(《老古玩店》)时,又把书名译为《孝女耐而传》了。因为在翻译过程中,译者不可能仅仅简单地将原语文化介绍和纳入到译语文化当中,就当作大功告成,译本还要接受译入语文化的相应改造,从而适应译语读者的阅读视野。

综上所述,文化研究逐渐占据学术活动的重要地位有其历史的必然。从文化的角度切入,翻译自然也是一种文化活动或跨文化交际。这一角度同只强调语言在翻译中地位的观点不同之处在于,它既重视语言的功能,又突出了文化的制约作用,从而将文化对翻译的影响引入理论视野。文化对翻译的制约既表现在拟译文本的选择上,也表现在翻译策略的确定中。传统译论在谈及影响译者的策略选择的因素时,就把注意力放在目标语言自身的发展、译者个人的审美或文体偏好、相关语言学理论以及占主导地位的翻译规范等上面。从文化的视角来研究翻译问题,探讨译者特定翻译策略的影响因素,是翻译理论研究的一个重要组成部分。因此,在文化视角下对影响译者翻译策略的各种因素进行动态研究与把握,能够深化我们对翻译活动的认识,从而更好地揭示翻译活动的规律,丰富翻译理论的研究。

第四节 歇后语的翻译方法

语言是文化的载体,文化是语言的土壤,翻译是跨文化交流的桥梁。众所周知,语言和文化密不可分。语言是文化的有机组成部分,而且是极其重要的一部分,它记录着人类文化发展的历史,反映着社会文明进步的成果,是交流、传播、延续和发展文化的工具。但语言不能脱离文化而存在,总是生长在一定的文化背景之中。文化是语言活动的大环境,各种文化因素都必然体现在语言文字之中。在语言活动过程中,处处都有文化的烙印,时时可见文化的踪迹。我国语言学家罗常培先生说过:"语言文字是一个民族文化的结晶,这个民族过去的文化靠它来流传,未来的文化也仗着它来推进。"

歇后语具有强烈的文化特征。歇后语的翻译要同时处理语言和文化的矛盾,不仅要译出原语歇后语的形象、喻义、修辞,还要译出其民族特色和地域色彩,这样才能达到最佳程度的文化交流。歇后语翻译的好坏直接影响到翻译的质量和文化交流的程度,因此如何保证原语文化信息传递的信息度,同时保证原语歇后语文化信息传递的有效度,这是歇后语翻译的关键。

汉语歇后语是"由两部分组成的一句话,前一部分像谜面,后一部分像谜底,通常只说前一部分,而本意在后一部分"。① 也就是说,前一部分是一个形象的比喻,可称为喻体,后一部分是对前一部分比喻的解释和说明,可称为本体。歇后语是人民大众喜闻乐见的一种熟语,在口语中运用十分广泛,就是在古典和现当代文学作品和一般文章中也随处可见。从修辞角度分析,歇后语基本上是利用比喻和双关语构成的。对于比喻部分的翻译,大体上可运用形象处理的方法进行翻译,有时甚至可省略不译,而对于后一部分特别是含有双关语的翻译,则是歇后语翻译的难点。双关语一般认为是不可译的,虽然钱歌川先生曾把"委员"和"桂圆"成功地妙译为"committee"和"common tea",但从总体上看原语中的同音异义形成的谐音双关或一词多义形成的谐义双关,通常不大可能在译语中找到相应的词语。②

汉语歇后语具有独特的结构形式,又深深地植根于民族文化之中,这种具有独特的语言表达形式又蕴含丰富民族文化内涵的歇后语翻译,需要克服语言和文化的双重障碍,无疑是歇后语翻译中的一大难题。译者迎难而上,积极寻找翻译对策,力求较好地完成"难以完成"的工作。

一、保留形象直译

对于大多数喻义歇后语,比喻部分生动形象,喻义部分是比喻的合乎事理的逻辑推理结果,不包含一词两意的双关语或谐音词语,因此通常采用直译法,既传达原语的内容,也保留原语的形象,便于译语读者阅读和欣赏。如:

例1. 这件事,除了他三儿子和几个经手的人以外,谁也不知道。他也不对任何人提起。哑巴吃黄连,有苦说不出。(周而复《上海的早晨》)

A. C. Barnes:No one knew of these transactions apart from his youngest son and the few people who had handled them, nor was he going to mention the matter to anyone else. He was like the dumb man eating the bitter herb:he had to suffer the bitterness of it in silence.

---

① 中国社会科学院语言研究所词典编辑室编. 现代汉语词典[M]. 北京,商务印书馆,1984.

② 包惠南. 文化语境与语言翻译[M]. 北京:中国对外翻译出版公司,2001.

例 2."……那个宝玉是个'丈八的灯台——照见人家，照不见自己'的，只知嫌人家脏。这是他的房子，由着你们糟蹋。越不成体统了。"（曹雪芹《红楼梦》）

As for Baoyu, he's like a ten-foot lampstand that sheds light on others but none on itself. He complains that other people are dirty, yet leaves you to turn his own rooms topsyturvy.

例 3.去设埋伏我们都没有信心，想他一定在昨天晚上就早溜了，今天去也是瞎子点灯白费蜡了。（曲波《林海雪原》）

We had to confidence in today's ambush because we were sure he had escaped last night. It seemedas useless as a blind man lighting a candle.

例 4.卢沟桥的石狮子——数不清。

Перевод：Каменные львы на мосту Лугоуцяо_не сосчитать.

二、保留形象节译

有些歇后语的喻义比较明显，译语读者可从喻体的形象中或歇后语所在的上下文中直接推知喻义，英译时可只需译出比喻部分。如：

例 1.（张金龙）突然来找小小子。小小子知道黄鼠狼给鸡拜年，没安好心眼；可又不能接待他。（袁静等《新儿女英雄传》）

Sidney Shapiro：Chin-lung called on him, alone. Hsiao realized that it was a case of the weasel coming to pay his respects to the hen. He was very uneasy, but he had to entertain his unwanted visitor. [①]

例 2.用心固然良苦，但前车可鉴，到头来终究只能是竹篮打水一场空。（《红旗》）

But as their previous experience showed, they can get nothing out of it for all their pains; as a Chinese saying puts it, their efforts will be like ladling water with a wicker basket. (Peking Review)

---

① Daughters and sons, tr by Sidney Shapiro, Foreign Languages Press Peking：1979.

三、转换形象意译

由于英汉两种语言的差异和不同的民族文化背景,无法保留原语中的比喻形象,而转换为译语读者所熟悉的形象进行翻译,这实际上是一种套译,尽管形象各异,但喻义相似或对应,也能达到语义对等的效果。如:

例1.姨奶奶犯不着来骂我,我又不是姨奶奶家买了。"<u>梅香拜把子,都是奴才</u>"罢咧!这是何苦来呢!(曹雪芹《红楼梦》)

You've no call to swear to me,madam. You didn't buy me. We're <u>all birds of a feather — all slaves here</u>. Why go for me?

例2.怪不得人说你们"诗云子曰"的人难说话!这样看来,你好像"<u>老鼠尾巴上害疖子,出浓也不多!</u>"(吴敬梓《儒林外史》)

Yang Hsien-Viand Gladys Yang:No wonder they say you bookworms are hard to deal with:one might just as well <u>try to squeeze water out of a stone.</u>[1]

例3."老混蛋,你吃的河水,<u>倒管的宽</u>,这是你说话的地方?"(周立波《暴风骤雨》)

Xu Mengxiong:"Old bastard,<u>poking your nose into things that don't concern you</u>! Who wants your opinion?"[2]

四、舍弃形象意译

有不少歇后语带有浓厚的中华民族文化色彩,在比喻部分包含有中国古代人名、地名、典故,有的源于中国特有的风俗习惯或佛教等,如直译出来,译文烦冗拖沓,对于不了解中华文化背景的译语读者很难理解,因此舍弃形象对喻义进行意译,译文反而显得言简意赅,简洁明了。如:

例1.他必审问我,我给他个"<u>徐庶进曹营——一语不发</u>"。(老舍《骆驼祥子》)(含有中国古代人名和典故)

He's sure to ask questions but I'll <u>hold my tongue to begin with</u>.

例2.李老太太听了一片奖励自己的话,不由得高兴起来,觉着自己到底

---

① The Scholars,tr,by Yang Hsien-Yi and Gladys Yang,Foreign Language Press Peking,1973.

② The Hurricane,tr by Xu Mengxiong,Peking Foreign Languages Press,1955.

是比丈夫大着两岁,应当容让他,虽然想起丈夫的一天到晚撅着嘴,<u>徐庶入曹营一语不发</u>,也确是心里堵得慌。(老舍《离婚》)

俄文译文:Перевод: Услышав бесчисленные похвалы в свой адрес, госпожа Ли так возрадовалась, что ощутила вдруг свое превосходство над мужем и решила быть снисходительной, хотя он все время молчал и хмурился, <u>словно Сюй Шу, входящий в лагерьд Цао Цао.</u>

翻译无定论,此处的俄语译文,则是直译保留形象。

例 3. 穷棒子闹翻身,是<u>八仙过海,各显其能</u>。(周立波《暴风骤雨》)(含有中国古代神话)

Xu Mengxiong:When we pass from the old society to the new, each of us shows his true worth.

例 4. 等他们赶来增援时,已是"<u>正月十五贴门神——晚了半月啦</u>。"(冯至,《敌后武工队》)(含有中国习俗)

Shen Yao-Yi:But they were <u>too late for a rescue</u>. ①

汉语中存在着同音异字或谐音词语,而在英语中很难找到与之对应的词语,所以在翻译谐音双关歇后语时往往只得舍去歇后语这一独特的语言形式和喻体形象,而仅译出其喻义。如:

例 5."我哪里管得上这些事来! 见识又浅,嘴又笨,心又直,'<u>人家给个棒槌,我就拿着认真(针)</u>'了。"(曹雪芹《红楼梦》)

"I'm incapable of running things. I'm too ignorant, blunt and tactless, <u>always getting hold of the wrong end of the stick</u>. "

例 6."再试纺,顶多忙一阵子,过了几天,还不是<u>外甥打灯笼——找舅(照旧)</u>。"(周而复《上海的早晨》)

A. C. Barnes:"And if we're now going to have a check spinning, it'll only mean that we'll be busier than ever for a spell and then after a few days <u>thing will be back to what they were before</u>. "(Morning in Shanghai)

例 7. 生活的海里起过小小的波浪,如今似乎又平静下去,一切跟平常一样,一切似乎都是<u>外甥打灯笼,照舅(照旧)</u>。(周立波《暴风骤雨》)

Xu Mengxiong:The even tenor of their life had been disturbed, but things seemed to be settling down again. The villagers felt <u>themselves back in the old rut</u>. (*The Hurricane*,北京外文出版社 1955 年)

---

① Behind enemy lines,tr, by Shen Yao-Yi, Foreign Languages Press Peking, 1979.

这两个例句都用了一个同样的歇后语"外甥打灯笼——照舅(照旧)"。显然,这个歇后语也是无法孤立地译成英语的。现有英译本结合原文整体的内容,并在译文中配合所在句的句法,灵活处理,还是把它的思想内容交代得一清二楚,所失掉的也是无关紧要的个别因素——歇后语的同音现象和语义上的双关。

从理论上讲,任何翻译都是可能的,歇后语难译,但经由译者的主观努力,仍然可以得到较好表达,歇后语的翻译史就证明了这点,此类成功译例不胜枚举。如:

例1."朱斌这个人就是狗咬耗子,多管闲事!"(吴强《红日》)

"Chu Pin! He's like a dog worrying a mouse, can't mind his own business!"

例2.各位同志,各位父老,各位姐妹们,你们要八仙过海,各显神通……。(周立波《山乡巨变》)

Comrades, elders and sisters, you must be like the Eight Immortals soaring over the ocean, each of you showing your true worth...

例3.蒋介石本人是泥菩萨过江,自身难保。(周立波《暴风骤雨》)

Xu Mengxiong: Even Chiang Kai-shek can't save himself any more than a clay idol can save itself while swimming across a river.

例4.这时候呀,干部们是泥菩萨过河——自身难保。(周而复《上海的早晨》)

A. C. Barnes: At the moment the cadres themselves are like the clay idol fording the river — it's as much as they can do to preserve themselves from disaster.

例5.千里送鹅毛,礼轻仁义重。(姚仲明、陈波儿等《同志,你走错了路!》)

To send the feather of a swan one thousand li: the gift in itself may be insignificant, but the good-will is deep.

例6.那胡正卿心头"十五个吊桶打水,七上八下"。(施耐庵《水浒》)

Hu Cheng-ching was very much upset by this, and his heart was beating like fifteen buckets being hurriedly lowered into a well for water — eight going down while seven were coming up. (杰克逊译本)

例7.我们有些同志喜欢写长文章,但是没有什么内容,真是"懒婆娘的裹脚,又长又臭"。(《毛泽东选集》)

Some comrades love to write long articles，but such articles are exactly like the foot-bandages of a slut，long and smelly.

例 8. 如果我们连党八股也打倒了，那就算对于主观主义和宗派主义最后的"将一军"，弄得这两个怪物原形毕露，"老鼠过街，人人喊打"，这两个怪物也就容易消灭了。（《毛泽东选集》）

If we also abolish the Party eight-legged essay，we shall checkmate both subjectivism and sectarianism，and these two monsters，once shown in their true colours，can be easily killed，just as a rat crossing the street is chased by all passers-by.

例 9. 到了此刻，看见被囊开了，才晓得被人偷了去。真是哑子梦见妈，说不出来的苦！（吴敬梓《儒林外史》）

Yang Hsien-Yiand Gladys Yang：He had only just realized that his bag had been opened and he had been robbed. Now，like a dumb man dreaming of his mother，he could not express his despair!

例 10. 民国十二年他们就来过，光见他们在龙涎河边上举着文明棍晃了三晃。当时就肉包打狗，一去再没回头。（段承滨、杜士俊《降龙伏虎》）

We had some here in twenty-three. They just stood there on the river bank flourishing their walking-sticks for a minute，and then they left and，like the meatpudding thrown at a dog，they never came back. ①（Taming the Dragon and the Tiger，北京外文出版社 1961 年版）

例 11. 金钏儿睁开眼，将宝玉一推，笑道："你忙什么？'金簪儿掉在井里头，——有你的只是有你的。'连这句俗话难道也不明白？……"（曹雪芹《红楼梦》）

The girl opened her eyes then and pushedhim away. "What's the hurry？'A gold pin may fall into the well，but if it's yours it remains yours.' Can't you understand that proverb?"

例 12. 凌鼒翔心里虽也不免有点难过，但又觉得人家都输，反正是盟兄弟交恕一个人赢了，于是说："横竖肉烂了在汤锅里，还不是一样。"（李六如《六十年的变迁》）

Chu-hsiang was naturally somewhat upset，but the fact that all the others lost and his sworn brother was the only winner made him feel a little better，so he said，"well，it's like 'meat cooked in the same pot'，there is no difference between brothers."

例 13."嘿！你真傻,牛口里的草,扯不出来的。"张树声说了这几句。(李六如《六十年的变迁》)

"What a naive idea! It's just as impossible as taking fodder from a cow's mouth!" snapped Chang Shusheng.

例 14.说得不好听的,就给他一个"实棒槌灌米汤,来个寸水不进",我算是满没有听提,这才能过日子。(曹禺《日出》)

... when he says something nasty, let it run off you like water off a duck's back, just pretend he hasn't said a thing. That's the only way to keep sane.

歇后语"实棒槌灌米汤,寸水不进"英译时如以直译法去处理,必然啰里啰唆,说不清道理,徒劳无功;如意译之又会平淡无力,所以译者借用英语同义习语 Like water off a duck's back(如鸭背淌水)来表达,同是寸水不进(即听不进去),一个用"实棒槌"和"米汤"来做比喻,一个用"鸭"和"水"做比喻,同义习语的借用把原文的隐意交代得十分清楚。

例 15.反正是一句话:"王八看绿豆",是对了眼了。(曹禺《日出》)

Anyway, it's a case of "When Greek meets Greek."

歇后语"王八看绿豆,对了眼"也是无法直接翻译成英语的,意译的话又会失去原文引用俗语的味道,所以译者借用同义习语 When Greek meets Greeks(希腊人遇希腊人,即"两雄相对"之意)来表达,形象不同,意义相同。

例 16."对新药业,老实讲,我是擀面杖吹火———一窍不通,并且,自己的精力也有限……"(周而复《上海的早晨》)

A. C. Barnes:"To be quite honest with you, I don't know the first thing about the modern drug business and also my energies are rather limited..."

歇后语"擀面杖吹火———一窍不通"兼用比喻和双关语,无法直译。译者把它意译为 don't know the first thing about.

例 17.可是谭招弟心中却想:骑着毛驴看书———走着瞧吧,看究竟是什么原因。(周而复《上海的早晨》)

A. C. Barnes:But Tan Chao-ti was still thinking to herself:"Let's wait and see what the reason for it turns out to be in the end."

歇后语"骑着毛驴看书———走着瞧"也兼有比喻和双关语,无法直译。译者把它意译为 wait and see.

例 18.朱延年一听提起朱暮堂,直摇头道:"他吗,棺材里伸出手来———死

要钱。他哪会借钱给我？我死了也不去找他。"（周而复《上海的早晨》）

A. C. Barnes：At the mention of this name he shook his head with conviction and said："No，he's still after my blood. How can you imagine he'd lend me anything? I'd die rather than ask him for a loan."

歇后语"棺材里伸出手来——死要钱"也难以直接翻译成英语。译者把它意译成 is still after my blood.

例 19. 他这一阵心头如同十五个吊桶打水，七上八下，老是宁静不下来。（周而复《上海的早晨》）

A. C. Barnes：His mind was in a turmoil these days and he was quite unable to think straight.

歇后语"十五个吊桶打水，七上八下"在此也不宜以直译法处理。译者把它意译为 was in a turmoil.

例 20. "你要有本事，就甭听我的话，去跟工作队串鼻子，咱们骑在毛驴上看唱本，走着瞧吧！"（周立波《暴风骤雨》）

Xu Mengxiong："If you're so clever, you needn't listen to me. Go ahead and fool about with the work team — we'll see who's right!"

歇后语"骑在毛驴上看唱本，走着瞧"在此也不能以直译法处理。译者结合上下文把它意译为 see who's right。

例 21. "你别狗咬吕洞宾，不识好人心。我是好心好意劝你，倒粘到我身上来了，这才是笑话哩……。"（周而复《上海的早晨》）

A. C. Barnes："Don't snap and snarl at me when I'm trying to do my best for you. I give you my advice with the best will in the world and you turn round and lay the blame on me，which is ridiculous..."

歇后语"狗咬吕洞宾，不识好人心"也不宜直译。译者结合上下文的内容把它意译为 Don't snap and snarl at me when I'm trying to do my best for you。

例 22. 又气得忽扇着嘴唇说，"打开天窗说亮话，政治犯，请你们自行归案吧！"（梁斌《红旗谱》）

Gladys Yang：He puffed out his lips angrily. "Let's speak frankly. Regarding those political criminals，we hope they will come with us voluntarily!"①

歇后语"打开天窗说亮话"也很难直译。英语中虽有习语 To put all cards on the table 和它同义,大概为了使对话更简短有力,译者未予选用,把它意译为 Let's speak frankly.

例 23.这是黎统领"<u>哑子吃黄连,有苦说不出</u>"的事情咧!(李六如《六十年的变迁》)

This has caused our Commander Li real grief, yet he finds it so <u>difficult to express.</u>

歇后语"哑子吃黄连,有苦说不出"也兼用比喻和双关语,不宜按字面直译。译者应用意译法,结合译文所在句的结构,把这歇后语的内容交代得一清二楚。

例 24.现在是<u>哑巴吃蚕豆</u>——黎元洪心中有了数。(李六如《六十年的变迁》)

But then Li Yuan-hung had begun to <u>understand the whole thing.</u>

歇后语"哑巴吃蚕豆——心中有数",由于兼用比喻和双关语,也不好按字面直译。译者根据上下文,把它意译成 to understand the whole thing。

例 25.茗烟又嘱咐道:"不可拿进园去,叫人知道了,我就'<u>吃不了兜着走</u>'了。"(曹雪芹《红楼梦》)

"Don't take them into the Garden," Ming-yen warned him. "If they were found I'd be in <u>serious trouble.</u>"

"吃不了兜着走"是歇后语"吃不了兜着走——吃不消"的前半截,也不好按字面直译。译者结合上下文,把它意译成 be in serious trouble。

例 26."他们没有十万八万,还敢进威虎山,哼! 那叫<u>猫舔虎鼻梁,找死</u>!"(曲波《林海雪原》)

"If they dared to come near us with anything less than a hundred thousand men, it would be <u>like a kitten clawing a tiger's nose — sure death.</u>"

歇后语"猫舔虎鼻梁,找死"译成 like a kitten clawing a tiger's nose — sure death,其中除 clawing(用爪子搔)是"舔"的意译外,其余都是直译。译者未把"舔"直译成 licking,是由上下文的内容决定的。用 clawing 能突出"挑

---

① Keep the Red Flag Flying, tr, by Gladys Yang, Foreign Languages Press, Beijing, China, 1980.

舔"的含义,而 licking 所表示的却是"爱抚"的动作。

例 27."……我说二三百两银子,你就说二三十两!'戴着斗笠亲嘴,差着一帽子'!……"(吴敬梓《儒林外史》)

Yang Hsien-Yiand Gladys Yang："When I say two or three hundred taels，you say twenty or thirty! It's like kissing in straw helmets — the lips are far apart!"

"戴着斗笠亲嘴,差着一帽子"是歇后语。译者以直译的方法处理前半截,以意译的方法处理后半截。

例 28."那哪能都知道? 他们一东一伙,都是看透《三国志》的人。要我说,那一耳刮子,也是周瑜打黄盖,一个愿打,一个愿挨的。"(周立波《暴风骤雨》)

Xu Mengxiong："Hard to say. The two of them are hand in glove，and they've both read the Romance of the Three Kingdoms. I should say that box on the ear was skilfully given by a Chou Yu and gladly taken by a Huang kai."

歇后语"周瑜打黄盖,一个愿打,一个愿挨"的译文是：skilfully given by a Chou Yu and gladly taken by a Huang Kai,但如不加注释把"周瑜打黄盖"的历史故事略加交代,外国读者仍会看不懂,所以现有英译本另加注释：A fourteenth century novel based on events which took place in the third century A. D. Chou Yu of the Kingdom of Wu had Huang Kai，another Wu general，cruelly beaten，and then sent him to the enemy camp in order to deceive the enemy.

例 29."穷棒子闹翻身,是八仙过海,各显其能……。"(周立波《暴风骤雨》)

Xu Mengxiong："When we pass from the old society to the new，each of us shows what stuff he's made of — like the Eight Fairies when they crossed the sea..."

译者把"八仙过海"直译成 the Eight Fairies when they crossed the sea 后另加注释说明八仙：The eight immortals of Taoism in Chinese folklore.

例 30.一个有力、能干,肩上扛上两百斤麻袋跑几里路都不喘气的人,现在却像掉在枯井里的牛犊一样,有力无处使。(知侠《铁道游击队》)

He had great strength and could carry a load of two hundred catties several li without panting. Now he felt as powerless as a calf trapped in a dry well.

例 31. 咱们俩的事，一条绳上拴着两只蚂蚱——谁也跑不了。（老舍：《骆驼祥子》）

We're like two grasshoppers tied to one cord, neither can get away!

例 32. 我看你这个人的话，真是大牯牛的口水，太长！（郭沫若《屈原》）

Your words are like the slobber of a buffalo — too long!

例 33. 你要去批评他忘恩负义，那是猫舔虎鼻梁——找死。

You should like to criticize him for his being ungrateful and leaving his benefactor in the lurch, which is like a kitten clawing a tiger's nose — sure death.

例 34. "不要失了你的时了！你自己只觉得中了一个相公，就'癞蛤蟆想吃起天鹅肉'来！"（吴敬梓《儒林外史》）

YangHsien-Yi and Gladys Yang："Don't be a fool!" he roared. "Just passing one examination has turned your head completely — you're like a toad trying to swallow a swan!"

例 35. 你这些怜惜佃户的话，都是猫哭老鼠——假慈悲。

All your piteous words for the tenants are no more than to shed crocodile tears.

例 36. "我是想：咱们是孔夫子搬家，净是书（输），心里真有一点点干啥的。"（周立波《暴风骤雨》）

Xu Mengxiong："Only I feel bad when we lose every fight."

例 37. "我在店里呢，是灯草拐杖，做不了主（柱）的。"（周而复《上海的早晨》）

A. C. Barnes：My position in the company doesn't permit me to make a decision individually.

例 38. "我这个人你也知道，说话向来是'袖筒里入棒槌'——直出直入！"

"You know me — I speak frankly and to the point."

例 39. 你在会上说的那番话让我觉得丈二和尚——摸不着头脑。

What you said at the meeting made me feel completely at a loss.

例 40. 周进听了这话，自己想："瘫子掉在井里，捞起来也是坐。"有甚亏负我？随即应允了。（吴敬梓《儒林外史》）

Yang Hsien-Viand Gladys Yang："Even if a paralytic falls into a well, he can be no worse off than before," thought Chou Chin. "It can't hurt me to go. " So he consented.

例 41.我就怕你是一个<u>没骨头的伞</u>——<u>支撑不开</u>。（袁静《新儿女英雄传》）

Sidney Shapiro：I'm afraid you are <u>a ribless umbrella</u>. You <u>won't be able to stand up in the storm</u>.

从以上例句可以看出，对大多数喻义歇后语，由于比喻部分生动形象，喻义部分逻辑推理合乎情理，通常采用直译法，既传达源语的内容，又保持源语的形象，便于文化传播，也便于读者阅读和欣赏。而翻译文化负载较重的歇后语时，大多采用解释法，或增补，或替代，以揭示源语文化内涵和特色。

第五章　歇后语汉英辞典翻译综述

　　歇后语是社会各阶层喜欢使用的一种熟语,上至社会政要,下至黎民百姓,常会在谈话和文章中用上一两句歇后语,就是在正统文学作品中也随处可见。因此,对歇后语的正确理解和翻译,无疑是十分重要的。1986 年美国芝加哥伊利诺大学的语言学教授、汉语学家罗圣豪先生(Prof. John S. Rohsenow)萌发了编写一部《汉英歇后语词典》的构想。1991 年,《汉英歇后语词典》由亚利桑那大学出版社出版。歇后语翻译不仅是要向学习者解释每条歇后语的意义,而且希望通过译文有助于学习者学习和了解歇后语所反映的文化背景,这就要求翻译时"不能改换比喻的形象或比喻本身,也不能避而不译。"①因此,歇后语翻译既要提供歇后语的字面意义又要提供隐含意义。

第一节　比喻和双关歇后语的汉英辞典翻译

　　汉语歇后语基本上是利用比喻和双关语形成的。Dagut 认为,原语中比喻的可译性,并不取决于比喻的"想象力"(boldness)或"创造性"(originality),而是取决于目的语读者在文化经验和语义联想这两方面与原语读者的差异②。歇后语的民族性,正是原语读者文化经验的反映;而其语义联想则体现在"喻体+本体"的这一特殊的结构形式上。

　　关于比喻翻译的方法,纽马克作了最全面的总结:在目的语中重视原语比喻的形象;用符合目的语习惯的形象替代原语比喻中的形象;用明喻译隐喻;用明喻+意义译隐喻(或明喻);译意;调整比喻;舍弃比喻不译;用原语比喻+

---

　　① 郭建中. 汉语歇后语翻译的理论与实践:兼谈《汉英歇后语词典》[J]. 中国翻译,1996(2).

　　② Dagut M B. Can Metaphor Be Translated? Babel, Vol. 22, No. 1(1976) pp. 21 - 23.

意义译原语比喻。①

双关语一般都认为是不可译的,因为原语中的同音异义形成的谐音双关或一词多义形成的谐意双关,一般不可能在目的语中找到相应的词语;另外,语法结构上的歧义,目的语与原语也不可能有对应的形式。②

因此,在翻译中,对双关语的处理,一般只能译意。正如福斯特所指出的:"翻译出来的双关语,尽管译笔巧妙,但并不是原来的那个双关语,而只是反映原作使用了双关语这一事实。原语中的那个双关语可能是无法翻译的。"③

翻译的目的和读者的对象,往往决定了翻译标准和翻译方法的选择。《汉英歇后语词典》主要是为学习汉语的英语民族的人编写的,目的不仅是要向学习者解释每条歇后语的意义,而且,希望通过译文有助于学习者学习汉语和了解歇后语所反映的文化背景。这就决定了我们的翻译标准和方法。作为一本学习汉语的工具书,我们既不能改换比喻的形象或比喻本身,也不能避而不译;明喻与隐语的区别也不存在任何意义,因歇后语都是以明喻的形式出现的。双关语不仅要译意,还要体现汉语中双关之所在,因而不能采取巧译的办法。

从《汉英歇后语词典》可以看出编者基本上采用了以下几条基本原则和方法:

(1)基本上采用直译法,并尽可能在译文中体现汉语歇后语的词义和语法结构,不少地方近乎对照翻译。

(2)直译法意义含糊时,再辅以意译法说明本意。

(3)所有比喻一律译出,在其寓意不清或难解时,再译意补充说明。

(4)对双关语采取直译和意译相结合的办法,并指出谐音或谐意的双关所在。

(5)对具有民族特色的典故、神话故事、经典出处,略作文化背景的注释。

从翻译的角度而言,歇后语的翻译一般可分四种方法处理:

(1)比喻和喻义属一般事物和情理,其间的关系各民族人民都能理解。

---

① Newmark P. The Translation of Metaphor, in the Ubiquity of Metaphor: Metaphor in Language and Thought, edited by Wolf Paprotte and RenéDirven [M]. Amsterdam /Philadelphia: John Benjamins,1985:295 – 329.

② Catford J C. A Linguistic Theory of Translation[M], London, Oxford University Press,1965,93 – 103.

③ Forster E M. Translation: An Introduction, In Aspects of Translation, edited by A. H. Smith[M]. London: decker and Warburg,1958.

例如：

老虎吃天——不知从哪儿下口/无从下口

A tiger wanting to eat the sky—not knowing where to start.

黄鼠狼给鸡拜年——不怀好意

A weasel wishing Happy New Year to a chicken——harboring no good intentions.

这一类歇后语，只需采取直译，其寓意便能为英语民族的人所理解。

(2)尽管比喻和喻义属一般事物和情理，其间的关系对汉民族来说可能不言而喻，但对英语民族来说，就难以理解。这儿牵涉到思维方法和习惯，汉语特有的习惯用法(语义联想)和生活经验等多方面的问题。例如：

丈二金刚/和尚——摸不着头脑

A Buddha s warrior guardian〔statue〕/ a monk one zhàngand twochi〔4·5 meters〕tall—(lit) can t touch his head; too tall to have his head touched; (coll) at a loss; unable to make head or tail of something.

上例中的"摸不着头脑"其语义联想对汉民族而言是不成问题的，但对英语民族而言，就不可能产生同样的语义联想。故直译之后再加意译，并注明"摸不着头脑"是汉语中的习惯用法。又如：

兔子的尾巴——长不了

The tail of a rabbit—(lit) can t be long; (fig) won t last long.

尽管人人都知道，兔子尾巴是不长的，但"长不了"的语义联想则只是汉民族所特有的，故直译之后再加意译，以显其寓意。

(3)另一些歇后语具有强烈而浓厚的民族特色，往往涉及汉民族的历史文化、神话传说，经典著作，乃至封建迷信等。对这类歇后语，往往意译还不能说明问题，必须加注交代文化背景。例如：

刘备卖草鞋——①本行②有货

Liu Bei selling straw shoes—① his original profession or calling; ② (lit) having (the) goods; (coll) having some special knowledge on a certain subject; learned; competent〔Liu Bei, one of the three rulers in R3k (the Romance of the Three Kingdoms) originally was a peddler of straw shoes〕

有些歇后语涉及汉民族风俗习惯的，有时也必须加注说明。例如：

八月十五的月饼——一盒子来，一盒子去

Moon cakes〔traditionally given to all one s friends and relatives at the

Mid_Autumn Festival〕on the fifteenth of the eighth lunar month—(lit) one plateful being brought in and one being taken out；(fig) coming and going.

(4)双关式歇后语不论是谐音还是谐意,只能直译＋意译,再点明双关之所在。例如:

打破砂锅——问(纹)到底

Breaking an earthenware pot—(lit) cracked to the bottom；(pun) interrogate thoroughly；get to the bottom of a matter.

上例是谐音双关。

棺材上画老虎——吓死人。

Painting a tiger on a coffin—(lit)〔to〕frighten the dead；(pun/coll) frighten(ed) to death.

上例是谐意双关。

《汉英歇后语词典》是为学习汉语的英语民族编写的,上面谈及的翻译原则和方法,不一定适用于其他文体的翻译。主要是为兼顾学习者对汉语词汇和语法的理解,译文过于质直。例如:

肉包子打狗——有去无回

Beating a dog with a meat dumpling—gone, never to return.

译文显然是为了与汉语的表层结构相对应,但译文所表达的形象与原文所表达的形象是不一致的。译文同样可以基本采取直译的方法,表达相同的形象:

Chasing a dog by throwing meat dumplings at it—gone, never to return

对翻译工作者而言,对歇后语的释义显然是有用的;不少译文也可直接拿来应用。考虑到文体和上下文,译者应参考《词典》的释义和译文作灵活变通。《词典》对翻译工作者有较大的参考价值,这一点应该是毫无疑问的。

第二节　汉英辞典中歇后语的文化信息处理

一、历史典故

带有历史典故的歇后语的翻译难点在于历史背景的处理,这里分析几种可行的方法。

司马昭之心——路人皆知

Everyman in the street is aware of Sima Zhao's intent——a covetous desire known to all. /Literary allusion: the history of the Three Kingdoms records. (《英汉汉英习语大全》)

司马昭是中国历史上的人物，只有对三国历史有所了解才会知道这个歇后语的意思，于是一些辞典在歇后语后面加上如上的文化注释，以帮助理解。但是这种注明方法并不很适于辞典中的歇后语翻译，辞典由于篇幅所限几十字冗长的文化背景注释不可能全部给出，否则会喧宾夺主。再举一个耳熟能详的歇后语"周瑜打黄盖——一个愿打一个愿挨"在几种词典中的翻译：

A severe flogging was consciously givenby a Zhou Yu and gladly taken bya Huang Gai——both parties agree offree will/the punishment is skillfully given by one and gladly accepted by another.（《英汉汉英习语大全》）

The punishment is skillfully given by one and gladly accepted by another.（《汉英大辞典》）

Strategy adopted by Zhou Yu hof logged Huang Gai with the latter's consent——both parties are willing.（《新时代汉英大词典》）

《汉英大辞典》中的翻译显然舍弃了歇后语的直译，直接给出了意译，反而严重遗漏了周渝、黄盖的历史人物信息；第一种和第三种的翻译都比较完整，先直译再意译，提供了歇后语的表面意义和暗含意义，但比较之下第一种更为妥当，因为词典中并没有上下文来提供周渝和黄盖的人物信息，这个时候陌生的人名用"a Zhou Yu, a Huang Gai"的提法更合乎英语的习惯，这也不失为是一种较好地处理歇后语中出现的历史人物的方法。

二、宗教神话

宗教信仰是人们精神生活的一个方面，在中国，佛教、道教和儒家思想都深深地影响着民族文化和人民的生活，在这样的环境下，很多歇后语中也出现了宗教神话传说中的形象（如鬼、神、道士等）。目前，对于这些歇后语的处理标准不统一，有直接意译的，也有借用英文习语套译的，例：

太岁头上动土——寻死

Breaking ground on Jupiter's head (i. e. provoking somebody who is superior in power or strength) counting disaster; Inviting death（《英汉汉英习语大全》）

这个歇后语中的太岁译做 Jupiter，如果读者不了解 Jupiter 是希腊罗马神话中的神，这个形象就不能使人联想到神圣不可侵犯的意思，而在《汉英综合大辞典》中译为 Tai Sui(legendary God)，相比之下，拼音加注释的方法更为直接妥当。

三、动物的感情色彩

　　一些歇后语是用动物来做比喻,如老鼠、黄鼠狼、癞蛤蟆等,处理动物歇后语的时候主要集中在处理它所带有的感情色彩。有些动物在英美文化中有着和汉文化相同的感情色彩,如老鼠在东西方文化中都是用来骂人的贬义词;但是一些动物在中英文化中意义迥然,如狗也是歇后语中常出现的贬义形象,如"狗拿耗子——多管闲事"这句歇后语是表示嘲笑骂人的。而在英语中,"狗"却常常是褒义的,宠物狗的一个常用名字就是 Buddy(伙计)。因此带有"狗"的歇后语西方国家的读者可能无法理解它的贬义的感情色彩。所以,可在直译的时候直接用带有感情色彩的词,从而充分表达歇后语的表意和本意。这句歇后语可以翻译为 A dog trying to catch a mouse — can not mind his own business/too meddlesome。Meddlesome 最直接地体现了管闲事的感情色彩。这样英语读者就不会误解"狗"的比喻和形象,而会按照中国的思维习惯接受狗在这句歇后语中贬义的文化意向。

附　录

附录一　《歇后语汉英词典》翻译精选

挨揍打呼噜——装糊涂

Pretending to snore while being beaten — （coll）pretending not to know；feigning ignorance

挨了棒的狗——气急败坏

A dog beaten with a club — （coll）flustered and exasperated；utterly discomfited and angry

矮子里拔将军——矮中挑长

Selecting a general from among dwarves — （lit）choosing the tallest among dwarves；（coll）choosing the best person available（from a limited selection）（used deprecatingly，often of oneself）

矮子骑高马——上下两难

A dwarf riding a tall horse — （lit）has difficulty both mounting and dismounting；（coll）difficult to advance or retreat；in a dilemma

矮子上楼梯——步步登高

A dwarf going upstairs — getting higher step by step；（coll）rising in position or rank

矮子坐高凳——够不着

A dwarf trying to sit on a tall bench — （lit）isn't tall enough to reach it；（pun/coll）can't reach [something]

矮子坐末排看戏——随人家喝彩

A dwarf watching a play from a last-row seat — （lit）applauds along with the others；（coll）follow others' suit

爱吃萝卜不爱吃梨——各有所好

Liking to eat turnips, but not pears — (coll) individuals have their own preferences

爱叫的鸟儿——不做窝

A bird that loves to sing — (lit) does not make a nest; (fig) all talk and no action

爱克斯光照人——看透了

X-raying a person — see right through [someone]

案板上的肉——任人宰割

Meat on a chopping block — can be butchered by others at will; at the mercy of others

按下葫芦浮起瓢——此落彼起

Pressing down one gourd while another gourd [ladle] floats up — (lit) rise here and fall there; (cy) as one falls, another rises; rise one after the other [a variant of the Chengyu]

八百钱掉在井里——难摸哪一吊

Eight [strings of one] hundred coins falling into a well — (lit) hard to get hold of any particular string (pun) hard to get the [right] tune or musical key; (coll) having a hard time understanding what someone is talking about or wants [In old Beijing dialect]

八个油瓶,四个盖儿——缺这少那

Eight oil bottles with only four tops — (coll) insufficient; nothing matches

八哥啄柿子——拣软的欺

A parrot picking at a persimmon — (lit) picking the softones; (fig) bullying the weak

八哥儿的嘴巴——人云亦云

A mynah bird's tongue — (cy) echoing the views of others

八级工拜师父——精益求精

A top-grade worker taking a teacher — (cy) keep improving

八戒啃猪蹄儿——自残(餐)骨肉

[Zhu] Bajie [Pigsy] eating pig's feet — (lit) eating one's own fleshand bones; (fig) [members of the same group] or party killing each other; fratricidal strife

八十老公挑担子——心有余而力不足

An eighty-year-old man using a carrying pole [i. e., serving as a porter] — (yy) the spirit is willing, but the flesh isn't up to it [The second part is a yanyu rhyme.]

八十岁的老头吹喇叭——上气不接下气

An old man of eighty blowing a suona [Chinese trumpet] — out of breath

八仙过海——各显神通

The Eight Taoist Immortals crossing the sea — each displaying his or her special powers; individuals have their own ways of dealing with things

八仙桌上放盏灯——明摆的

Placing a lamp on a square table — obvious or apparent

八仙桌子盖井口——随方就圆

A square table covering the mouth of a well — (lit) adapting the round to the square; (cy) adapting to circumstances; adaptable [person]

八月的棉花——越老越红

Cotton seedsin August — (lit) the older, the redder; (fig) the older, the more progressive minded [political]

八月的荷花——一时鲜

A lotus flower in the eighth lunar month — fleeting beauty

八月里的黄瓜棚——空架子

Cucumber frames in August/September — (lit) bare frames; (fig) no content; a mere skeleton; a bare outline; imposing in appearance only

八月(里)的石榴——满脑点子

A pomegranate in August/September — (lit) [a head] full of seeds; (coll) a mind full of ideas

白麻纸上坟——哄鬼(呢)

Visiting a grave carrying white hemp paper (as spirit money to offer the dead instead of the proper yellow paper) — (lit) deceiving (only) ghosts; (coll) a cheat who has become so obvious he could only fool the dead

白娘娘吃了雄黄酒——现原形

Bai Niangniang (the young woman's form taken by the White Snake Spirit) drinking red orpiment wine — (thus) her true form appears (Legend of the White Snake) is a popular story portrayed in many traditional operas, films, etc.]

白糖加蜜糖——甜上加甜

Sugar plus honey — sweetness added to sweetness. [i. e. ,even happier]

白天见鬼——心病

Seeing ghosts in the daytime — having secret troubles

白天做梦——胡思乱想

Dreaming in the daytime — (cy) going off into wild flights of fancy

白眼儿狼戴草帽——变不了人

A wolf wearing a straw hat — can never become a human being (derogatory; said of a person)

白衣秀士王伦当梁山寨主——容不得人

The "White-Robed Scholar" Wang Lun acting as the head of Liang Mountain stockade — (lit) can't tolerate others [Cf. WM.]; (fig) narrow-minded

白纸上落黑字——更改不掉

Black characters on white paper — can't be changed; things done can't be undone; the die is cast

《百家姓》不念第一个字——开口就是钱

Beginning to read the "List of One Hundred Chinese Surnames" without reading the first name (Zhao) on the list (thus starting with the second name,"Qian", which means "money") — speaking of money first

百年松当柴烧——大材小用

Burning a hundred-year-old pine tree as fire wood — (lit) putting fine timber to petty use; (cy) using talented people for trivial tasks; a waste of talent

拜佛走进了吕神庙——找错了门

Entering Lu Temple to worship the Buddha — (coll) have found the wrong place (Lu Congbin, one of the Eight Taoist Immortals, was a Taoist priest.)

斑鸠吃萤火虫——肚里明

A turtledove eating up a glowworm or firefly — (lit) bright in the belly; (coll) have a clear understanding of things

班门弄斧——不看对象

Wielding an axe before the door of [Lu] Ban [the master carpenter] — ①（coll）showing off in the presence of an expert. ② making a fool of oneself. [The first part is a Chengyu]

百灵鸟儿碰到鹦鹉——会唱的遇上会说的

A lark coming across a parrot — a singer meeting a talker; two quick-tongued persons together

搬起石头砸自己的脚——自讨苦吃

Lifting a rock only to drop it on one's own foot — bringing trouble upon oneself

半天云里打灯笼——高明又高明

Hanging a lantern in the sky — (lit) brightness on high; (pun) more and more intelligent

半天云里挂口袋——装疯（风）

Hanging a bag on the clouds — (lit) put wind into; (pun/coll) pretending to be insane

半天云里伸巴掌——高手

Stretching out one's palm in the sky — (lit) a high hand; (pun/coll) highly skilled

半夜打雷心不惊——问心无愧

Not being frightened by the midnight thunder — (cy) feeling no qualms upon self-examination; a clear conscience

半夜里的被窝——正在热乎劲儿上

Being in one's bed quilt at night — (lit) nice and warm; (fig) warm and friendly; chummy

擀杖吹火——一窍不通

Blowing into a fire (to give it oxygen) with a club (instead of with a blowpipe) — (lit) [the air] can't go through; (pun) ① not make sense ② won't work ③ can't figure out why

包黑脸断案子——六亲不认

"Black-faced Bao" [Bao Wenzheng, or Bao Gong (q. v.), a Northern Song magistrate famous for his fairness] judging a case — refusing to be influenced by or show favoritism toward any of one's relatives or friends

包脚布当头巾——高升了

Using foot-binding bandages as a kerchief — (coll) promoted to a high position (sarcastic)

饱带干粮,暖带衣——做好准备

Carrying (extra) food when full and (extra) clothes when warm — well prepared (The first part is a Yanyu)

保温瓶的塞子——赌气（堵汽）

The cork of a thermos bottle — (lit) keeps air from going out; (pun) feel wronged and act rashly

宝玉的通灵玉——命根子

Bao Yu's jade talisman — his very life; (fig) very important (Jia Baoyu, the central character in DRC, had this jade talisman from birth.)

抱薪救火——反惹祸害

Carrying faggots to put out a fire — adopting a wrong method to save a situation and ending up by making it worse

抱着木炭亲嘴儿——碰了一鼻子灰

Embracing and kissing charcoal — running into a noseful of soot; meeting with a rebuff

抱着元宝跳井——舍命不舍财

Jumping into a well with a shoe-shaped (gold or silver) ingot — (cy) caring for money more than for one's own life

背纤断绳——拉倒

The rope of a boat hauler breaking — (the boat hauler) falls down; (coll) forget about it; drop it

背石头上山——越背越重

Going uphill, carrying rocks on one's back — getting heavier and heavier

背着儿媳妇过河——费力不讨好

Crossing a river carrying one's daughter-in-law on one's back — doing a thankless task

背着棺材上阵——豁上命

Going to the battle front carrying a coffin on one's back — ready to risk one's life

背着米讨饭——装穷

Begging while carrying rice on one's back — pretending to be poor

背靠米囤饿死——懒得出奇/太懒了

Starving to death while leaning against a grain bin — too lazy for words

背上镜子——只照别人，不照自己

Having a mirror on one's back — only reflects others，but not oneself；criticize others，but not oneself

被窝里放屁——独吞

Breaking wind under a bed quilt — inhale the bad smell oneself；monopolize；keep something all to oneself

笨鸟先飞——早入林

A clumsy bird starts earlier — (lit) the first to enter the wood (The first part is yanyu；usually said modestly of oneself to explain one's making preparations earlier than others. Contrast "the early bird gets the worm.)

嘣嘣响的西瓜——熟透了

Watermelon that gives a [deep] thumping sound when tapped — (lit/fig) quite ripe

逼着公鸡下蛋——办不到

Forcing a rooster to lay eggs — impossible to accomplish

鼻子里插葱——装像（象）

Sticking a (ling green) onion in (one's) nose — (lit) pretending to be an elephant；(pun/coll) feigning ignorance；playing the fool

比着箍儿买蛋——哪有那么合适的？

Buying eggs by measuring them with a ring — where on earth are you going to find anything that suitable？

壁上挂魁星——鬼话（画）.

A picture of Kui Xing hung on the wall — (lit) a picture of a ghost；(pun) sheer lies (In ancient Chinese astrology，Kui Xing was the star-god in charge of literature. He is usually depicted as a ghost-like figure.)

病好打太医——恩将仇报

Beating the physician as soon as one's illness is cured — mercy repaid with hate；requite kindness with enmity（Taiyi originally referred to an imperial physician.)

拨好的闹钟——不到时候，不打点

An alarm clock [already] set — (lit) won't ring until the appointed time; (fig) won't take action until the appropriate time

玻璃灯笼——内外都明

A glass lantern — (lit) bright both within and without; (fig) understood clearly by insiders and outsiders

玻璃瓶里的苍蝇——处处碰壁

A fly in a glass bottle — (lit) running up against walls everywhere; (coll) rebuffed everywhere

脖子上挂镰刀——危险！

A sickle hung around the neck — dangerous!

铙子翻转敲——唱反调

Reversing the cymbals and beating them together — (coll) singing an opposing tune

跛子的拐杖——顶条腿

A cripple's crutch — (lit) equivalent to a leg; (coll) an important support or contributor

不保温的热水瓶——坏蛋（胆）

A thermos bottle that cannot keep warm — (lit) the glass liner is broken; (pun) a "bad egg"; scoundrel

不吃羊肉惹膻气——自背臭名

Having gotten the rank smell of mutton without having eaten it — (cy) having gotten a notorious name for oneself

不出芽的谷子——坏种

Rice seed that can't germinate — (lit) bad seed; (pun/coll) a bad sort

不见兔子不放鹰——抓得紧

Won't loose the hawk until a rabbit comes in sight — a tight hold; pay close attention to something; make the best use of one's time

不入虎穴——焉得虎子

If one does not enter the tiger's lair — how can one obtain tiger cubs? "nothing ventured, nothing gained"

布袋里的菱角——尖儿的出头儿

Water caltrop in a cloth bag — (lit) the points (of the water caltrop)

will stick out；(pun) cleverness or cunning will show itself or be promoted

布袋里装石榴皮——一个子儿也没有

Putting pomegranate skins in a cloth bag — (lit) there is not a single seed in it；(coll) penniless

财神爷叫门——天大的好事

The God of Wealth knocking at the door — a heavenly boon

裁缝的尺子——量人不量己

A tailor's ruler — measures others but not himself；applying the rules only to others

踩着凳子够月亮——手太短

Stepping up on a bench to grasp the moon — (lit) arms too short；(coll) a far cry (from something)

踩着乌龟,叫它伸头——越逼越不行

Stepping on a turtle and telling it to stick its head out — the more you force (something)，the more it can't be accomplished

踩着银桥上金桥——越走越亮堂

Walking from a silver bridge to a gold bridge — [one's prospects] become brighter and brighter

菜刀哄孩子——不是玩的

Coaxing a child with a kitchen knife — not a game

菜刀切豆腐——两面光

Cutting bean curd with a kitchen knife — (lit) smooth on both sides；(coll) pleasing to both parties

菜园里的苦瓜——越老心越红

A bitter melon in a vegetable garden — the older, the redder the core；the older, the more progressive minded

蚕宝宝吃桑叶——胃口越来越大

A silkworm eating mulberry leaves — its appetite gets bigger and bigger

沧海一粟——非常渺小

One grain afloat on a vast ocean — (lit) very tiny；(fig) "a drop in the bucket"

苍蝇抱鸡蛋——找缝儿下蛆

A fly holding an egg — (lit) looking for a crack to lay maggots in; (fig) looking for a chance to launch an attack

苍蝇飞进花园里——装疯[蜂]

A fly flying into a flower garden — (lit) pretending to be a bee; (pun) pretending to be insane

苍蝇跟屎壳郎做朋友——臭味相投

A fly making friends with a dung beetle — (lit) bad smells attract each other; (cy) like attracts like

苍蝇嗅(闻)到臭味儿——如获至宝

A fly sniffing a stink — (cy) as if having found a priceless treasure

[(曹操)吃]鸡肋——弃之可惜,食之无味

[(CaoCao) eating] chicken ribs — (lit) to eat it is tasteless, to throw it away would be a pity; (fig) things of little or no value; something one just keeps around to "make do" with [Cf. the chengyu, wei ru ji lei, "as tasteless as chicken ribs." Based on an incident in San Guo Zhi (The History of the Three Kingdoms)]

曹刿论战——一鼓作气

Cao Gui [a warrior in the state of Lu during the Spring and Autumn Period] expounding the strategy of war — (lit) beat the drum, and get ready; (cy) press on without letup; get something done in one sustained effort

草船借箭——满载而归

Straw boats borrowing arrows — (cy) come back with fruitful results (Zhuge Liang and Lu Su obtained additional arrows by sending boats filled with straw dummies across the Yangzi River in a heavy fog, where Cao Cao's forces shot at them. Cf. R3K)

草帽烂了边儿——顶好

A straw hat with its brim worn out — (lit) the crown is all right; (pun) the best. (See the following entry)

草帽子当锣——想[响]不起来

A straw hat serving as a gong — (lit) no sound can be produced; (pun) can't recall or think of something or somebody. (See the preceding entry)

草坪上丢了绣花针——难寻

Losing an embroidery needle in the lawn — difficult to find; "a needle in a haystack"

草上的露水——不长久

Dew on the grass can't last long

厕所里埋地雷——激起公愤（粪）

Burying a mine in the lavatory — (lit) the public shit will be disturbed; (pun) public indignation will be aroused [Cf. "the shit will hit the fan."]

搽粉进棺材——死要面子

Powdering one's face before being put into a coffin — (lit) concerned to death with "face"; (coll) overly concerned with appearances

搽粉上吊——死要脸

Powdering one's face [before] hanging oneself — (lit) concerned with one's face unto death; (coll) determined to keep up appearances at any cost

茶馆里谈天——想到哪儿,说到哪儿

Chatting in a teahouse — talking about whatever comes to mind

茶壶里煮饺子——肚里有,嘴上倒不出

Cooking dumplings in a teapot — (lit) something is inside the belly that can't be poured out from the mouth; (fig) ① a learned, but not eloquent man; ② awkward to speak of; hard to express what is on one's mind (See the following entry)

拆房放风筝——只图风流,不顾家

Dismantling one's house in order to fly a kite — (lit) concerned only with wind currents, not with one's home; (pun) engage in dissolute activities at the expense of one's family

拆庙散和尚——各奔东西

A (Buddhist) temple torn down and the monks dispersed — (cy) each going his own way; each pursuing his own course

馋嘴巴走进中药店——自讨苦吃

A glutton entering a traditional Chinese medicine shop — (lit) asking to taste bitterness; (cy) looking for trouble

长竹竿进城门——转不过弯儿来

A long pole taken into the city gate — (lit) unable to make a turn; (coll) stubborn or literal minded

肠子不打弯儿——直性子

A person with straight intestines — frank and straight forward

唱老生的生气——吹胡子，瞪眼睛

The Old Man character (in Beijing opera) flying into a rage — frothing at the mouth and glaring (with his eyes opened wide)

唱戏的没主角——胡闹

No leading role in an opera — (lit) (just) reckless noise making (like a bit player); (coll) running wild; making trouble

朝天放枪——空想(响)

Shooting at the sky — (lit) a high (or wasted) sound; (pun) empty, pointless thoughts

朝廷爷吃煎饼——均(君)摊

An imperial court official eating a thin fried pancake — (lit) distributed by the monarch; (pun) share equally

潮水过了才下网——迟了

Spreading out a fish net after the tide has receded — too late

炒豆发芽,铁树开花——好事难盼

Roasted beans sprouting shoots, the Iron tree in blossom (rare occurrences) — (cy) it is difficult to realize one's high aims or expectations

炒虾等不得红——真猴急

Can't wait for the shrimps to turn red — too impatient to wait; extremely anxious

车到山前——必有路

The cart being driven to the foot of a mountain — there must be a way

车干塘水捉脚鱼——干(干)到底

Pumping dry a pond to catch turtles (which hide in the mud) — (lit) dry right to the button; (pun) carrying through or persisting to the end

撑外墙的木柱——死顶

A pillar bracing a crooked wall — (lit) firmly braced; oppose to the death; (coll) not carry out orders from above (political)

成熟的稻穗子——垂着头

Ripening rice ears — (lit) with head hanging; (coll) sad; unhappy; depressed

成天想蚕茧儿——只顾私（丝）

Thinking about silkworm cocoons all day long — (lit) only caring about silk; (pun) caring only about oneself

城隍庙搬家——神出鬼没

The temple of the City God moving (its location) — (lit) gods going out and ghosts disappearing; (coll) coming and going like a shadow; appearing and disappearing mysteriously

城隍庙里的鼓槌——一对

Drumsticks in the temple of the City God — (lit) a pair; (fig) a couple; a pair

城隍庙里内讧——鬼打鬼

Internal strife within the temple of the City God — (lit) devils beating devils; (fig) strife among one's enemies

城隍爷戴孝——白跑（袍）

The City God in mourning dress — (lit) [in a] white robe; (pun/dial) have made a fruitless trip

城门楼上吊嗓子——唱高调儿

Practicing singing scales on top of the tower of a city gate — singing a high tune; talking big; making a high-sounding statement; high-flown talk

城门楼上挂猪肉——架子大

Hanging a piece of pork up on the tower over a city gate — (lit) the frame is large; (coll) haughty in manner

城墙上出丧——死出风头

Holding a funeral procession on the city wall — (lit) seeking the limelight (even) in death; (pun/coll) trying desperately to be in the limelight

城墙上的草——风吹两边倒

A blade of grass atop the city wall — swaying right and left with the winds

城头上放风筝——出手就不低

Flying a kite on the top of the city wall — starting on a high level

城头上跑马——①兜圈子②难回头

Riding a horse on top of the city wall ① going around in circles;

② impossible to turn round

乘飞机钓鱼——还差一大截

Fishing from an airplane — still a long distance away

程咬金的斧头——①头三下子狠②就这两下子

Cheng Yaojin's ax — ① (lit) only the first three (strokes) are fierce; (fig) he has only this one skill ② (lit) possessing only these two (sic) strokes; (fig) his only skill; a "one-punch" fighter [Cheng Yaojin was a general who, although strong, was not accomplished in the martial arts; cf. Sui Tang Yanyi (Romances of the Sui and Tang Dynasties).]

秤砣打秤砣——实打实

The sliding weight of a steelyard scales is struck by another sliding weight — (lit) a solid striking a solid; (fig) honest, full, and solid

秤砣落井——一落到底

A sliding weight ofa steelyard scales dropping into a well — (lit) sinking right to the bottom; (coll) (a cadre) demoted to the lowest rank

秤砣虽小——压千斤

The sliding weight of a steelyard scales although small — can balance a thousand catties; a small person can accomplish great feats (great feats) (a yanyu in two parts)

吃曹操的饭,干刘备的事——人在心不在

Getting one's food from Cao Cao while serving Liu Bei [two opposing leaders in R3K] — present in body but not in spirit; one's mind, heart, or loyalty is elsewhere

吃的盐不少——净管闲[咸]事

Having eaten a lot of salt — (lit) only concerned with salty matters; (pun) always concerned with matters that do not concern oneself

吃饭不想种田人——忘本

Not thinking of the farmers while having one's meals — forgetting one's benefactors; forgetting one's class origin

吃饭泡汤——喝粥的命

Soaking (i. e., thinning one's) cooked rice in soup [or water] — (lit) having the fate of eating rice porridge; (fig) fated or destined to be poor

吃海水长大的——管得宽

Having been brought up on a diet of sea water — (lit) widely concerned；(fig) making everything one's business

吃了豹子胆——天王老子都不管

After having eaten leopard gallbladder — not even afraid of the Heavenly King's father (a rhyme；the gall-bladder is said to be the seat of courage)

吃了扁担——横了心（肠）

Having eaten a carrying pole — the heart (or intestines) made straight；[one who has made up his mind and] become determined or desperate

吃了墨汁——黑了心肠

Having drunk Chinese ink — (lit) the heart and the bowels both blackened；(fig) evil

吃了账本儿——心中有数

Having eaten an account book — (lit) have numbers in one's heart；(coll) have a pretty clear idea；know what's what；really know how things stand

吃了猪下巴——爱打嘴儿

Having eaten pig's jaws — (lit) liking to stick one's snout in；(coll) fond of interrupting others；(dial) bragging, or talking and making a fool of oneself

吃麻油唱曲子——油腔滑调

Singing songs while eating sesame oil — (lit) oily tunes；(coll) glibly；having a slippery tongue；a slippery, oily person

吃咸鱼,蘸酱油——多此一举

Dipping salted fish in soy sauce — (cy) an unnecessary move

吃着碗里,望着锅里——贪得无厌

Eating what is in the bowl while looking at the cooking pot (to see how much is left) — (cy) insatiably avaricious

池塘里的浮萍——随风飘

Duckweed (floating) in a pond — going with the wind

赤膊戴领带——穷要好看

A bare-chested man wearing a tie — [a poor person vainly] attempting to look nice

抽刀断水——白费劲

Drawing one's sword to cut off the flow of water (the first half of a line of poetry by the famous Tang dynasty poet Li Bai) — (coll) a vain effort

抽烟烧了枕头——怨不着别人

Setting one's pillow on fire while smoking [in bed] — can't blame anyone but oneself

丑媳妇儿见公婆——迟早有一次

An ugly looking daughter-in-law (going to) see her parents-in-law—(lit) sooner or later the time will come; (fig) there's no escaping

出洞的老鼠——东张西望

A rat (just) out of its hole — (coll) peering around

出笼的鸟儿——收不回

A bird out of the cage — impossible to get in back

出门逢债主——扫兴

Going out from home only to run into one's creditor — have one's spirits dampened

出门坐飞机——远走高飞

Going out to take a trip by air — (lit) going far and flying high; (coll) off to distant parts

出其不意,攻其不备——奇袭

Surprising and attacking someone unawares — a surprise attack [Cf. Sunzi Bingfa (Sunzi's The Art of War).]

出头椽子——先烂

The rafter that sticks out — gets rotten first (an admonition not to "stick one's neck out")

出土文物——老古董

Unearthed cultural relics — antiques (said of things or people)

出窑的砖——定型了

Bricks (taken) out from the kiln — having been finalized in form; set; firmly cast

穿钉鞋,拄拐棍儿——步步小心

Wearing spiked shoes and carrying a walking cane — being [deliberately] careful at every step; double security

穿冬衣,戴夏帽——不知春秋

Wearing a winter coat and a summer hat (at the same time) — (lit) not knowing whether it's spring or autumn; (coll) not understanding the current political situation or history; muddle headed

穿没底的鞋——脚踏实地

Wearing a pair of shoes without soles — (lit) have one's feet planted on solid ground; (fig) earnest and down to earth

穿新鞋走老路——因循守旧

Taking the old road wearing new shoes (a political slogan often used during the Cultural Revolution) — (cy) sticking to old ways; following the beaten path

穿着坎肩儿作揖——露两手儿

Wearing a sleeveless jacket and bowing (with hands clasped) — (lit) two hands are exposed; (coll) exhibiting one's abilities; showing off ("to show off")

穿着孝衣拜天地——悲喜交加

Going through the wedding ceremony dressed in mourning — grief and joy intermingled

穿着雨衣打伞——多此一举

Using an umbrella while wearing a raincoat — (cy) engaging in unnecessary procedures

船到中流碰暗礁——散板儿了

A boat colliding with a submerged reef in midstream — (hit) breaking up; coming apart; (coll) extremely tired; "bone tired"

船老大坐后艄——看风使舵

A helmsman sitting at the stern helm [of a ship] — (yy) trimming his sails to the wind [usually political]

床头上跑马——走投无路

Riding a horse on the bow of a ship — have nowhere to go

串起来的螃蟹——横行不了

Crabs tied together with a string — cannot run wild; cannot ride roughshod over others

窗户里伸腿——没找到门儿

Sticking one's leg out through the window — (lit) not able to find the door; (fig) unable to find a way to do something

窗户的纸——一捅就破

Paper on a [latticed] window — (lit) a mere poke tears a hole in it; (fig) [rumors or lies] easily exposed

床底下吹喇叭——低声下气

Blowing a trumpet under the bed — (lit) (with a) low voice and breathy tones; (fig) soft-spoken and submissive; humble; ingratiating

床底下放风筝——再高也有限

Flying a kite under a bed — how high, there's a limit

吹了灯瞪眼睛——出了气,也没得罪人

Blowing out the lamp in order to glare at some-ont — (fig) giving vent to one's anger without offending anyone

吹唢呐——哪里,哪里

Blowing a Chinese trumpet — (lit) "na-li-na-li" (the sound the trumpet makes); (coll) "it's nothing" (a polite disclaimer)

春笋破土——节节升

Spring bamboo shoots breaking up through the ground — (lit) shooting up joint by joint; (fig) a continuous rise (e. g. , in rank, standard of living, social position)

搭戏台卖螃蟹——(买卖不大)架子不小

Setting up an opera stage to sell crabs — (lit) (the business is small) (but) the setup is big; (fig) putting on grand airs (although one's social status is lowly)

打半边鼓——旁敲侧击

Beating only one side of a drum — (lit) a flank attack; (cy) make oblique references; beat about the bush

打掉了牙齿咽到肚里——忍气吞声

Swallowing the teeth one has just had knocked out of one's mouth — swallowing an insult

打翻测字摊儿——不识相

Overturning a fortune-teller's desk — (lit) not reading physiognomy; (pun/dial) insensitive to circumstances; making ill-time dremarks, actions, and so on (Shanghai)

打架揪胡子——谦虚（牵须）

Seizing someone's beard while fighting — (lit) pulling a beard；(pun) be modest

打开棺材治好病——起死回生

Opening a coffin and curing the sickness — (cy) bringing somebody back to life

打着手电筒——照人家,不照自己

Using a flashlight — (lit) lighting up others (but) not oneself；(fig) asking much of others but not of oneself

打肿脸充胖子——①假充富态②死要场面

Having one's face slapped until it's swollen — ① (lit) (hiding one's loss of face by) pretending to have gotten fatter；(fig) pretending to be rich ②going in for ostentation and extravagance to one's own detriment (The first part is a yanyu)

当兵的叫街——没想（饷）了

Soldiers calling in the street — (lit) out of rations；(pun) no expectations. (Before 1949, troops often had to forage for their food.)

端午节吃饺子——与众不同

Eating [ordinary] dumplings during the Dragon Boat Festival [when glutinous rice dumplings are normally eaten] — out of the ordinary；not commonplace

端着金碗讨饭——装穷

Begging with a golden bowl — pretending to be poor

额角上放扁担——头挑

Placing a carrying pole on one's forehead — (lit) "head carrying"；(pun/dial) the best (Shanghai)

大姑娘做媒——有嘴说别人,无嘴说自己

A young girl serving as a matchmaker — her mouth mentions only others, not her own

大海捞针——没处寻

Dredging for a needle in the sea — nowhere to find it；finding a needle in a haystack

大年三十盼月亮——痴心妄想

Looking for a full moon on Lunar New Year's Eve — wishful thinking (once in a blue moon)

担雪填井——白费力气

Carrying snow to fill a well — wasting one's energy

断了线的风筝——收不回

A kite with a broken string — can't be got back

对牛弹琴——白费功夫

Playing a lute for a cow — wasted time (or effort); casting pearls before swine

鳄鱼掉泪——假惺惺/假慈悲

A crocodile shedding tears — hypocritical or false sympathy; "crocodile tears"

二,三,四,五,六,七,八,九——缺衣(一),少食(十)

Two, three, four, five; six, seven, eight, nine — (lit) lacking one and ten; (pun) without clothes and food; in extreme poverty〔A dissatisfied peasant wrote this and pasted it as a sign framing the two sides and top of a doorway during the disastrous Great Leap Forward of 1958 – 1960.〕

《二十四史》——不知从哪里说起

"The Twenty-Four Histories" (a set of dynastic histories compiled in the Qian Long period of the Qing dynasty covering remote antiquity up to the Ming dynasty) — (It's such a long and complicated story.) one hardly knows where to start (a Yanyu)

房梁上挂暖壶——高水平

Thermos flask hanging on the roof beam of a house — (lit) a high water bottle; (pun) high level; high standard

放长线——钓大鱼

Throwing out a long line — (lit) (to) catch a big fish; (fig) to find out who's really behind something

放虎归山——必有后患

Releasing a tiger back to the mountains — sure to be a source of trouble later (a yanyu rhyme)

放屁呷着脚后跟——倒霉

Letting a fart and hitting oneself in the heel — bad luck

房子上生孩子——高产

Giving birth to a child on board an airplane — (lit) high birth; (pun) high yield (economics)

飞行员的降落伞——随机应变

A pilot's parachute — (lit) following the airplane in case of an accident; (pun/coll) acting according to circumstances

肥猪跑到屠夫家——送上门

A fat pig walking itself to the butcher's house — serving oneself up

风吹墙头草——两边倒

The wind blowing the grass atop a wall — wavering on both sides; fence-sitting

风箱里的老鼠——两头受气

A mouse in a bellows — (lit) getting pressure from both sides; (fig) getting blamed from both sides; caught in the middle

凤凰飞上梧桐——自由旁人话短长

A phoenix perching atop a (tall) Chinese parasol tree (i. e. when a person of beauty or talent displays him or herself) — naturally some people's tongues will wag (an image based on a folk belief)

赶鸭子过河——呱呱叫

Driving ducks across the river — (lit) quack-quacking; (coll) top-notch; very good

赶鸭子上架——吃力不讨好

Driving a duck onto a perch (ducks do not normally roost on perches) — expending one's effort to no good result

橄榄屁股——坐不住

The bottom of a Chinese olive — (lit) cannot sit firmly; (fig) cannot sit still; hyperactive

擀面杖吹火——一窍不通

Using a rolling pin to blow into a fire — (lit) no aperture is open; (coll) lacking the slightest knowledge of something

刚出山的猛虎——威风不小

A ferocious tiger just out of the mountains — (coll) awe

inspiring; majestic

刚打好的渔网——①心（新）眼多；②百孔千疮

A just-completed fishing net — ① (lit) full of new holes; (pun/coll) full of unnecessary misgivings; oversensitive ② (lit) a thousand holes, a hundred sores; (cy) riddled with gaping wounds; afflicted with myriad ills

刚过门的媳妇儿——扭扭捏捏，羞羞答答

A newly married bride — (lit) shilly-shallying; coy and shy; (fig) not taking a clear-cut position

刚开坛子的老酒——冲劲儿足

Wine in a newly opened earthen jar — having a strong "essence" or "spirit" (said of noe who has a strong drive or temper)

高山有好水，平地有好花——各有所长

There's good water in high mountains, there're beautiful flowers on the plain — (cy) each has its own advantages

高射炮打坦克——水平降低

Using an antiaircraft gun to shoot tank — (cy) lowering one's level; (fig) retrogressing; falling behind

高字边上加一手——你想搞啥？

Adding a "hand" radical to the [left] side of the Chinese character gao [high] — (pun) what are you thinking of doing?

割草打兔子——捎带干的

Killing a rabbit while cutting grass — incidentally

胳膊折了——袖里藏

A broken arm — (lit) hidden in the sleeve; (coll) brave or stalwart (usually used by criminal gang elements); not letting on that one has been cheated, deceived, or taken in

胳膊往里弯——只顾自己

Turning one's arms inward — only caring for oneself

胳膊肘儿——朝里弯／拐

Elbows — (lit) (naturally) turning inward; (fig) naturally considering one's own people or relatives first; "blood is thicker than water" [Cf. the followingentry.]

隔着门缝儿瞧人——把人看扁啦

Looking at someone through the crack between the door and its frame — (lit) looking at people in a narrow way; (coll) underestimate people (See the previous entry.)

隔着一层窗户纸——一捅就破

Separated by only a layer of window casement paper — (lit) easily broken by a poke (of the finger); (fig) easily exposed; a (mutually agreed upon) feigned ignorance (a yanyu)

隔着云雾看山头——不清楚

Looking at the top of a hill through clouds and mist — not clear

给了九寸想一尺——得寸进尺

Wishing for one chi (foot) after being given nine cun (inches) — (cy) "give him an inch and he'll take a mile" (One chi, one third of a mater, is equal to ten cun.)

给三岁娃娃说亲——还差二十年

Arranging a marriage for a three-year-old child — (lit) still twenty years away; (fig) a long way off in the future; not now

跟和尚借梳子——找错了人

Asking to borrow a comb from a monk — gone to the wrong person (Buddhist monks traditionally shaved their heads.)

公鸡打架——对头

Roosters fighting — (lit) opposing heads; (pun) rivals; opponents

狗吃豆腐——闲(衔)不住

A dog eating bean curd — (lit) could not get hold of it in its mouth; (pun) always keeping oneself busy

狗戴嚼子——胡勒

A dog wearing a bridle — (lit) promiscuously cinched; (coll) nonsense

狗戴帽子——装人

A dog wearing a cap — pretending to be a human being (an insult)

狗嘴里吐不出象牙——没好话

Ivory will not grow in a dog's mouth — having an uncivil tongue (The first part is a yanyu)

狗拿耗子——多管闲事

A dog catching rats — too meddlesome; wasting one's time on trivial matters that do not concern one

姑娘做媒人——自己作保

A young woman serving as a matchmaker（for herself）— standing guarantor for oneself

谷地里的高粱——出人头地

Chinese sorghum growing in a rice（or millet）field —（coll）standing out among one's fellows; head and shouters above others

（刮风扫地,）下雨泼街——假积极

（Sweeping the streets while it is blowing and）sprinkling water while it is raining — pretending to be politically active

关公面前耍大刀——自不量力

Brandishing the broad sword before Cuan Gong — not having a correct estimation of oneself; making a fool of oneself（Guan Gong was skilled in the martial arts. Cf. R3K. ）

关公战秦琼——①乱了朝代②七错八搭

[General] Guan Gong [of the Three Kingdoms Period（A. D. 221 – 63）] fighting [General] Qin Qiong [of the early Tang dynasty（A. D. 618 – 907）] — ①（lit）mixing up the dynasties;（fig）muddling things up ②（lit）"at sixes and sevens"; completely mixed up;（fig）confusing two things that are completely unrelated [The first part is the title of a famous xiangsheng comedy dialogue by Hou Baolin. Chi cuo ba da is Shanghai dialect.]

关老爷阅兵书——秉烛达旦

Guan Lao Ye（Guan Gong）reading a book on the art of war —（lit）holding a candle until dawn;（coll）burning the midnight oil [Cf. R3k; see Guan Gong]

关着门做皇帝——自尊,自贵

Acting the emperor behind closed doors —（cy）self-dig-nification and self-glorification

棺材里伸手——死要钱

Stretching one's hand out of a coffin —（lit）asking for money after one dies;（fig）trying to get money by any possible means

广东人唱京戏——南腔北调

A cantonese singing Beijing opera —（lit）a mixed accent of north and south；（coll） talking with a broad accent；nondescript talk with a mixed accent

鬼门关出告示——鬼话

A notice put up at the Gates of Hell — （lit） all devilish words；（cy） a pack of lies

滚汤泼蚂蚁——一窝都是死

Throwing boiling water on ants — the whole nest is dead

滚油锅里捡金子——难下手

Pickling gold out from a pot of boiling oil — （coll） difficult ot put one's hand into

锅膛里吹火——碰一鼻子灰

Blowing at the fire in a stove — （lit） （have） one's nose smudged with ashes；（coll） get snubbed or rejected

过年娶媳妇儿——双喜临门

（one's son） Getting married while celebrating the Lunar New Year — a double blessing descends upon the house

过了时的黄历——翻不得

An out-of-date （imperial） calendar — （lit） no point in turning （its pages）；（coll） no point in consulting，quoting，or citing it （because it's old and out-of-date）

蛤蟆跳井——不懂（扑通）

A frog jumping into a well — （lit）"ker-splash"；（pun） don't understand （Budong is a onomatopoeic pun on pu-tong. ）

号兵张嘴——吹了

The bugler opening his mouth — （lit） blow off；（coll） break off （relations）；break up；fall through

耗子吃猫食——悄悄地干

A rat eating a cat's food — doing quietly；doing somethingfurtively

耗子掉进米坛子——机会难得

A rat falling into a vat of rice — （coll） a rare chance

耗子逗猫——没事找事

A mouse teasing a cat — looking for trouble

耗子给猫捋胡子——溜须不要命

A mouse stroking a cat's beard — willing to risk one's life to butter someone up (Shanghai dialect)

耗子爬秤杆儿——自称自

A rat crawling up on a steelyard balance scales — (lit) weighing oneself；(fig) having an overinflated image of one's own importance

耗子舔猫鼻子——找死

A mouse licking the nose of a cat — looking for death

耗子钻进书箱里①识（食）本②咬文嚼字

A rat getting into a bookcase — ① nibbling the books；(pun) losing one's capital；② (lit) chewing essays and gnawing characters；(cy) paying excessive attention to wording

和尚打伞——无法（发）无天

A monk opening an umbrella — (lit) without hair，without sky；(pun/coll) having [regard for] neither [earthly] law nor heaven [ly principle]

黑板上写字——能写能抹

Writing on a blackboard — (what) can be written can (also) be erased

猴子捞月亮——空忙一场

A monkey trying to fish [the reflection of] the moon out of the water — a vain attempt

壶中无酒——难留客

(When) there's no wine in the pot — (it's) difficult to ask the guests to stay (a yanyu in two parts meaning one has nothing to attract others)

虎头上拍苍蝇——①胆大②找死

Swatting flies on a tiger's head — ① very daring；plenty of courage ② courting death

怀里揣着个小兔子——①怦怦直跳；②惴惴不安

Hugging a small rabbit to one's chest — ① (lit) struggling with one's heart pounding all the while；(fig) excited；frightened；② alarmed and on tenterhooks；anxious and fearful

怀里的东西掉进靴子里——还是自己的

Something in one's arms falling into one's boot — still belongs to one

黄汉升的箭——百发百中

Huang Han Sheng's arrows — (lit) a hundred shots, a hundred bull's-eyes；（cy）a crack shot；clairvoyant（Huang Han Sheng was a veteran general under Liu.）

黄连树下弹琴——苦中取乐

Playing a lute beneath a Chinese goldthread tree — （lit）finding happiness amidst bitterness；（coll）finding happiness in adversity

皇帝打架——争天下

Emperors fighting（each other）— contending for the world；scrambling for begemony

黄鼠狼给鸡拜年——不怀好意

A weasel wishing Happy New Year to a chicken — harboring no good intentions

皇帝的女儿——不愁嫁

The emperor's daughter — will never worry about getting married

皇帝的别名儿——孤家寡人

The emperor's personal pronouns — （lit）the sovereign；the royal "we"；（pun）a person in solitary splendor；a person who has no mass support；a loner

回民赶集——诸（猪）事不问

People of the Hui nationality［i. e., Chinese Muslims］going to market — （lit）do not ask for things related to pork；（pun）not attending to anything；not caring about anything

昏官断案——各打五十大板

A fatuous magistrate setting cases — （lit）each（party is sentenced to be）beaten fifty strokes；（fig）punishing the innocent and the guilty alike；blaming both sides without discrimination；"a pox on both your houses"

豁牙吃西瓜——道道儿多

A person with missing or scraggly teeth biting a watermelon — （lit）（leaving）many lines（of tooth marks on the melon）；（coll）having many "ways"；resourceful

火烧红莲寺——妙哉（庙灾）

The Red Lotus Monastery on fire — （lit）the temple suffers a disaster；（pun）wonderful！The Red Lotus Monastery is a temple of evil monks portrayed in the twentieth-century popular noveljianghu qixia zhuan by pingjiang buxiaosheng. Part of China's first martial arts (silent) film huo shao hong lian si (Fire Destroys the Red Lotus Monastery), made in the 1920s, was based on this novel.

鸡孵鸭子——白忙

A hen (trying to) hatch out ducks — (coll) pointlessly busy (Fu is a colloquial pronunciation.)

鸡给黄鼠狼拜年——自找倒霉

A chicken paying a New Year's call on a yellow weasel — (coll) looking for trouble; bringing trouble on oneself (See huangshulang gei ji gainian)

鸡毛当令箭——假传将令

Using a chicken feather as (though it were) an official warrant to give commands — (fig) give false orders using pretended authority; low level official(s) overzealous in implementing orders from above (The first part is a chengyu)

鸡毛过大秤——没有分量

Feathers weighed on a scale — (lit) of noweight; (fig) insignificant

鸡飞蛋打——一场空

The hen has flown away and the eggs are broken — all in vain

鸡娘哺鸭子——爱管闲事

A (mother) hen feeding ducks — liking to interfere in (trivial) matters that do not concern one

急雨打在水缸里——心里翻起了泡泡

A driving rain beating down into a water vat — (lit) bubbles rise in the center; (fig) perturbed; disturbed; uneasy; fidgety

鲫鱼下油锅——死不瞑目

A carp fried in oil — (lit) won't close its eyes even in death; (cy) dying with a grievance or everlasting regret

家雀变凤凰——越变越好

A sparrow turned into a phoenix — becoming better and better

家有十五口——七嘴八舌

There are fifteen people in the family — (lit) seven mouths and eight tongues; (coll) all talking at once; a lively discussion with everybody trying to get a word in

（贾）宝玉的通灵玉——命根子

The jade talisman of （Jia） Baoyu ［the hero of DRC］ — （fig） one's lifeblood

拣了芝麻, 丢了西瓜——因小失大

Picking up the sesame seeds, overlooking the water-melons — concentrate on minor matters to the neglect of major ones.

剑拔弩张——一触即发

With swords drawn and bow bent — （lit） may break out at any moment; （cy） an explosive situation ［The first part is also a chengyu］

见了大官儿叫舅——高攀

Calling a high official "uncle" — making friends or claiming ties of kinship with someone of higher social position; social climbing

见了强盗喊爸爸——认贼作父

Calling a bandit "papa" — （lit） take a robber for one's father; （cy） regard the enemy as kith and kin

见了蚊子就拔剑——大惊小怪

Drawing one's sword at the sight of a mosquito — （cy） making a fuss over nothing; making a mountain out of a molehill

见了丈母娘叫大嫂——无话找话

Calling one's mother-in-law sister-in-law instead — （coll） finding a pretext for conversation

江边卖水——多余

Selling water by the riverside — superfluous

姜子牙算命——买卖兴隆

Jiang Ziya going into the fortune-telling business — business is brisk （Jiang Tai Gong （q. v.） was said to be adept at telling fortunes. See Feng Shen Yanyi, chap. 16.）

蒋干访周瑜——①窥察动静②自找倒霉

Jiang Gan paying a visit to Zhou Yu — ① to spy ② bring trouble upon oneself （Jiang Gan, an adviser under Cao Cao, was sent south to spy in the camp of Zhou Yu, the enemy general. As Zhou Yu knew this, he prepared a letter for Jiang Gan to find, falsely implicating one of Cao Cao's generals, who was put to death. See the following entry; cf. R3K.)

浇树浇根——交人交心

(when) watering a tree, water the roots — (when) making friends, know someone's heart (a yanyu; technically a rhyme)

嚼着甘蔗上楼梯——节节甜,步步高

Going up stairs chewing sugarcane — (lit) tasting greater sweetness joint by joint while going up step by step; (fig) life gets sweeter and sweeter as one advances in rank or position

脚踩两只船——①一个也不落实;②三心二意

Straddling two boats — ① (lit) neither one is firmly planted; (fig) a foot in either camp; "fence-sitting" ② of two minds; hesitant

脚踩(踏)西瓜皮——滑到哪里是哪里

Stepping on a watermelon rind — (lit) wherever one slips to, that's where one is;

叫花婆子谈嫁妆——穷人说大话

A woman beggar talking about a dowry — a poor person talking big

叫花子不留隔夜食——一顿光

A beggar keeping no leftover food for the next day — (lit) eating in all up (at one meal); (coll) spendthrift; not saving; improvident

叫花子打算盘——穷打算

A beggar using an abacus — budgeting in poverty

叫花子碰上要饭的——穷对穷

A beggar meeting a pauper — both are poor

叫林黛玉抡板斧——强人所难

Asking Lin Daiyu [the fragile heroine of DRC] to brandish an ax — (cy) making somebody do something that he or she won't or can't

金漆马桶——外面好看,里面臭

A gold-edged night stool — fine-looking in appearance, stinking inside (an insult)

进站的火车——叫得凶,走得慢

A train entering a station — (lit) makes a terrible noise, runs slow; (fig) much talk and little action

近视眼看告示——迫在眉睫

A nearsighted person reading a (public) notice — (lit) so close that his eyebrows and eyelashes almost touch (it); (cy) imminent; extremely urgent

近视眼看麻子——观点模糊

A nearsighted person looking at a pockmarked face — (lit) viewing the spots in a muddled way;(pun) confused viewpoint

近水楼台——先得月

The balconies (or towers) nearest the water — get the moon (light) first; those with "connections" to an organization (or person with power) get preferential treatment [a quotation from Qing Ye Lu by Yu Wen bao]

晋襄公放败将——放虎归山

Lord Xiang of Jin (of the Spring and Autumn Period) setting the defeated officers free — (lit) letting the tiger return to the mountain; (fig) cause calamity for the future

九月的甘蔗——一节比一节甜

Sugarcane in the ninth (lunar) month (October) — (lit) getting sweeter with every section; (fig) greater happiness with every passing day

酒杯里能洗澡——小人

Able to bathe inside a wine cup — (lit) a small man; (coll) not a gentleman; a petty person

酒糟鼻子不喝酒——白担虚名

A man with a "brandy nose" (who) does not drink — (coll) carrying an undeserved reputation

韭菜——割了一茬又一茬

Chinese chives — as soon as you cut them down, they grow right back up again (This is an image used by Mao Zedong in criticizing the killings during the bad years following the Great Lean Forward: "Human heads are not like Chinese chives")

砍柴人下山——两头担心（薪）

A woodcutter descending from a hill — (lit) with fire wood dangling before and after him (on a carrying pole); (pun) both parties worried

看人上菜——势利眼

Presenting (guests with) different dishes (according to their different social positions) — snobbish (attitude)

看"三国"掉眼泪——替古人担忧

Shedding tears while reading the Romance of the Three Kingdoms [R3K] — (lit) worrying about the ancients in vain; (fig) pointlessly worrying about something beyond one's purview or control

空心萝卜,绣花袍——中看,不中用

A hollow turnip (or) an embroidered robe — impressive looking, but useless (person)

空蒸笼上锅台——争(蒸)气

Putting empty steamers on the stove — (lit) (to) steam air; (pun) trying to make a good showing; trying to bring credit

孔夫子搬家——净是输(书)

Confucius moving his home — (lit) it's all books; (pun) lose all the time (at gambling)

拉着老虎尾巴喊救命——自找危险

Crying for help while pulling a tiger's tail — getting oneself in danger

蜡烛点火——一条心

Lighting the candle — (lit) only one wick; (pun) of one heart and one mind; cooperating

癞蛤蟆打哈欠——好大的口气

A toad yawning — how big the breath is! (pun/coll) big talk; a pompous tone

狼吃东郭先生——恩将仇报

The wolf trying to eat Master Dongguo — (cy) requiting kindness with enmity

老包断案——脸黑心不黑

Lao Bao hearing a case — black in face but not in heart (Bao Gong, well known as an honest and upright official in the Song dynasty, is usually portrayed with a black face.)

老公公背儿媳妇儿——出力不讨好

An old grandpa carrying his daughter-in-law — (coll) effort expended in vain; a thankless job

老虎念经——假装正经

A tiger chanting (Buddhist) scriptures — pretending to be decent or respectable or serious（a rhyme）

老虎屁股——摸不得

A tiger's backside — cannot be touched（a yanyu used sarcastically by Mao Zedong to describe cadres who thought they were untouchable, immune from criticism; a popular slogan used during the Cultural Revolution）

老鼠上灯台——明偷

A mouse jumps up on a lampstand —（lit）stealing in the light;（coll）stealing openly

老鼠同猫睡——练胆量

A rat sleeping with a cat —（coll）trying to build up one's courage

老鼠眼睛——一寸光

A mouse's eyes —（lit）an inch of light（or sight）;（coll）shortsighted; see only what is under one's nose（Cf. the chengyu, shu mu cun guang, "a mouse's eyes can only see an inch."）

老太太的裹脚(布)——又臭又长

An old woman's foot bindings — stinking and long

老鸦笑猪黑——自丑不觉

A crow laughing at the swarthy（skin of a）pig — not aware of one's own defects;（fig）"the pot calling the kettle black"

附录二 歇后语在文学作品中的翻译实例

(一)《芙蓉镇》——《A small town called Hibiscus》, tr, by Gladys Yang

"什么？什么？你老伯喝了<u>红薯烧酒讲酒话</u>，怎么拿唐僧上西天取经来打比，那是封建迷信，我们这是农业革命！你这话要叫上级听去了，嘿嘿……"

"What's that? <u>Are you tipsy</u>, uncle, dragging in Tripitaka? That was feudal superstition, their pilgrimage. We want to revolutionize agriculture! If the higher-ups heard you, you'd be in for it."

杨书记不知出于无心还是有意，每顿饭都派民政干事到厨房里打了来一起吃。民政干事隐约听人讲过，区委书记的外甥女在县里搞恋爱像<u>猴子扳苞谷，扳一个丢一个</u>，生活不大严肃。

And Secretary Yang, deliberately or by chance, always sent for Mangeng to join them. Mangeng had heard that this niece of Yang's was fast. She had chased men <u>like a monkey picking corn-cobs, dropping one</u>

after another.

"老表,你闻出点什么腥气来了么?"老谷性情宽和,思想却还敏锐。

"谷主任,胡蜂撞进了蜜蜂窝,日子不得安生了!"满庚哥打了个比方说。

"Smell anything fishy, brother?" Old Gu might be easy-going, but he was shrewd.

"Manager Gu, a hornet has broken into beehive. We shan't be left in peace." was Mangeng's answer.

王秋赦苦思苦想,渐渐地明白了过来,今后若想在政治上进步,生活上提高,还是要接近李国香,依靠杨民高。就像是宝塔,一级压一级,一级管一级。他不是木脑壳,虽是吃后悔药可悲,但总比那些花岗岩脑壳至死不悔改的好得多。

After racking his brains it dawned on him that his only hope of getting ahead politicallyand rising in the world was by sucking up to Li Guoxiang and relying on Yang Min'gao. They were above him in the power structure. He was no numskull. Though remorse was bitter it paid better than being pigheaded.

秦癫子三十几岁,火烧冬茅心不死,是个坏人里头的乐天派。他出身成分不算差,仗着和黎满庚支书有点转弯拐角的姑舅亲,一从剧团开除回来就要求大队党支部把他头上的右派分子帽子改作坏分子帽子。

Crazy Qin, now over thirty, was content with his lot. His family origin was not too bad and he was a distant relative of Li Mangeng, whom he had persuaded to change his label from "Rightist" to "bad element".

这可把那些等着吃米豆腐的人惹恼了,纷纷站出来帮腔:"她摆她的摊子,你开你的店子,井水不犯河水,她又没踩着哪家的坟地!""今天日子好,牛槽里伸进马脑壳来啦!""女经理,还是去整整你自己的店子吧,三鲜面莫再吃出老鼠屎来就好啦! 哈哈哈……"

The people waiting for beancurd were provoked into taking her side. "She has her stall, you have your eating-house. Why butt into her business? It's not as if she'd trampled anyone's grave." "Don't poke your nose everywhere! Get away from here!" "Why not clean up your own shop, get rid of all that rat shit in your noodles. Ha, ha..."

后来就连他的女人"五爪辣",都被他的神色吓住了,担心他真的得下了什么病。"五爪辣"这女人也颇具复杂性。胡玉音"走运"卖米豆腐那年月,她怕

男人恋旧，经常<u>舌头底下挂马蹄</u>，嘴巴"踢打踢打"，醋劲十足。（四章五）

Finally even his wife Peppery was afraid that he was ill. Peppery herself was a complex character. When Yu-yin did so well with her beancurd stall and Peppery suspected her husband of still hankering after her, <u>jealously kept her scolding like a shrew.</u>

"哈哈哈！我就是富农婆！卖米豆腐的富农婆！你这个坏人，你是想吓我，吓我？""不是吓你，我讲的是真话，<u>铁板上钉钉子</u>，一点都不假。"（二章七）

"Ha, ha, so I'm the wife of a new rich peasant! A beancurd pedlar the wife of a new rich peasant! Are you trying to scare me, youwretch?"

"I'm not, I'm <u>telling the truth, not making this up.</u>"

"<u>乌龟不笑鳖，都在泥里歇。</u>都是一样落难，一样造孽。"

"<u>Tortoises don't make fun of turtles, they're all in the mud.</u> In the same fix."

王秋赦就像一眼缺了口子的池塘，清水浊水哗哗流。提起旧事，辛酸的热泪扑扑掉，落在楼板上滴答响。"……我亏了你主任的苦心栽培……我对不起上级。我这一跤子跌得太重……我如今只想着向你和杨书记悔过，请罪……我真该在你面前掌自己一千回嘴……"

This speech poured out <u>like muddy water from a breach in a pond</u> while his tears plopped on the floor. "You went to such pains to train me, but I let the higher-ups down. Came a great cropper... Now I want to apologize to you and Secretary Yang and ask for punishment... I should slap my mouth a thousand times before you..."

（二）《敌后武工队》——《Behind enemy lines》, tr, by Shen Yao-Yi

"怎么，你可咋呼啊！真是<u>锛得木子死在树窟窿里，吃了嘴的亏</u>！"辛凤鸣幸灾乐祸的在一旁小声地敲打贾正的鼓边。贾正听到辛凤鸣的奚落，狠劲朝他捣了一胳膊肘子："去你的！真是<u>三天不打，就要上房揭瓦</u>！看，等我以后收拾你！"

"Why, you've let your tongue slip again. You can never control your mouth, never see what trouble it gets you into!" said Hsin softly, exulting over Chia's discomfort. Chia gave him a vicious shove in the ribs. "Get lost. <u>You need a good drubbing every three days.</u> I'll settle with you later."

"怎么活像个伤口？他就……"卫生员说着拿起绷带来缠。赵庆田一听到这儿，知道要坏事，就给卫生员使眼色。卫生员不理睬地缠了一遭，缠两遭，缠到第三遭,装作使劲地一勒……它要是伤口,还经得住绷带这么煞? 快走吧!
别鼻子插葱,跑这儿充象来啦。

"Looks like a wound, does it? Why he..." The medic stopped talking
as hebandaged Chao's arm, for at this point Chao gave him a sharp stare so
that after three more rounds with the bandage he pretended to pull it tight.
"If this was a wound, could he stand that?" said the medic. "Now, go.
What do you know about doctoring anyway?"

周大拿这下没钻好,又想别的法门。他觉得范村离保定这么近,八路军绝
不会老来住,眼下就答应减,真减假减,你八路军走了就得由我。他认为这是
"掺糠喂鸡哄蛋"的好办法,哄走了武工队,目的也就达到了。顺嘴说了句:"减
吧,你们说怎么减,我就怎么做!"

When this plan didn't work, Chou thought of another. He felt that
since Fantsun was so close to Paoting, the Eighth Route Army would not
visit it often. A real or phoney reduction, how could they tell after they'd
gone? His agreement would send the work team away, and he would be
master again. "Okay let's reduce it then. You just tell me how much. "

"怎么老划洋火呀?"中心炮楼上的哨兵问道。"五黄六月烟反潮,抽着又
灭了,不划洋火还行? 你是吃河水长大的,干什么要管这么宽?"临时仓库房顶
上的岗哨也不示弱地朝回顶撞。

"What do you keep striking matches for?" demanded a sentry from the
central fort. "Because in this damp weather they keep going out before I get
my cigarette lighted. What's it to you!" countered the man on the roof
uninhibitedly.

"对这种变节事故,吃了秤砣铁心的家伙,就得这么办!"刘文彬挥动着手
掌说,"河东里昨天处决了叛徒马鸣,咱们今天就公审铁杆汉奸刘魁省!"

"This is the only way to deal with the kind of person who turns
traitor!" said Liu Wen-pin with an appropriate gesture. "Yesterday Ma
Ming was executed. Today we will try the long-time traitor Liu Kuei-
sheng!"

根据战斗的需要,经杨子曾批准,缴获鬼子的一块带保险壳的夜光表由魏
强使用。戴手表,在魏强说来是大姑娘坐花花轿,头一遭的事。

Wei Chiang had been issued a luminous watch in accordance with the
needs of the war and as authorized by Yang Tau-tseng himself.

小黄庄的联络员说："算啦,大年初一吃饺子,都一样。现在请所长做主,看怎么办吧?"

The contact from Hsiaohuang said:"Forget it! The same is true of all the other villages. Now let's hear from the police superintendent what's to be done."

从此,夜袭队算和南关车站的人们拴上了仇,作上了对。宪兵队长松田亲自出马调停过几次,也没从根上解决问题。两边天天见面,见面就找碴挑错;谁见谁都是"二饼"碰"八万",斜不对眼!

From that time there was a feud between the Night Raiders and the policemen of the South Gate railway station. Matsuda had to personally intervene several times to keep them from each other's throats, but failed each time. The two sides met every day, glowered at each other every day, each trying to pick fault with the other.

赵庆田从灶膛里拿块烤熟的红薯,烫得两手来回捯换,嘴里一个劲地"嘘嘘"。"来,秃子,二一添作五!"说着用劲一掰,热气腾腾的、瓤儿红红的一大块红薯递给了小秃。郭小秃接过来,张嘴闹了一大口。

Chao Ching-tian sucked in his breath as he tossed a piping hot sweet potato from hand to hand, then said:"Hey, Hsiao Tu, let's share it." Chao broke the sweet potato in two, steam rising from it, then threw half to Hsiao Tu, who caught it and immediately took a king-size bite out of it.

"别隔着门缝看人。我要是个五尺高的男子汉,早跟俺家宝生一块给国家效劳去啦。说真的,咱们的人在我这里住着,我是怕有个闪错。"

"Don't look at people narrowly, as if through a crack in the door. If I were a six-foot man, I'd have gone long ago with my son Pao-sheng to join the resistance. To tell the truth, I'm just afraid that something may happen to those people of ours living in my house."

"绱鞋不使锥子,针(真)好;狗赶鸭子,呱呱叫。比我强一百倍。抗战胜利了,你可以当个教写字的先生。"贾正开着玩笑地夸赞了一番。

"A hundred times better than mine. After the war you can teach calligraphy," Chia Cheng kidded.

"对,对。这仁人是黄杏熬北瓜,一色货。用不到同志你说,老百姓早把他仁拴到一堆啦。我刚才念叨的,只不过粮食堆里的一个谷子粒;要查起来,我这里就记上了半本。"

"Right，right. Those three are like the colour of apricots mixed with pumpkin — you can't tell them apart. The comrades don't need to say it，everybody knows that the three are birds of a feather. What I have just told you is no more than a drop in the ocean. If you want to check，I have a list that fills half a notebook. "

火烧眉毛得顾眼前。松田根据青纱帐的串起、武工队的活动、部下的吃亏、大皇军的南调……察觉到分兵把守碉堡、据点，像个五指伸开的手掌，总不如攥成拳头有力。

But，in the situation of the "green screen" of concealment for the Eighth Route having grown high，the armed work team moving about freely，his underlings suffering repeated defeats，and the Japanese troops being transferred south，Matsuda concluded that dividing his troops to defend the strong holds would be like a hand with the five fingers spread — not so powerful as a fist.

魏强一听，知道这是想敲他的竹杠，心里捉摸："这可是叫花子碰上个要饭的，穷对穷啦。"但是他为了应付着过去，还是装模作样地将右手伸到怀里去摸钱，他摸着摸着忽然起急地说："看我这记性，明摆着是自己装的钱，怎么摸不着啦。掖到哪儿去啦……"

Wei Chiang knew that he was being touched for money，and he said to himself："So，pauper meets beggar，poor up against poor. " But he must keep up the pretence，so he reached into his gown with his right hand as though for money，after a while looked suddenly worried，then said："How forgetful I am. I was sure I'd put my money here，and now I can't find it. Where did I put it?"

"这叫阎王爷贴告示——鬼话连篇。"刘太生笑着指指报纸。"不，他是屎壳郎打喷嚏——满嘴喷粪！"贾正挥动拳头朝炕沿上一砸，气呼呼地抓过摊在炕上的伪报纸，揉成蛋扔在炕桌上。"叫我说，他这是扣着腚眼上房——自抬自。"李东山瞅着桌上被揉搓成一团的伪报纸。"他真会打肿了脸充胖子！刘太生的那顶白毡帽，他怎么不写成赫赫战果？"赵庆田又将揉搓成团的伪报纸拿起，慢慢舒展开来看。

"That's what you might call a proclamation by the King of Hell — devils' words from start to finish，" replied Liu Tai-sheng pointing at the paper，extremely amused.

"He's just making himself look fat by slapping his own face! Why didn't they write up Liu Tai-sheng's white felt cap and call it a handsome trophy?" observed Chao Ching-tien, who took up the newspaper and began reading it slowly.

侯扒皮气得眼珠子瞪圆。他左手朝大腿一拍："警告爷们，爷们是老虎推磨——不听那套，对老百姓是外甥打灯笼——照舅（旧）！武工队你有能耐就施展吧，我姓侯的豁出去啦！"

Skinflintglared round-eyed with anger. He slapped his thigh with his left hand. "Giving us an ultimatum. We'll never listen to any of that stuff! Our treatment of civilians will not change one bit. Just see if your armed work team can do anything about it! Anyway, I, Hou, will pay no attention."

"一分奈何你当我愿意缴枪？我也是叫人家逼得没法啦！叫你说，"马鸣像个剃了尾巴的猴，腾地又从八仙桌上跳下，右手揎揎左胳膊的衣袖，没一点廉耻地比划："好几个枪口都逼住了你，你怎么动？你怎么掏枪打？上下嘴唇一碰，说什么都不费劲，遇上真的，恐怕谁也得老毛子看戏——傻了眼！"

"Do you think I was willing? I was forced. I had no other way! What would you do?" He sprang cat-like from the table and bared his left arm. "With so many guns pointing at you, can you move? Can you shoot? Brave talk is easy enough, but when you meet the real thing, well, I'm afraid you'll be knocked out just the same."

拿棍子捅，够不着；让人上去拿，谁也老牛拉车朝后鞧，干咋唬，不动弹。哈叭狗想在这儿充充能耐。连朝手心啐了两口唾沫，搂着椿树就朝上攀。

He picked up a stick to poke at it but couldn't reach it and asked someone to climb the tree after it. The others all drew back, like unwilling oxen hitched to a waggon, making noises but doing nothing. The Pekinese, who wanted to show off, spit into both palms and started up the tree.

马鸣确实是个稀泥软蛋，别看他是个年轻小伙子，却受不了鬼子的一顿毒打，别看他身上挎着三号驳壳枪，这只是聋子的耳朵——摆设。

Ma Ming was a weakling and a coward. He looked stalwart enough, but he was unable to bear the blowsof the Japanese. That Mauser hanging by his side was purely ornamental.

"罗锅子的腰——一就了。我看，就这么办！回去操筹钱吧！"黄玉文的身子离开板凳,说完,便朝外走去。人们觉得他多会儿给炮楼上办事也是磨磨蹭蹭地对付,今天反倒痛快地答应下,心里都挺奇怪。在胡乱猜疑的时候,也都脚前脚后地跟了出来。

"As I see it, that's the only way. We'll go back after the money." Huang Yu-wen got up from the bench he was sitting on and went out. The others had the impression that Huang was never one to be in a hurry to carry out the puppets' orders. Today, however, he had readily promised, and they thought this strange. Making wild guesses as to the reason why, all went out one after another.

"要那样,干脆把给我做的那口六寸厚的柏木棺材抬去罢!"梁洛群话是那么说,心里并不真愿意。他觉得用这么上好的棺材装殓特务的老娘,简直是毛驴备上银鞍鞯,有点不配。于是不愉快地闹了句:"不过,要争取不过梁邦来,给他娘这个棺材就是有点冤!"

"In that case, take the six-inch-thick white pine coffin I made." These words were not what Lo-chun really had in mind, for he felt it would be a waste of a fine coffin on a secret agent's mother — like throwing good money after bad. "What a pity to waste this material if we can't win over Liang Pang," he said somewhat resentfully.

侯扒皮和哈叭狗带领他们的喽罗们来到黄庄,侯扒皮凭借他的门头硬,一下变成据点的太上皇;哈叭狗虽说跟他是棉花、线子——两样的事,倒底侯扒皮有权势,也得紧着巴结随和。两人仍旧一唱一随,还是臭味相投的好朋友。

When the two took their men to Huangchuang, Hou became overlord of the village stronghold through the influence of his powerful backing, while the Pekinese became his underling currying his favour. The two remained close in ill fame, as alike and as different as cotton wool and cotton thread, with Skinflint the top man.

"同志们别笑,我学的这是碾砣砸碾盘,实打实的事。"没容得洛玉把话说完,有的人又要笑,魏强连咳咳了两声,人们才把嘴并住。

Luo-yu gestured as he mimicked, throwing everybody into convulsions of laughter. Then Wei Chiang calmed them down.

以往肚里存不住话的快嘴二婶,今天却和往日大不相同。虽然她来回地搜寻几遍人群,可是,叽里呱啦爱说的嘴巴,如今好像贴上封条,一声也不吭。她每次目光瞅准刘文彬、汪霞,都迅速滑过去,好像他俩没在场。死亡靠近了她,她并没有让死亡吓得想出卖良心。"一个人为国家要宁折不弯,别做墙头草。"这是徐政委在公民誓约大会上讲的话。

But Gabby today was not at all like on other days. Although her eyes had swept the crowd several times, her mouth which was usually busy chattering away seemed to have a lock on it. Not a sound did she utter. And every time she glanced at Liu Wen-pin or Wang Xia she seemed to have seen nothing. Although she knew death was near, she was not afraid, nor did she ask for sympathy.

村里虽然万分沉静,村西北角的炮楼里,却吹拉弹唱闹得挺凶。铁墙根站着的贾正,不耐烦地朝炮楼的方向一瞥:"妈的,看你这秋后的蚂蚱,还能蹦几蹦?"

Though the village was deathly still, the fort at its northwest corner was noisy enough. Chia Cheng, standing with his back to the wall, looked impatiently in the direction of the fort. "You're like grasshoppers in autumn, dammit, not very many more hops to go!"

果然,在魏强他们离开周大拿家第二天,周大拿立刻变了卦。他像秋天的野兔子——又撒起欢儿来。他扬言吹风:"别看昨夜我领头减,今天我还领头免!"

As was to be expected, the very next day after they had left, Chou did an about-face, jubilantly declaring:"I led the rent reduction last night, but I'm leading the change back today!"

"你知道,你知道,知道怕你偷吃了。谁问你啦,真仨鼻子眼多股子气。"辛凤鸣戏谑地说。

"Nobody asked you. Stop letting off steam as if you had an extra nostril," teased Hsin Feng-ming.

"情况怎么样?洛玉。"刘文彬没有容洛玉走到跟前,就问起来。"屎壳郎搬家,都滚他娘的蛋啦。""哪里下来的?""西边入舟村的。"

"What's the situation, Lo-yu?" Liu Wen-pin asked before Li came up to him. "When a dung beetle moves house, the whole caboodle gets out." "Where did they come from?" "Tajan Village, west of here."

为争取他,上级曾给甄友新一个任务,专在他身上做工作。哪知他是块死榆木头,想劈个缝儿都很难。

Chen Yu-hsin had been given the task of winning Black Bear over, but who was to know that the latter would be such a diehard. He <u>simply refused</u> <u>to open up a crack.</u>

……在分区,出发前队长不是说,上级要咱们当先遣部队急速回来吗?当时我琢磨,武工队什么时候都是先遣部队,队长不说,谁心里也像个明镜,哪知,这是四扇屏里卷灶王——画(话)里有画(话)。我说咱们队长这些天对情报抓得那么紧呢,三天两头牌人进据点侦察,有时还亲自出马,闹半天是在做准备,准备撒大网,逮些大鱼吃!

"When we were at the sub-district, didn't the commander say just before we left that we were under orders to hurry back as an advance unit? At that time I thought this was just another routine assignment, because the work team has always been vanguard. But this time there is <u>something more</u> <u>to what he said.</u> Look at our commander. He is paying great attention to the intelligence reports, sends someone to scout out the strongpoint every two or three days. Sometimes he goes himself. We are out to catch a big fish!"

"你要不是派些吃里爬外的人,我那几十万斤麦子也不能丢。这个责任比十几杆枪、十几个人都大,你不负能行吗?"

"我负?"侯扒皮青筋暴露地问。

"当然是你!"哈巴狗一口咬定说。

"我是<u>铁路巡警,管不着你那一段</u>!"

"不用嘴头硬,到时候你会知道锅是铁打的。"

"If you'd sent a squad worth its salt I wouldn't have lost those wheat. That's more than losing a dozen guns and men. Can you deny that? How can you hold me responsible?" Skinflint demanded, the veins on his forehead swelling.

"Of course you're responsible!" the Pekinese barked.

"I <u>belong to the garrison corps and I can't be bothered with your</u> <u>affairs!</u>"

"Harsh words are no use. When the time comes you'll know that a kettle is beaten out of metal."

"到炮楼找你哥去?那真是<u>王麻子的膏药,没病找病</u>。我可不去!"吆唤小秃来歇着的家伙,装做好人的样子说,"你俩谁去?"

"Go and see your cousin? <u>That would be looking for trouble.</u> I won't go." The one who had invited Hsiao Tu over now pretended to be above that.

"Any of you want to go?" he asked the others.

"侯扒皮又催红松檩款子的事了。今天是五天头,他说无论如何过六不过
七。过十七号,拿保长是问。真是望乡台上打莲花落,不知死的鬼!"黄玉文撇
着嘴说。

"Skinflint's pushing for the money for the red pine beams. Five days
have passed. He said that the sixth day might pass too, but the seventh
wouldn't. After July 17 the Pao chiefs will be punished," add Huang Yu-
wen making a face.

坂本少佐瞎驴撞槽地忙了多半宿,待一切都造成了事实,他才察觉到自己
上了武工队的当。这下肚子气得鼓鼓的,活像个癞蛤蟆,干瞪眼直劲搓搓手
心,真是哑巴吃黄连,有苦难说。事情传到北平,老松田急得就像热锅里的螃
蟹,心里蹿火,爪子紧抓挠;天没晌午,忙坐上急行车赶回保定城。

It took Major Sakamoto several hours to make head or tailor the
situation. Then he realized he had been played for a sucker by the work
team and fumed inwardly like a mad puffedup toad. Still, all he could do was to
stare bleakly and rub his hands together, swallowing his rage and
bitterness. When news of the incident reached Matsuda in Peiping, he was
like an ant on a hot griddle, and before daylight he took the express train
back to Paoting.

哈巴狗硬着头皮来到了中间镇,和侯扒皮驻在一个据点里。他俩,一个是
糟害群众的祸首,一个是欺压百姓的魔王,二人站到一块,坐在一起,真是妖魔
对丑怪,没挑的一对坏。

The Pekinese, much against his will, went to Chenglu market town and
took up quarters in the building where Skinflint Hou also stayed. They were
really a pair — one being chief bully of the people, while the other was a
demon riding on their backs.

不过,汪霞送来的这份关于梁邦的情报,却引起了他好大的兴趣。他仔细
地思考好大一会儿,总觉得为了了解各村的秘密情报员,去争取或是去捕捉回
家办丧事的梁邦,简直像用一搂粗的木料做镰把,有点大材小用。

On the other hand he was extremely pleased about Wang Hsia's
information concerning Liang Pang. After mulling it over for a while he
tentatively concluded that it was not enough just to set ferreting out the

enemy's in the villages as the sole purpose of winning over or capturing Liang Pang，who would be returning home for his mother's funeral.

侯扒皮是个钱串子脑袋，觉得征麦又是个拢钱的好机会，就"润田兄"长、"润田兄"短地紧着溜舔奉承，和哈巴狗套近乎；哈巴狗觉得手下虽有二十几个警察，但，个个都是鹰嘴鸭子爪，能吃不能拿的手，催讨小麦的事，只能依靠侯扒皮。

Skinflint Hou with his nose for money deals considered this another chance for him to grab one more fistful，and he called the Pekinese "Brother Jun-tien" all day long，buttering him up so as to get nearer to him. The Pekinese had the feeling that though he had more than 20 police under him，all of them were good-for-nothing-like ducks with long beaks made for gobbling，but also with webbed feet unable to pick up anything. He would have to depend entirely on Skinflint Hou to lay hold of the wheat.

在敌占区作战，必须打得干脆，撤得利落，走得诡秘。结束了战斗，魏强简单迅速地向杨子曾报告了战绩，然后按照指示，领着小队的同志，带着胜利品，朝东北方向，不过村不进庄地转移待老松田陪同津美联队长，带领四五百名鬼子，坐着土黄色的卡车，风是风，火是火地从保定城里赶来增援时，已是"正月十五贴门神——晚了半月啦。"

As a rule，battles in enemy territory were fought to a quick conclusion and followed up by veiled withdrawal. After the battle，Wei Chiang gave Yang Tau-tseng a quick briefing on the results. Then，following instructions，he led his team with their trophies northeast，by passing all villages.

Matsuda，accompanied by the Japanese regimental commander Tsuji，quickly arrived with about 500 Japanese troops from Paoting by clay-coloured trucks. But they were too late for a rescue.

随着院里的瓦响，刘茂林立即转为强硬的口吻："那你们有多少枪?"他认为韦青云他们已经成了钻进他这翻笼里的黄雀，瞎扑腾也逃不出去。

Liu Mao-lin's voice was like flint now. "How many guns haveyou?" he asked，considering Wei Ching-yun and his men as canaries unable to escape from his cage once they had flown in.

敌人正用全力对付贾正，猛地又从背后树林子里射来几颗枪弹。这下，敌人又丈二和尚，摸不着头脑了。"怎么回事?""八路到底有多少?"这时，敌人真像钻进风箱的老鼠,两头受气,再也不愿意在这神秘的黑夜里,十分不利作战的地形上多停留一秒钟,像被打得狗儿夹起尾巴朝江城逃遁了。

The enemy's fire was all concentrated on Chia Cheng when sudden shots came from the grove hehind them. The enemy was quite puzzled. Jammed and beaten from two sides, the enemy had no desire to stay in that unfavourable terrain in the dark for another second, and they took off for Chiangcheng crestfallen.

(三)《儒林外史》——《The Scholars》, tr, by Yang Hsien-Yi and Gladys Yang

严贡生发怒道:"放你的狗屁!我因素日有个晕病,费了几百两银子合了这一料药;是省里张老爷在上党做官带了来的人参,周老爷在四川做官带了来的黄连。你这奴才!猪八戒吃人参果,全不知滋味,说的好容易!是云片糕!方才这几片,不要说值几十两银子?'半夜里不见了轮头子,攮到贼肚里!'只是我将来再发了晕病,却拿什么药来医?你这奴才,害我不浅!"叫四斗子开拜匣,写帖子。"送这奴才到汤老爷衙里去,先打他几十板子再讲!"

"You dog!" roared Yen. "Because I have these fits of dizziness, I spent several hundred tael of silver to buy this medicine. Mr. Chang of the provincial capital bought the ginseng in it for me when he was an official in Shangtang, and Mr. Chou bought the gentian when he was magistrate in Szechuan. You had no business touching it, you scoundrel! Walnut wafers, indeed! Nearly a hundred tael' worth of medicine has disappeared down your throat! And what am i to take next time I have an attack? You've played me a dirty trick, you dog!"

差人道:"马老先生,而今这银子,我也不问是你出,是他出,你们原是'毡袜裹脚靴',但须要我效劳的来。老实一句,'打开板壁讲亮话',这事,一些半些几十两银子的话,横竖做不来,没有三百,也要二百两银子,才有商议。我又不要你十两五两,没来由把难题目把你做怎的?"

"Now, Mr. Ma," said the runner, "I don't mind whether you pay the money or he pays it. Being in the same line, you're as close as sock and boot. But you've got to make it within my power to help. Let's be frank and put all our cards on the table: a few dozen tael are not going to settle anything. I tell you straight out: if you haven't got three hundred you must have at least two hundred before we can talk. It's not that I want to make things difficult for you; but what use are five or ten taels"

差人恼了道:"这个正合着古语:'漫天讨价,就地还钱。'我说二三百银子,你就说二三十两,'戴着斗笠亲嘴,差着一帽子'!怪不得人说你们'诗云子曰'的人难讲话!这样看来,你好像'老鼠尾巴上害疖子,出脓也不多'!倒是我多事,不该来惹这婆子口舌!"说罢,站起身来谢了扰,辞别就往外走。

"This is just like the proverb: The price is as high as the sky and the offer as low as the earth," said the runner angrily. "When I say two or three hundred tael, you say twenty or thirty! It's like kissing in straw helmets — the lips are far apart! No wonder they say you bookworms are hard to deal with: one might just as well try to squeeze water out of a stone. Well, I should have minded my own business instead of coming here to let himself in for this old wives' gabble."

He stood up, apologized to Mr. Ma for troubling him, said goodbye and started out.

秦中书听见凤四老爹来了,大衣也没有穿,就走了出来,问道:"凤四哥,事体怎么样了?"凤四老爹道:"你还问哩!闭门家里坐,祸从天上来。你还不晓得哩!"秦中书吓得慌慌张张的,忙问道:"怎的? 怎的?"凤四老爹道,"怎的不咋的,官司够你打半生!"秦中书越发吓得面如土色,要问都问不出来。凤四老爹道:"你说他到底是个甚官?"秦中书道:"他说是个中书。"凤四老爹道:"他的中书还在判官那里造册哩!"秦中书道:"难道他是个假的?"凤四老爹道:"假的何消说! 只是一场钦案官司,把一个假官从尊府拿去,那浙江巡抚本上也不要特参,只消带上一笔,莫怪我说,老先生的事只怕也就是'滚水泼老鼠'了。"

When Chin heard that Feng had come, he hurried out without stopping to put on his outer gown.

"What's happened now, Fourth Brother Feng?" he asked.

"You may well ask! Here you are sitting at home while disaster descends upon you! Haven't you heard?"

"Heard what? Heard what?" Chin was thrown into a panic.

"Nothing much — just a charge that will take you half a life-time to disprove!"

Chin's face turned the colour of earth. He was much too frightened to speak.

"What is his rank really?" asked Feng.

"He says he's a secretary of the Imperial Patent Office."

"He may become one in hel — he isn't one here."

"Do you mean to say he's bogus?"

"Of course he is. A man who is charged with a serious crime has been arrested in your house as an impostor. The Governor of Chekiang doesn't need any special indictment against you, sir. He has merely to mention the matter and, if you'll pardon me for saying so, you'll find yourself like a rat in scalding water!"

次日,范进少不得拜访拜访乡邻。魏好古又约了一个同案的朋友,彼此来往。因是乡试年,做了几个文会。不觉到了六月尽头,这些同案的人约范进去乡试。范进因没有盘费,走去同丈人商议,被胡屠户一口啐在脸上,骂了一个狗血喷头:"不要得意忘形了!你自己只觉得中了一个相公,就'癞蛤蟆想吃起天鹅屁!'我听见人说,就是中相公时,也不是你的文章,还是宗师看见你老,过意不去,舍给你的,如今痴心就想起老爷来!这些中老爷的,都是天上的文曲星;你不看见城里张府上那些老爷,都有万贯家私,一个个方面大耳。像你这尖嘴猴腮,也该撒泡尿自己照照;不三不四,就想天鹅屁吃!"

The next day Fan Chin had to call on relatives and friends. Wei Hao-ku invited him to meet some other fellow candidates, and since it was the year for the provincial examination they held a number of literary meetings. Soon it was the end of the sixth month. Fan Chin's fellow candidates asked him to go with them to the provincial capital for the examination, but he had no money for the journey. He went to ask his father-in-law to help. Butcher Hu spat in his face, and poured out a torrent of abuse. "Don't be a fool!" he roared. "Just passing one examination has turned your head completely — you're like a toad trying to swallow a swan! And I hear that you scraped through not because of your essay, but because the examiner pitied you for being so old. Now, like a fool, you want to pass the higher examination and become an officials. But do you know who those officials are? They are all stars in heaven! Look at the Chang family in the city. All those officials have pots of money, dignified faces and big ears. But your mouth sticks out and you've a chin like an ape's. You should piss on the ground and look at your face in the puddle! You look like a monkey, yet you want to become an official. Come off it!"

六老爷首席,那嫖客对坐。六老爷叫细姑娘同那嫖客一板凳坐,细姑娘撒娇撒痴定要同六老爷坐。四人坐定,斟上酒来,六老爷要猜拳,输家吃酒赢家唱。六老爷赢了一拳,自己哑着喉咙唱了一个《寄生草》,便是细姑娘和那嫖客猜。细姑娘赢了。六老爷叫斟上酒,听细姑娘唱。细姑娘别转脸笑,不肯唱。六老爷拿筷子在桌上催着敲,细姑娘只是笑,不肯唱。六老爷道:"我这脸是<u>帘子做的</u>,要卷上去就卷上去,要放下来就放下来!我要细姑娘唱一个,偏要你唱!"王义安又走进来帮着催促,细姑娘只得唱了几句。

Sixth Master sat in the seat of honour, the customer facing him; but when Sixth Master told Miss Hsi to sit on the customer's bench, she insisted skittishly on sitting with him. When the four of them had sat down, wine was served. Sixth Master made them play the finger game, with the loser drinking and the winner singing. When he won he sang in a husky voice; then Miss Hsi and the customer played, and the prostitute won. Sixth Master called for more wine to drink, while they listened to her singing. When she turned her face away with a laugh and refused, he rapped on the table with his chopsticks to urge her on. Still she just laughed, and would not sing. "My face is a <u>bamboo blind</u>," Sixth Master warned her. "<u>A blind lets up and down, and I can pull a long face whenever I please.</u> If I want you to sing, my girl, you'll sing!" Wang Yi-an came in as well to help persuade her, and at last she sang a few lines.

来家那年,却失了馆,在家日食艰难。一日,他姊丈金有余来看他,劝道:"老舅,莫怪我说你:这读书求功名的事,料想也是难了!人生世上,难得的是这碗现成饭,只管粮不粮莠不莠的到几时?我如今同了几个大本钱的人到省城去买卖,差一个记账的人,你不如同我们去走走;你又孤身一人,在客伙内,还是少了你吃的、穿的?"周进听了这话,自己想:"'<u>瘫子掉在井里,捞起来也是坐</u>。'有甚亏负我?"随即应允了。

Having lost his job, Chou Chin went home. He was extremely hard up. One day his brother-in-law, Chin Yin-yu, came to see him and said, "Don't take offence at what I say, brother. But all this study doesn't seem to be getting you anywhere, and a bad job is better than none. How long can you go on like this — neither fish, flesh nor fowl? I am going to the provincial capital with some other merchants to buy goods, and we need someone to keep accounts. Why don't you come with us? You are all on your own，and in our group you won't want for food or clothes." "Even if a paralytic falls into a well，he can be no worse off than before," thought Chou Chin. "It can't hurt me to go." So he consented.

丈人见他十分胡说，拾了个叉子棍赶着他打

瞎子摸了过来扯劝。丈人气的颤呵呵地道："先生！这样不成人，我说说他，他还拿这些混账话来答应我，岂不可恨！"陈和甫儿子道："老爹，我也没有甚么混账处，我又不吃酒，又不赌钱，又不嫖老婆，每日在测字的桌子上还拿着一本诗念，育甚么混账处！"丈人道："不是别的混账，你放着一个老婆不养，只是累我，我那里累得起！"陈和甫儿子道："老爹，你不喜女儿给我做老婆，你退了回去罢了。"丈人骂道："该死的畜生！我女儿退了做甚么事哩？"陈和甫儿子道："听凭老爹再嫁一个女婿罢了。"丈人大怒道："瘟奴！除非是你死了，或是做了和尚，这事才行得！"陈和甫儿子道："死是一时死不来，我明日就做和尚去。"丈人气愤愤地道："你明日就做和尚！"瞎子听了半天，听他两人说的都是"堂屋里挂草荐——不是话"，也就不扯劝，慢慢地摸着回去了。

Enraged by such foolish talk，the father-in-law picked up a forked stick and belaboured his son-in-law with it. The blind man groped his way over to make peace. "Sir!" cried the old man，quivering with rage. "He simply isn't human! When I give him a piece of my mind，he answers me back like an idiot. It's enough to make anyone wild!" "I didn't talk like an idiot，dad," protested Chen Si-ruan. "I don't drink，gamble or go whoring，do I? I read a volume of poems every day between my fortune-telling. What's wrong with that?" "We can leave everything else out of it；but you're wrong to neglect your wife and expect me to look after her. I can't afford it!" "If you're sorry your daughter's my wife，dad，take her back." "Curse you! Why should I take my daughter back?" "To let her marry again" "A plague on you!" The father-in-law was furious. "Unless you die or become a monk，how can she marry again?" "I shan't be dying just yet，but I'll become a monk tomorrow." "Go and become a monk then!" The old man was in a towering rage. After hearing all the nonsense they were talking，the blind man gave up trying to reason with them and groped his way back to his room.

凤四老爹同众人忙问道："客人，怎的了？"那客人只不则声。凤四老爹猛然大悟,指着丝客人道:"是了! 你这客人想是少年不老成,如今上了当了!"那客人不觉又羞地哭了起来,凤四老爹细细问了一遍,才晓得:昨晚都睡静了,这客人还倚着船窗,顾盼那船上妇人,这妇人见那两个客人去了,才立出舱来,望着丝客人笑。船本靠得紧,虽是隔船,离身甚近,丝客人轻轻捏了他一下,那妇人便笑嘻嘻从窗子里爬了过来,就做了巫山一夕。这丝客人睡着了,他就把行李内四封银子二百两,尽行携了去了。早上开船,这客人情思还昏昏的,到了此刻,看见被囊开了,才晓得被人偷了去。真是哑子梦见妈──说不出来的苦!

"What's the matter?" asked Feng and the rest. The young man did not answer. Suddenly it dawned on Feng, who pointed at him. "I know!" he cried. "You're young and green, so you fell into a trap." Tears poured down the shamefaced buyer's cheeks. Feng questioned him closely and learned that the night before, when everyone else was sleeping, he had leaned out of the cabin to watch the girl in the sampan. When she saw the two others had left, she came out of the cabin and smiled at him. The two vessels were lying alongside, and although on different boats they were very close, so the young man petted her till she smiled and climbed into his cabin, and they had a night of love. Once the buyer was asleep, the woman stole four packages of silver worth two hundred tael from his baggage. When the junk cast off at dawn, the young man was still half-asleep. He had only just realized that his bag had been opened and he had been robbed. Now, like a dumb man dreaming of his mother, he could not express his despair!

牛浦道:"我虽则同老爹是个旧邻居,却从来不曾通过财帛;况且我又是客边,借这亲家住着,那里来的几两银子与老爹?"石老鼠冷笑道:"你这小孩子就没良心了,想着我当初挥金如土的时节,你用了我不知多少,而今看见你在人家招了亲,留你个脸面,不好就说,你倒回出这样话来!"牛浦发了急道:"这是那里来的话! 你就挥金如土,我几时看见你金子,几时看见你的土! 你一个中年人,不想做些好事,只要'在光水头上钻眼──骗人'!"石老鼠道:"牛浦郎你不要说嘴! 想着你小时做的些丑事,瞒的别人,可瞒得过我? 况且你停妻娶妻,在那里骗了卜家女儿,在这里又骗了黄家女儿,该当何罪? 你不乖乖的拿出几两银子来,我就同你到安东县去讲!"牛浦跳起来道:"那个怕你! 就同你到安东县去!"

"We may be old neighbours," said Niu, "but we never did business together. Besides, I am a stranger here, staying with my father-in-law. What money can I give you?" "You ungrateful cub!" The Rat gave a sneering laugh. "Think how much you had from me when I was spending money like water! Yet now that I try to save your face — since I see you've married a second wife here and it wouldn't be quite the thing to expose you — you still talk to me like that!" "What do you mean?" retorted Niu angrily. "When did I ever have money from you? I've never seen you spending money like water! An old man like you should be thinking of doing good deeds, instead of cheating people all the time." Niu Pu! warned The Rat. "Be careful what you say! Think of all the crooked things you did in your early days! You may still be able to fool others, but you can't fool me. You're guilty of bigamy, you know. You've deserted your Pu family wife over there and deceived your new Huang family wife here. If you don't hand over a few tael quietly now, I'll report you to the Antung yamen!" "Do you think I'm afraid of you!" Niu leapt to his feet. "Let's go to the yamen!"

(四)《暴风骤雨》——《The Hurricane》, tr, by Xu Mengxiong

"穷棒子闹翻身,是八仙过海,各显其能。老爷子,别说你岁数大了,太公八十遇文王。咱们五十上下的人,也算年纪大? 上年纪的人,见识广,主意多。不瞒老哥说,萧队长有事还问咱。这回上三甲开会,咱说,有了牲口,就说车子最当紧,老初偏说,碾盘顶要紧,临了,萧队长还是说老孙头我说的对呢,老初算啥呀? 咱过的桥比他走的道还多……"

"When we pass from the old society to the new, each of us shows his true worth. Don't say that you're too old. At eighty, Tai Gong＊ met Emperor Wen and took up an important post. How can we call ourselves old at fifty? Elderly people are experienced and can give good advice. To tell the truth, sometimes even Team Leader Xiao asks my opinion. Only yesterday, at the meeting at Sanjia, I said that once we had horses the next thing to get was carts, while Old Chu insisted that grindstones were more important. Who was right, after all? Team Leader Xiao agreed with me. What is Old Chu anyway? In my lifetime, I've crossed more bridges than he has streets"

"韩家还能有枪吗?""能算出来。韩老六拉大排的时候,连捡洋捞,带收买,有三十六棵钢枪,一棵匣枪。他兄弟韩老七上大青顶子,带走二十来棵,韩长脖、李青山上山，又带走几棵，韩老六的大镜面匣子也给带走了，加上外屯起出的几棵，我看韩家插的枪，没露面的，有也不多了。"

"唐抓子有吗？""他是<u>抱元宝跳井，舍命不舍财的老财阀</u>，不能养活枪。他胆儿又小，瞅着明晃晃的刺刀，还哆嗦呢……"

"Can his family still have guns hidden away in this village?" "That can be figured out. When Han kept private guards, he had 36 guns of all sorts, which he had bought or seized from the surrendered Japanese military store. He had a Mauser too. When his barit brother took to the mountains, he carried away about 20 of these guns; and when Long Neck and Li Qingshan went up after the bandit chief, they took several more with them, including the Mauser. Now several guns have been found in neighbouring village too; so there can't be many left."

"Has Snatcher Tang any guns?"

"He's one of those men who would <u>jump into a well with silver ingots tied to their waist-bands sooner than gove up their money</u>. He wouldn't buy guns. Besides, he's a coward; the sight of a bayonet makes him shake in his boots…"

大伙就在合作社开起会来。屋里院外，一片声音叫嚷道："咱们要跟他们算算细账。"郭全海坐在柜台上，嘴里噙着小蓝玉嘴烟袋，没有说话，留心着别人说话。合作社里一片嘈杂，老初的大嗓门压倒所有的声音，他说："这算什么合作社？这些家伙，布袋里买猫，尽抓咱们老百姓的迷糊。"几个声音同时说："咱们要跟他们算账。"

Then and there, the villagers called a meeting. Inside the co-operative and outside in the courtyard a shout went up: "We must settle accounts with them!" Guo Quanhai perched on the counter, silent, smoking his pipe with the jade mouth-piece, watching the scene and listening to the animated discussion. In the din, Old Chu's voice boomed out above the rest: "Do you call this a co-operative store? These fellows are selling cats in bags. Do they think we're fools?"

也有些人，跟韩家既不沾亲挂拐，也没有磕头拜把，单是因为自己也有地，也沾着些伪满的边，害怕斗争完了韩老六，要轮到他们头上。另外一种人，知道韩老六的儿子韩世元蹽到"中央军"那边去了，怕他再回来。还有一些人，心里寻思着，韩老六是该斗争的，但何必自己张嘴抬手呢？<u>"出头的椽子先烂"</u>，

"慢慢看势头"。这三种人，都不说话。

Some people were not particularly enthusiastic about the struggle, not because they were Han's relatives or sworn brothers, but because they owned land themselves and had had dealings with the Japanese. They were afraid that after Han had been dealt with it would be their turn. Others thought that Han's son, who was with the Kuomintang army, might one day stage a comeback and take reprisals. Still others thought Han deserved to be tried, but did not intend to speak against him themselves. After all, exposed rafters are the first to rot. These three kinds of people decided to wait and see which way the wind would blow, and kept silent.

富裕中农胡殿文，划成小富农，割了尾巴。胡家四匹马，农会征收了两匹。这么一来，谣言又像黑老鸹似的飞遍全屯。有的说："中农是过年的猪，早晚得杀。"有的说："如今的政策是杀了肥猪杀壳囊。"这些谣言起来以后，全屯的中农都来农会，自动要求封底产，有的说："把我家也封上吧。"有的说："反正都得分，趁早把我家封上吧。"还有的跑到老初家里，要求他道："老初，我家还有一条麻花被，你们登记上吧。"人们谣传着，有两匹马的，要匀出一匹，有两条被子的，要匀出一条。开贫雇农大会，中农都不叫参加，他们疑心更盛了。中农娘们走到隔壁邻居去对火，站在造屋里，就唠开了。

A well-to-do middle peasant by the name of Hu Dianwen was mistakenly classified as a small rich peasant and deprived of two of his four horses. This gave rise to rumours, which soon spread through the whole village. Some remarked, "Middle peasants are like porkers on Lunar New Year's Eve — their end is just a question of time." Others added, "The policy is to kill fat pigs first and then the sucklings." Every middle peasant who heard this gossip went to the Peasants' Association with a request to have his property confiscated. "Please take my belongings," they would say. Some suggested: "If you're going to seal up my things sooner or later, why not sooner?" One dropped in on Old Chu and demanded that his cotton quilt be confiscated. Rumours continued to spread: of every two horses, one must be surrendered, and of every two cotton-padded quilts one must be given up. When poor peasants and farm labourers met, middle peasants were not asked to join and so they became more suspicious, while their wives gossiped.

"我干过啥呢？大伙选我当主任，我一个初步也不敢迈呀，老是小小心心，照规矩办事。"

老孙头冲着他脸说："谁推你当主任的？你们几个狐朋狗友，耗子爬秤钩，自己称自己。你们三几个朋友，喝大酒，吃白面饼，吃得油淌淌，放个屁，把裤子都油了，这使的是谁的钱呀？"

Zhang grimaced. "What have I done wrong? They elected me chairman. And I always watched my step, was careful and conscientious and did my duty according to the rules." Old Sun was quick to rebut this. "Who elected you? Your shady pals did it, and called you chairman. Your gang got together to eat and drink. Your guts were so greasy you were afraid to cough for fear of the whole thing slipping. Who paid for it all?"

"你拿去吧，新年大月包两顿饺子吃吃。你看这肉，膘不大离吧？"韩老六说，"这比街里的强，到街里去约，还兴约到老母猪肉哩。"郭全海一想，黄皮子给小鸡子拜年，他还能安啥好肠子吗？他不要。"你不要，就是看不起人。"韩老六说，一脸不高兴。"好吧，就提了吧。"郭全海心想，把肉提到他的朋友老白家，包了两顿饺子吃。

"Take it and make pork dumplings for New Year's Day. See what fine pork it is! Much better than what's sold on the market. They palm off old tough stuff on you." Quanhai was reminded of the weasel that paid a courtesy call on a hen. He tried to decline this gift. "If you refuse, that would be treating me with contempt," threatened Han, pursing his lips in displeasure. "All right, I accept your gift," Quanhai force himself to say. So he took the pork to his friend Bai's home and they made dumplings with it.

萧队长问道："你们小组讨论过吗？他们对党的认识怎么样？""讨论过，白玉山回来过年，跟白大嫂子谈到参加组织的事，跟她解释了共产党是干啥的。"萧队长说："她现在的认识呢？""她说，共产党是为全国老百姓都翻身，为了大家将来都过美满的日子，不是火烧眉毛，光顾眼前。她认定了这个宗旨，决心加入共产党，革命到底。"

"Have you discussed this in your small group?" Xiao asked. "Do the applicants have a proper appreciation of the Party's cause?" "Yes. While Bai was home for the New Year holiday, he told his wife about the Communist Party and what it meant to be a member." "How does she look at it now?"

"She says the Communist Party aims to help all the people in the whole country to emancipate themselves, so that everybody can live a happy life in future. Communists don't just care about their immediate interests. She understands this principle and wishes to join the Party and go all out to do revolutionary work."

我爹说:"您家拿出两个布的钱,不过是牛去一毛,仓去一粟呀,却是成全咱们小子一辈子的好事了。"怎么说,杜善人也是不错,那门亲事就这样黄了。女家老人也说得有理,不收你彩礼,姑娘衣裳总得做一身,不能露着肉来拜天地呀。兄弟姐妹们,在旧社会,穷人娶媳妇,那真是空中的雁,水底的鱼,捞不着的呀,穷人的姑娘也不能许配穷人。"侯长腿说到这儿,停了一下。

"My father said, You can easily spare me the money for two lengths of cloth. For you, it's like a hair on the back of a cow or a grain in a barn, and you would be helping to arrange the most important affair in my son's life. Du refused to listen. So the marriage fell through. And we couldn't blame the girl's father. He didn't want any money, only asked for a jacket and trousers. After all, a bride couldn't very well appear in rags. Brothers and sisters! In the old society, for a poor man to find a wife was as hard as catching a wild goose in flight, or a fish at the bottom of the river. Not even a poor girl would marry a poor man." Hou stippen to wipe his eyes with the back of his hand.

萧队长说:"积极分子不是官,是老百姓当中敢作敢为的头行人。你要不干,不做这好人,不用来辞,不来就行了。""不是不来,我一开头,就随队长,还能半道妥协吗?我是想:咱们是孔夫子搬家,净是书,心里真有一点点干啥的。"萧队长安慰他几句,叫他回去还是跟知心人唠嗑,跟老百姓聊天,说大地主好几千年树立起来的威势,不是一半天就能垮下的,不能心急。

"An activist isn't an official," Team Leader Xiao told him. "He's just a common citizen who dares to take part in a good cause and lead a group of people. If you don't care to carry on as an activist, you can just stop being one. There's nothing to resign from." "It isn't that I don't want to come here any more. You know I've been with you since you came. I've put my hand to the plough and don't want to turn back. Only I feel bad when we lose every fight." Team Leader Xiao tried to comfort him and told him to talk it over with his friends, saying that it was impossible overnight to break the power of the landlords, which had existed for thousands of years. Impatience was no use.

"郭主任真行,我看比赵主任还有能耐。"溜须的人都叫他主任:"上我家去串串门子吧。""人家当主任了,还看不起咱们民户,咱们搬梯子也够不上了。"嫉妒的人说。"这才是拉拉蛄穿大衫,硬称土绅士。"粮户讽刺他。"别看他那熊样子,'中央军'来了,管保他穿兔子鞋跑,也不赶趟。"藏在屯子里的干过"维持会"的坏根们背地里说。

"Our Chairman Guo is great, I think he's even more capable than Zhao." All the flatterers called him chairman instead of vice-chairman. "Drop in to see us some evening," they invited. "Can a chairman still remember common men? He's up on top; we couldn't reach him even with a ladder," jeered the jealous. "A mole cricket in a long gown calling himself a gentleman," a landlord described him sarcastically. "He may be swaggering about now, but wait till the Kuomintang army comes back — he won't be able to escape even if he runs like a hare," sniggered certain bad elements who had been members of the interim puppet village administration.

白大嫂子接着说:"咱们掌柜的,早先在乎兰受训,如今调双城工作,这回回来,又去抓差。'满洲国'他是个懒蛋,靠风吃饭。打工作队来,他变好了,人也不懒了。"一个男人声音打断她的话说:"老头卖瓜,自报自夸。"白大嫂子扬起她的像老鸹的毛羽似地漆黑的眉毛说:"怎么是自报自夸?你混蛋!"那人调皮地笑道:"说老头呀,不是说你老娘们。"主席挥手道:"静一静,听她说完。"

Mrs. Bai went on: "My husband studied in the Party school in Hulan, and words at Shuangcheng. He came back for New Year but he's gone off again on an errand. In the Manchukuo days he was a drone — never did a stroke of work. But since the land-reform workers came to our village he's different. He's not lazy any more." "A melon-seller advertising her own melons!" This was of course from a man. Mrs. Bai arched her black brows. "How can you say that? Get along with you!" "I meant your old man — not you," the man joked. "Don't interrupt her. Hear her out." The chairman waved his hand.

到会的老人都叫:"赞成。"大伙不嗑瓜子了,三三五五,交头接耳,合计成立老年团。萧队长记起郭全海说的老王太太来,他问老孙头:"老王太太来没

— 209 —

有?"车老板子张眼望一望人堆,便说:"她没有来。那是一根<u>老榆木疙瘩,挪不</u><u>动的</u>。"会开完了,人都散了,萧队长邀郭全海同去看老王太太。他们迈进王家的东屋,看见这老太太穿一件补丁摞补丁的青布棉袍子,盘腿坐在南炕炕头上,戴副老花眼镜,正在补衣裳。瞅他们进来,她冷冷地招呼一声:"队长来了,请上炕吧。"她仍旧坐着,补她那件蓝布大褂子。

"Yes!" The old people stopped cracking melon seeds and began to talk about the proposed league. Remembering old Mrs. Wang, Xiao asked Old Sun if she was present. The carter scanned the audience. "No. She's <u>like an</u><u>old elm stump, immovable.</u>" After the meeting, Xiao had Quanhai take him to call on old Mrs. Wang. They found her sitting cross-legged on the Kang in the east wing of her house, mending rags. She was in a patched, black cotton-padded long gown, a pair of spectacles on her nose.

"啥也没问题。老百姓只有一点不满意,说赵主任自己分得少。他们都问:'赵主任不是穷棒子底子吗?咋能不分东西呢?'我说:在'满洲国',咱们哥俩是一样的,都是<u>马勺子吊起来当锣打,穷得叮哩当啷响</u>。那时候,赵主任也不叫赵主任,叫赵——啥的,说出来可磕"。现下咱们穷人'光复'了,赵主任当令,为大伙儿办公,为大伙是该屈己待人的,可是啥也不要,叫锁住他妈还是穷得叮哩当啷响,也不像话,回头叫资本家看笑话。说咱们这四百人家的大屯子,连一个农会主任也养活不起。"老孙头说得屋里的人都笑了。

"The villagers have only one complaint to make — you've allotted yourself too little. They all ask, Isn't Old Zhao a poor man like us? Why, then, doesn't he deserve equal treatment? I say to them: 'In the puppen Manchukuo time, we were both alike, <u>both naked poor.</u>' The nickname you had then, Chairman Zhao, wasn't a beautiful title at all. Now the poor people have come to the top, and you run things in our village, yet you deny yourself everything. Your wife and son live no better than before. That's overdoing things. The capitalists will laugh at us behind our backs. They'll say the four hundred families in this village can't even give the chairman of their Peasant's Association a decent living." This brought a laugh from everyone in the room.

说到这里,韩老六想要提提老田头他姑娘的事,并且跟他说几句好话。但一转念,他想,还是不提好一些。老田头却早在想着他的姑娘,伤心起来。她死的哭呀!老田头两只眼睛里,停着两颗泪珠子,他的嘴唇微微地抖动,他在使劲忍住心上的难过。韩老六赶紧抓住田万顺的胆小心情，把假笑收住，冷冷地说："你要有本事，就甭听我的话，去跟工作队串鼻子，咱们骑在毛驴上看唱本，走着瞧吧!"说到这儿，韩老六抬起右手，往空中一挥，又添说一句："到时候，哼!"这一声哼，在老田头的脑瓜子里，好久还嗡嗡地响。这时候，院子里又有人问道："六爷在屋吗?"

At this point, the landlord remembered what he had done to the old tenant's daughter and was about to say a few words to reconcile him on this score, but thought better of it. Actually Old Tian's mind also went back to his daughter and the circumstances leading to her tragic death. Tears welled up in his eyes, and his mouth quivered, but he tried hard to keep a grip on himself. Taking advantage of Old Tian's timidity, Han wiped the smile off his face and said coldly: "You needn't listen to me but do as you choose. Just go ahead and dicker with the work team — we'll see who's right!" He cut the air with his right hand for emphasis. "Wait and see!" he snorted. While this final snort was still droning in Old Tian's ears, a voice came from the courtyard: "Is Mr. Han at home?"

韩老六威胁道："来信说，'谁要分了咱们房子地，就要谁的脑瓜子。'"韩老六又看他一眼，看着杨老疙瘩腿脚有一些哆嗦。他又添上一句："你不必怕，咱们一东一伙，这么些年头，还能不照顾? 往后别跟工作队胡混，别看他们那个熊样子，我看他姓萧的算是手里捧着个刺猬，摆也摆不下，扔也扔不掉。他斗我，看他能斗下，这不是斗了三茬了? 再来三茬，我姓韩的日子也比你们过得强，不信，你瞧吧。"听见鸡叫了，韩老六又改变态度，凑近一些，悄声地说："你帮我作一些个事，将来我可帮你的忙。他们这些天，下晚尽开会，谁谁都说一些什么? 你都告诉我，你有啥困难，上我这儿来。"

"He says, 'Just let them take our houses and land, and we'll take their heads.'" Seeing Yang quail, Han added, "but don't you worry. We've known each other all these years, and I'll protect you. From now on, don't get mixed up with the land-reform workers — don't let yourself be taken in by them. That fellow Xiao is like a man with a hedgehog in his hands — he can neither hold it nor shake it off. He wants to tackle me. See if he can! He's tried three times already, and I'm still safe and sound. Another three times, and I'll still be better off than all of you. If you don't believe me, just wait and see." It was cock-crow. Han waxed more intimate and confidential. "You help me now, and I'll help you later. There have been a lot of meetings recently. What are they up to? If you'll find out and report to me, I'll help you out to any of your difficulties."

"这马原先是老顾家的。"老初说,"'康德'十一年,老顾租了韩老六家五块地,庄稼潦了,租粮一颗不能少,老顾把马赔进去。这回分马,赵主任说是要把这儿马还他,'物归原主',他不要。""咋不要?"娘们问他。"人家迷信:<u>好马不吃回头草</u>。"老初说。"看你这二虎,人家不要的,你们捡回来。真是寿星老的脑袋,宝贝疙瘩。""你才二虎哩,人家迷信好马不吃回头草,我怕啥呢?这马哪儿去找?口又小,活又好,你瞅这四条腿子直直溜溜的,像板凳子一样,可有劲呐。"

"This horse used to belong to Old Gu," Old Chu said to his wife. "In 1944, Old Gu rented 75 mu of land from Han. The crop failed because of a flood, but the poor fellow had to pay the landlord the rent all the same — and he paid it with this horse. Chairman Zhao offered to give the horse back to its rightful owner, but Gu refused it." "Why?" "Old Gu is superstitious. He said, 'I don't want my horse back. As the saying goes, <u>a good horse doesn't turn back to eat grass.</u> '" "Then, why did you bring him home, you old fool?" "Who's the old fool, you or me? Old Gu is superstitious. Does that mean I should be superstitious too and give up such a good horse? Just look at him — young, muscular, fine straight legs, sleek and strong!"

韩长脖忙说:"不用,不用,六婶子你甭去拿。"嘴上这样说,却站着不动,等大枣核进去又出来,把一小卷票子塞进他的发黄的白布小衫兜兜里,他才哈腰道谢,退着往外走。韩老六说:"走了?捎个信给李振江、田万顺,叫他们来这一下。"说罢,他又躺在烟灯的旁边,大老婆子坐在炕沿,咕咕噜噜埋怨起来。她怨世道,怨人心,又怨这个穷本家一月两头来,成了个填不满的耗子窟窿眼。她说:"来一回又一回,<u>夜猫子拉小鸡,有去无回</u>。亏他这瘦长脖子还能顶起那副脸。"韩老六听到院子里的狗咬,鹅叫,接着屋外有脚步声音,骂他大老婆子道:"你懂啥?你就看见眼皮底下几个钱。快到里屋去。看有人来了。"

"Oh, ho, don't bother, please, Auntie," said Long Neck hastily. But he made no move to prevent his aunt from going into the room for the money. Presently she came back with a sheaf of banknotes which she shoved into the pocket of his dirty white cotton jacket. He thanked her with a bow, and was starting to go when Han said: "Tell Li Zhenjiang and Tian

Wanshun to come to see me." After his nephew had left, Han stretched out again beside the opium lamp. His wife sat down on the edge of the kang and began complaining of the way of the world and human nature, and of this poor relative in particular, who kept coming several times a month for loans. He was a perpetual drain on them. "Your nephew keeps coming, like a weasel filching chicks. I wonder how that long, scrawny neck of his can support his thick-skinned face!" Dogs barked, geese honked and then footsteps were heard in the courtyard. "You blockhead! Money is all you can see. Go in quick — somebody's coming."

"好吧,咱们来说说咱们的事情,"萧队长开口:"大伙凑拢来一点,今儿也不算开会,大伙唠唠嗑,伪满压迫咱们十四年,粮户苦害我们几千年,大伙肚里装满了苦水,吐一吐吧,如今是咱穷伙计们的天下了。""对,对,大伙都说说,八路军是咱们自己的队伍,三营在这儿,都瞅到了的。"刘德山抢着说,"萧队长在这,咱们今儿是灶王爷上西天,有啥说啥。""对,有啥说啥,一人说一样。"窗台附近有一个人附和,这人就是李振江,他把他的灰色毡帽掀到后脑勺子上,豆油灯下,露出他的光溜溜的秃头来。

"Very well then, shall we gather closer together and talk?" said Xiao. "This isn't a formal meeting, folks. We're just going to discuss things together. We suffered fourteen years under the puppet Manchukuo regime, while the landlords have ridden roughshod over poor people like us for thousands of years. We all have a bellyful of bitterness to pour out. And we can talk freely today — we poor folks have come into our own." "Quite right, quite right! The Eighth Route Army is our own. We all saw the way the Third Battalion behaved while they were here," Liu Deshan began. "Now we can depend on Team Leader Xiao. We can say what we like." "Right. We'll each tell something." This was from Li Zhen-jiang, who was standing by the window. He pushed his grey felt hat back exposing his bald head, which gleamed in the lamplight.

新媳妇脱下半新棉袍,准备烧火煮猪食,一面又道:"翻了天,就翻了天咋的?"老王太太嘴巴皮子哆嗦着说道:"萧队长你听,她这还算不算人?"婆媳两个针尖对麦芒,吵闹不休。歪在炕上的大儿子起来劝他妈道:"妈你干啥?你让着点,由她说去,反正在一起也待不长了。萧队长和郭全海也劝了一会,退了出来。在院子里,遇见西下屋的军属老卢家,笑着邀他们到屋里坐坐。老卢家对火装烟,就小声地一五一十,把王老太太暴躁的原因,根根梢梢,告诉了他们。

The new daughter-in-law was taking off her long gown to cook mash for the pigs, but she could not help answering: "Yes, it is a rebellion!" Old Mrs. Wang's lips were quivering. "Team Leader Xiao, did you hear that?" Mother-in-law and daughter-in-law started quarrelling. The son who was sprawled on the kang sat up. "Mother, what is it now? Can't you leave her alone?" he said. Xiao and Quanhai also put in a word or two to quiet things down. They then retreated into the courtyard, where they met an old man Lu, father of an armyman, who smilingly invited them to his room in the west wing. Old Lu, puffing at his pipe, started talking about old Mrs. Wang.

老孙头没有走,也没有说话。他蹲在后面一个墙角下。萧队长走来问他:"你咋不说话?"老孙头站起来说:"大伙都说过了呗。""依你说,李振江打韩老六,按的是啥心眼儿?"老孙头狡猾地笑着说:"斗争恶霸,不打还行?""这是真打吗?""那哪能知道? 他们一东一伙,都是看透《三国志》的人。要我说,那一耳刮子,也是周瑜打黄盖,一个愿打,一个愿挨的。"萧队长走到前边,跟工作队的人合计了一下,又叫郭全海、白玉山、赵玉林几个人一起,商量了一会。郭全海走到桌子的旁边,对大伙说:"会就开到这疙瘩。今儿天气好,大伙还着忙割小麦,拿大草,韩老六该怎么处置,大伙提意见。"

Old Sun remained behind, but he didn't say anything, just squatted in a corner at the back. When Team Leader Xiao came up and asked him why he didn't speak up, the carter replied, rising to his feet, "They took all the words out of my mouth. " "What do you think made Li Zhenjiang hit Han?" Old Sun smiled knowingly, but answered, "Well, a criminal landlord must be beaten. " "Was is real?" "Hard to say. The two of them are hand in glove, and they've both read the Romance of the Three Kingdoms*. I should say that bloody nose was skilfully given by a Zhou Yu and gladly accepted by a Huang Gai. " Team Leader Xiao stepped forward and spoke first to the land-reform workers and then to Quanhai, Bai and Zhao. After some discussion, Quanhai stepped back to the desk. "We'll close the meeting. It's a fine day, and everybody's got work to do. Before you leave, you can suggest what we should do with Han"

A 14th-century novel based on events which took place in the third century A. D. Zhou Yu of the Kingdom of Wu had Huang Gai, another Wu general, cruelly beaten and then sent to the enemy camp in order to deceive the enemy.

张富英提拔的小组长一看到郭全海生气，就吵吵嚷嚷："看他脸红脖子粗的，吓唬谁呀？""他动压力派呐？""这不是'满洲国'了，谁还怕谁？"有一回，老孙头喝了一棒子烧酒，壮了一壮胆子，到农会里来说了两句向着郭主任的话。这帮子人一齐冲他七嘴八舌，连吓带骂："用你废话？你算是啥玩意呀？""老混蛋，你吃的河水，倒管的宽，这是你说话的地方？也不脱下鞋底，照照模样。""他再胡咧咧，就开会斗他。"老孙头害怕挨斗，就说："对，对，咱说了不算，当风刮走了。"说完，迈出农会，又去赶车喝酒，见人也不说翻身的事了，光唠着黑瞎子，把下边这话，常挂在嘴上："黑瞎子这玩意，黑咕隆咚的，尽一个心眼。"

When Zhang's newly appointed group leaders saw Quanhai grow angry, they jeered at him. "His flushed face and tight throat can frighten no one. " "How dare he try to ride roughshod over us?" "This isn't Manchukuo; why should we be afraid of him?" One day Old Sun, emboldened by drink, spoke up for Quanhai, offending Zhang's gang and bringing a hornets' nest about his own ears. "What do you know? Who the hell are you?" "Old bastard, poking your nose into things that don't concern you! Who wants your opinion? Who are you anyway!" "Hold your tongue, or we'll call a meeting and have a showdown!" Cowed by this last remark, Old Sun muttered, "All right, all right! Forget it!" He strode off, back to his cart and cups. After that he stopped talking about the present struggle, but confined himself to his bear stories. "What a black hulk a bear is!" he would begin. "But how simple!"

(五)《上海的早晨》(由马恩斯翻译)

1."喔，"冯玉祥会意地说，"那是因为最近华东军政委员会发出了关于贯彻增产节约开展反对贪污反对浪费和反对官僚主义斗争的指示，陈市长特地在上海邮政局设置信箱，接受各界人民和公教人员等对于贪污、浪费和官僚主义行为的秘密检举和控告。三反运动这样大张旗鼓地雷厉风行地展开，你到啥地方去看到干部？这辰光，干部们是泥菩萨过河——自身难保。别说沪江纱厂，税务分局派来的那位方宇驻厂员，就是再大的官，他首先得顾顾自己，至于啥税款呀，那倒是次要的。"

"Ah," said Feng Yongxiang understandingly. "That's because the East-China Military and Administrative Commission has recently issued a directive about fully implementing the policy to increase production and practise economy and waging the struggle against corruption, waste and bureaucracy. The mayor has had letter-boxes specially installed in the Shanghai Municipal Post Office for secret denunciations and accusations by people in all walks of life and people in government offices and other public institutions about bribery, waste and bureaucracy. How can you expect to see any cadres about when the 'three Antis' campaign is being conducted on such a scale and with such thoroughness? At the moment the cadres themselves are <u>like the clay idol fording the river — it's as much as they can do to preserve themselves from disaster</u>. It's not just people like Fang Yu, the tax office representative in the Hu Jiang Mill, who are in this situation: all footicals, no matter how high-ranking they may be, are having first to look after themselves, and such things as the collection of taxes are now of secondary importance."

"对新药业,老实讲,我是<u>擀面杖吹火——一窍不通</u>,并且,自己的精力也有限,办厂都忙不过来,没时间考虑经营其他企业。倒是柳先生,听说利华药户生意不错,流动资金不少,正在找出路,你们两位是同行,又是老朋友,我看,可以合作合作。"

"To be quite honest with you, I <u>don't know the first thing about</u> the modern drug business and also my energies are rather limited: I can hardly find time for my own mills, let alone for considering branching out into other fields of enterprise. But from what I hear Mr. Liu, on the other hand, is doing very well with his Li Hua Pharmacy and has quite a lot of floating capital that he's seeking an outlet for at the moment. You two are in the same line of business and you're also old friends and it seems to me you might well get together on this."

谈正经的,我建议:请余静同志代表我们向资方交涉,查出原棉里面的问题,好不好?"好!"又是一阵热烈的掌声。这掌声表示大家认识一致,表示大家亲密团结,又表示大家要求解决这个问题的旺盛的斗志的意志。可是谭招弟心中却想:<u>骑着毛驴看书——走着瞧吧</u>,看究竟是啥原因。

"Let's be serious. I propose that we ask Comrade Yu Jing to take the matter up with the management on our behalf and find out what's wrong with the raw cotton. Agreed?" "Agreed!" There was another burst of enthusiastic applause, showing that they all saw the matter in the same light, and that their friendship and unity had been restored; it also demonstrated the irrepressible fighting spirit with which they were demanding that the trouble should be cleared up. But Tan Zhaodi was still thinking to herself: "Let's wait and see what the reason for it turns out to be in the end."

朱延年因为欠朱暮堂五十两金子过期没有归还，两人早就断绝了往来。朱延年一听提起朱暮堂，直摇头道："他吗，棺材里伸出手来——死要钱。他哪会借钱给我？我死了也不去找他。""不管怎么说，究竟是堂兄弟，一笔写不下两个朱字。暮堂最近来信还谈起你哩。"

Zhou Yannian and Zhu Mutang had long ceased to have anything to do with one another since Zhou Yannian had failed to repay Zhou Mutang's loan of fifty ounces of gold even after the period of the loan had expired. At the mention of this name he shook his head with conviction and said: "No, he's still after my blood. How can you imagine he'd lend me anything? I'd die rather than ask him for a loan." "After all's said and done, you're still brothers. You all belong to the Zhu family. And Mutang mentioned you in his last letter."

徐总经理想起通过梅佐贤和方宇的往还，在座谈会上梅佐贤虽然没说，可是方宇在税务分局里谈没有谈呢？他最关心的是这一点。他心头上的乌云越发聚集得多而且厚了。他这一阵心头如同十五个吊桶打水，七上八下，老是宁静不下来。他看看手表，已经九点半了，便问梅佐贤："韩工程师为啥还不来？"

Xu Yide thought of the transactions he had had with Fang Yu via Mei Zuoxian and although Mei Zuoxian had not mentioned them at the forum, might Fang Yu himself not have said something about them in the tax office? This was the one point that worried him most. The dark clouds were gathering thick and fast in his mind. His mind was in a turmoil these days and he was quite unable to think straight. He glanced at his watch and found that it was already half past nine, so he asked Mei Zuoxian: "What's keeping the engineer?"

"我的女儿在朱家，谁晓得她到啥地方去了？我正要问你们哩。你一定晓得,你告诉我。不告诉我,我绝不甘休!""你别狗咬吕洞宾,不识好人心。我是好心好意劝你,倒粘到我身上来了,这才是笑话哩。还是说出来算了吧,不说,老爷今天不会饶你的。""我不晓得,我说啥?"

"How should I know where she is when she's been here with the Zhu all the time? I was just going to ask you people where she is. You must know, so you'd better tell me. I won't give up until you do tell me." "Don't snap and snarl at me when I'm trying to do my best for you. I give you my advice with the best will in the world and you turn round and lay the blame on me, which is ridiculous. Now come on, out with it and let's have done. If you don't you'll get short shrift from the master." "How can I tell you when I don't know?"

(六)《红旗谱》(《Keep the Red Flag Flying》由戴乃迭翻译)

一句话没说完,严萍早出了大门。涛他娘走到门口,看了蓝黑暗的夜色。回来不见了江涛,对着严志和嘻地笑了一声。严志和说:"年头呀!革命革得开通了,大地方时兴男女自由。"涛他娘说:"看神色,他们俩不错了。"严志和暗喜,说:"许着,咱得给他们助点劲,别学了运涛和春兰那个,棒打鸳鸯两分离!"江涛踩着纱灯上射出的影子,走在苍茫的夜色里。乡村的淡墨色的轮廓像一堵墙,静静地站着。仰起头来看满天星星向他们眨眼笑着,微弱的青光从梨树叉上射下来。

But by now, Ping was already out of the gate. Mrs. Yan followed to peer through the dark night. When she came back she found Jiangtao had disappeared. She smiled at her husband. "It's the new way," explained Yan. "Revolution has freed them. In big places men and women mix quite freely." "They seem to be getting on well," said Mrs. Yan. "H'm. We must help them along. They mustn't be like Yuntao and Chunlan." By the light of the lantern, Jiangtao picked his way through the night. Darkness surrounded the village like a wall of silence. He looked up at the stars smiling down from the sky, and the pale glimmer that came through the pear trees.

那是一间精致的小屋,粉白墙壁,红油地板,天花板上雕镂着花纹。门前是小礼拜堂,屋子后面是一片墓地,荒坟上长满了枣棘和红荆。有一个穿灰色军装的士兵,扛着枪站在门口,探头探脑向屋里窥望。他看那个士兵,瘪皱的脸嘴,油污的枪,破军装被汗水浸透了,发着臭气。整个说起来,他站在医院里,和这气氛很不相称。张嘉庆一看见灰色兵就生了气,愣着眼睛骂:"你妈的!看什么?"岗兵见他凶煞似的,战战兢兢地说:"连长叫我们给你站岗。"张嘉庆冷笑了一声说:"嘿!给我站岗?背着门扇取布,我没有这么大牌子!"说着,他瞪起眼睛,头发直想乍起来。

The neat whitewashed room he was in had a red varnished floor and moulded ceiling. In front of it stood the chapel, while behind was a graveyard overgrown with wild dates and brambles. A grey-uniformed soldier with a rifle at the door now stuck his head into the room. The fellow's wrinkled face, greasy rifle and shabby, sweaty uniform were utterly incongruous in this hospital. Jiaqing scowled and swore: "Damn you! What are you staring at?" The soldier answered nervously: "The company commander told me to gard you." Jiaqing snorted. "To gurad me, ha! I hardly qualify for such an honour!" He glared and bristled with anger.

江涛、严萍、嘉庆,在院里洗衣服的时候,严知孝和老伴在北屋里有一场小小的争论。妈妈说:"闺女打了,也该有个安排。"又指着窗户外头说:"看!这样下去又好了吗?"严知孝说:"我看也没有什么不好。"妈妈把脖子一拧说:"你看不见?大闺女大小子们,成天价在一块耳鬓厮磨,好看吗?"严知孝说:"也没有什么不好看。"妈妈说:"我看老奶奶说的那个,你还是答应了吧!"严知孝说:"那是你的闺女,你答应下吧!也不跟孩子商量商量?"妈妈又说:"商量?要叫我是萍儿,巴不得的!登龙那孩子,长得白白儿的,精精神神的,多好啊……"严知孝说:"咳,你净装些个糊涂,你要是萍儿,你不愿和大小子们在一块玩?孩子们自然会选择自己的道路,打着鸭子上架不行,强拧的瓜儿不甜!"

While Jiangtao, Ping and Jiaqing was washing in the yard, Yan Zhixiao and his wife were arguing in the house. "The girl's growing up, it's time to arrange her marriage. Look!" Mrs. Yan pointed outside the window. "What good can come of this way of carrying on?" "I don't see any harm in it," retorted Yan. His wife tossed her head. "You wouldn't. A big girl spending all her time with those young fellows?" "There's nothing wrong with that." "I'm in favour of that boy granny suggested. Why won't you agree?" "She's your daughter! Why don't you talk it over with her?" "Talk it over? If I were Ping, I'd be only too pleased. Denglong is a fine-looking boy and full of spirit...." "Pah, don't pretend to have less sense than you have. If you were Ping, if you were a girl her age, wouldn't you want to have a good time with the boys? Leave the child to choose for herself. You can't force these things. Arranged marriages are no good. "

朱老星说："力气是随身带着的，好像泉眼一样，你只要用，它就向外冒。你要是不用它，它也就不冒了。你看大贵这身子骨，当了几年兵，在操场上摔打得多么结实，多么粗派。你看他那两条胳膊，一伸就象小檀条子似的。"大贵说："你说这个，我相信。"朱老星说："是呀！当兵对咱穷人固然没有好处，可是也落下个好身子骨。"大贵说："我还学会放机关枪哪！"朱老星笑了说："着啊！这放机关枪，对咱穷人本来没有好处。可是<u>大姑娘裁尿布，闲时做下忙时用</u>。将来咱要是用着这机关枪了，拿起来就能放。话又说回来，在这严冬腊月，下雪天本来可以闷在炕头上，抽个烟歇歇歇歇。我觉得总不如把这谷搓归结归结好。"

"Strength is something you have if you use it. It's like a fountain head. If you want it, it gushes out. If you don't it doesn't. Look at Dagui after a few years in the army. See how solid he is after drilling and exercising all this time! His arms look like regular cross-beams. " "I believe you!" said Dagui. "Yes," said Zhu Xing. "It's not good for us poor folk to be soldiers, but it builds a man up. " "I've learned to use a machine-gun too," said Dagui. Zhu Xing smiled. "Yes. All these machine-guns don't get us poor folk anywhere. <u>When a girl cuts out nappes she has no use for them, but there they are ready when she wants them.</u> A time may come when we need to use machine-guns, and then you'll be prepared. To come back to what we were saying: In the snowy winter, a man could sit on the kang and smoke, taking it easy. But that's not as good as fixing up these stalks. "

老套子盛上岗尖一碗山药粥，说："大侄子你先吃，我就是这一个碗。"江涛两手捧着，把碗递给他，说："我吃过了，大伯你吃吧！"江涛拿起笤帚，给他扫扫地，又扫了扫炕。老套子冻得浑身打战，两手捧着碗，蹲在灶火门前，拨出点火来烤着。一边烤一边吃。他说："常说，<u>大年初一吃饺子，没外人儿</u>。咱外族外姓的，怎么觍着脸去吃人家过年的饺子？"江涛说："你自个儿又不会捏。"

The Carter filled a bowl with potato stew. "You eat first, nephew," he said. "I've only the one bowl. " Jiangtao passed the bowl back to him with both hands. "I've eaten already, uncle. Go ahead. " Jiangtao picked up a brush and swept the floor and the kang. The Carter was shivering with cold as he squatted with his bowl by the stove, trying to warm himself. "<u>They say dumplings should be eaten in the family on New Year's day, with no outside there. I don't belong to their clan - how can I eat their New Year dumpling?" "But you don't know how to make them yourself."

江涛不等父亲说完,就说:"保定府有个第二师范,是官费,连膳、宿费都供给,只买点书、穿点衣裳就行了。"朱老忠说:"这对咱穷苦人倒挺合适。"这时,严志和又圪蹴下腿蹲在井台上,低下头拿烟锅划着地上,半天不说话。看朱老忠一心一意要叫江涛去上学,他猛地又急躁起来,说:"咱这过当儿,你还不知道? 那里能供得起一个大师范生呢?"朱老忠知道严志和是个一牛拉不转的脾气,一遇上事情,严志和就恨不得一头碰南墙,老是认为自己的理儿对。朱老忠说:"咱不能戴着木头眼睛,只看见一寸远。老辈人们付下点辛苦,江涛要是念书念好了,运涛再坐着革命的官儿,将来咱子子孙孙就永远不受压迫,不受欺辱了。你不能只看眼下,要从长远处着想。"严志和说:"照你说的,为了江涛上学,再叫你花点子钱,怎么对得起大贵二贵呢!"

Before his father could finish, Jiangtao cut in: "There's a No. 2 Normal School in Baoding, dad. It's state-subsidized. Board, lodging and tuition are free. All I'd need would be a few books and some clothes." "That's just the place for poor working folk like us!" cried Zhu. Yan squatted down by the well again. With bent head he knocked his pipe out on the ground, saying nothing for some time. Evidently Zhu was set on sending Jiangtao to school. "You know my means, don't you?" he demanded desperately. "How can I afford to keep a normal school student?" Yan could be as obstinate as a mule, as Zhu was well aware. He said: "Let's not light a lamp in the dark which shows only our own feet. We'll tighten our belts for a time. Once Jiangtao has finished his studies and Yuntao is an officer of the revolution, their sons and grandsons after them can live in comfort. The trouble with you is you see no further than your nose." Yan said :"Judging by what you say, you're going to spend more money on Jiangtao's schooling— but that isn't fair to Gagui and Ergui!"

涛他娘出了一口长气,自言自语:"唉! 为起个女人哪,真是难呀! 下辈子再托生的时候,先问问阎王爷,他要叫我托生个女人,我宁愿永远在阴间做鬼……"严志和听涛他娘嘟嘟哝哝,捅了一下她的被窝口儿,说:"这几天,你么怎么过来?"涛他娘把脖子一扭:说:"你甭理我,一个人漂流着去吧,回来干什么? 说走抬起腿脚就走了,上有老下有小,谁给你服侍?"严志和说:"你!"涛他娘说："我是你们使一辈子的丫头？我早就想过了，你要是不回来，我就嫁人。**爹走了娘嫁人，各人管各人，看孩子们怎么着？**"

His wife heaved a long, long sigh. "It's no joke to be a woman," she muttered. "Next time it's my turn to be born, I shall ask the King of Hell what I'm to be; and if he says a woman, I'll choose to remain a ghost in the underworld..." Hearing his wife muttering, Yan nudged her bedding and asked: "How have you made out these days?" "Never you mind!" She tossed her head. "Why should a man who drifts off trouble come back? If you want to go, go! There are old and yong at home — who's going to look after them for you?" "You!" "Am I a slave girl to wait on your family all my life? I'd made up my mind to marry again if you didn't come back. <u>With their father gone and their mother remarrying</u>, I wonder how they'd have managed!"

冯登龙又和严萍谈了一会子家庭琐事，他痛恨冯阅轩侵害他的家庭，他咒骂，他怨恨。一说到冯阅轩的名字，把牙齿咬得咯嘣咯嘣地响。为了这件事情，严萍也为他不平过，甚至是气愤。可是后来才觉得这场官司，打来打去，不过是两家地主为个女人争风吃醋，不由得暗笑，心想："**狗咬狗两嘴毛罢了！**"

Denglong gossiped with her for some time about family affairs. He cursed Feng Yuexuan, whom he hated for ruining his family. At each mention of Feng Yuexuan's name he ground his teeth. Though Ping was quite indignant on his behalf, when she remembered that it was simply two landlords who had fought all these lawsuits from one court to another over a woman, she could not help reflecting with amusement: "<u>When dog bites dog, each gets a mouthful of fur.</u>"

"蒋介石颁布割头税，增加百货捐，是为了搜刮一批银钱进行剿共。而这班子包商，大地主大资产阶级们，是为了赚一笔大钱养家肥己。农民们眼看一块猪肉搁进嘴里，土豪恶霸们硬要拽走。我们以反割头税为主，一包商冯老兰为目标，发动农民进行抗捐抗税。以后，还好发动抗租抗债，打倒土豪劣绅，铲除贪官污吏……**老鼠拉木锨，热闹的戏还在后头唱！**"说到这里，他弯下腰，斜起眼睛，转着眼珠想了老半天。又说："贫农养猪，中农养猪，富农养猪，中小地主也养猪。在这个题目下，可以广泛深入地发动群众，来一次公开合法的斗争。可是要注意一点！"

"Did you ever hear of such a tax? Never before in history has there been a tax on the pigs killed for New Year. This means that the pork dumplings eaten at New Year are taxed: people are no longer free to eat pork dumplings. The peasants want to eat a morsel of meat, but those others insist on snatching it away. Taking this pig slaughter tax as our chief concern, and the chief merchant Feng Lanchi as our main target, we'll arouse the villagers to resist their taxes and levies. Later on, we'll arouse them to resist rent and interest, to overthrow the local despots and get rid of dirty officials.... The fun is just beginning, there's more to come!" He stooped, looked sidewise, and rolled his eyes thoughtfully. Then he added: "Who keeps pigs? Poor peasants, middle peasants, rich peasants, small and middle-sized landlords. On a question like this we can mobilize a broad section of the populace. But there's one thing to remember!"

春兰说："我一天天地纺,铁打房梁磨绣针,功到自然成!"停了一刻又说:"我去找忠大伯和志和叔,叫他们给我备办。叫我去,我也得去,不叫我去,我也得去,我去定了!"停了一刻,又盯着江涛说:"看你也长成大人了,学得油嘴滑舌的,跟着瞎心的老人们谋算我。"江涛一下子气急了,说:"我那里……我是设身处地为你着想。"春兰鼓起嘴唇,瞟了江涛一眼,生气地说,"切"就再也不说什么。

"I dream of it every day. An iron rod can be sharpened into a needle. If I try hard enough I shall succeed." After a pause she went on: "I'll go and see Uncle Zhong and Uncle Zhihe and ask them to help me. I must go, whether they agree or not. I'm set on it!" She hesitated again, then looked hard at Jiangtao, "You've grown up too and learned the gift of the gab. You had the same plans for me as those wrong-headed old folk." "I never..." protested Jiangtao indignantly. "I was just thinking of you." Chunlan threw him a reproachful glance. "Well..." was all she said.

朱老忠从柜房里拿出把缨掸,掸着满身的尘土,说:"眼下东北倒还没有战事……咳!民国以来天天打仗,这年头有枪杆子的人吃香!今天你打我,明天我打你,谁也打不着,光是过来过去揉搓老百姓。"他一面说着,皱起眉泉笑,似乎军阀混战的硝烟,还在他们鼻子上缭绕。店掌柜的说:"各人扩充自个儿的地盘呗! 别的不用说,不管那个新军头一来,先是要兵,要兵人们就得花钱买。还叫人们种大烟,说什么'……谁敢种大烟一亩,定罚大洋六元。'你看看这个,不是捂着耳朵捅铃铛?"

Zhu had fetched a whisk from the office and was flicking the dust from his clothes. "Not at the moment" He sighed. "Since the Republic was founded, there's been fighting pretty well every year. This is a splendid time for the military. Today you fight me, tomorrow I fight you; but neither of us gets killed. It's the people who suffer." He wrinkled his nose as if he still smelt the acrid smoke of the warlords' guns. "Each is out for all he can get," agreed the innkeeper. "Soon as a new army arrives it stars conscripting men, and we have to pay to get off. They make us plant poppies too, but impose a six-dollar fine on all who grow poppies. Did you ever know anything like it? Talk about stopping your ears while you ring a bell!"

李德才气愤地瞪出眼珠子,待了一会,悄默默地转过身子去找朱大贵。一进大贵家门,忠大伯在门口站着,见了李德才,笑了说:"野猫子进宅,无事不来。李秀才轻易不到我家,来! 有什么事你说吧!"李德才说:"可就是,虽然是邻居,你没到过我院,我也没到过你院。今天来,倒是有一桩小事儿。"

Li Decai glared at him in angry silence, then made off in search of Dagui. He found Zhu Laozhong standing by his gate. "It's not often we have the honour of a visit from you, Mr. Li."said Zhu. "What brings you here?" "Yes, though we're neighbours, you haven't been to my house nor I to yours. Today I've come on a small matter of business."

朱老忠说:"依我说咱们说干就干,冯老兰,他净想骑着咱穷人脖子拉屎不行!"朱大贵一只脚蹬在炕沿上,揎起袖子抢着小烟袋,说:"左不过叫他们把咱压迫成这个样子。江涛兄弟! 你头里走,傻哥哥我后头跟着。"朱老忠眨巴眨巴眼睛,说:"一个耳朵的罐子,抢吧! 可是,这一次更要人多点。那场官司,联合了二十八家,还输塌了台呢!"

"I say, do it!" urged Zhu Laozhong. "We can't let Feng Lanchi spit in our faces." Dagui put one foot on the kang, rolled up his sleeves and brandished a small pipe. "He can't do anything worse to us than he has done. You take the lead, Jiangtao, and I'll follow you." Zhu Laozhong blinked and said:"All right! But we need more people. We had twenty-eight families to fight that lawsuit, but still we lost"

（七）《新儿女英雄传》——《Daughters and sons》，由 Translated by Sidney Shapiro 翻译

张金龙笑着说："没那事儿！我在倒腾买卖呢。你这会儿混得怎么样？"李六子说："唉，别提了！三麻子那个人还不知道？手又黑，心又狠，捞到什么，都是被窝里放屁——独吞！

他妈的，当地兄弟的连根毛儿也落不上！前儿个，他发了一笔大财，克了一个买卖人，说他私通八路，弄了几十匹绸缎，都不见了。他盘算我们都还不知道呢，哼！"

"Nonsense," laughed Chin-lung. "I'm doing a small trading business. How are things here with you?" "Ai, don't ask," sighed Li. "You know what Kuo is like — black hands and cruel heart. Any loot we grab disappears. Swallowed up. I don't even see a hair of it. The other day he made a small fortune. Nabbed a merchant and accused him of smuggling stuff to the Pa Lu. Shook him down for a couple of dozen bolts of satin. Now where are they? Huh, does he think we don't know."

大水好几夜翻过来，掉过去，睡不着觉，愁了个半疯子。他对小梅说："咱俩可是高粱地里的稆秸子（秸子是高粱的一种），一道苗儿。两个傻蛋，往后受罢训回去，百吗也不懂，可怎么着？"小梅也愁蹙蹙地说："谁说不是呀！咱们两个笨鸭子上不了架，受了一回子训，就装了一肚子小米饭，回去怎么见人哪？"大水说："咱不信！人家是人，咱也是个人，咱就学不会？"

Ta-shui tossed and turned for several nights, unable to sleep. "We're a couple of stupid hicks," one day he said to Mei, very distressed. "What'll we do if by the time the course is over, we still don't know anything?" Mei, too, was worried. "We stuff ourselves with the school's food every day, but when we go back home, how will we be able to face people? It looks like we can't keep up with the others." "I don't believe it," said Ta-shui staunchly. "If the others can learn, so can we!"

老乡们说，这回干部可卖了力气啦，都劝双喜、大水和村干部们回去歇歇。这三天三夜，真够他们受的！忙得饭也顾不上吃。赶上了，跟人家吃一口两口铛铛，赶不上，稀里糊涂地也过去了。又哪里合过眼呀！这会儿双喜大水你看着我，我看着你。大水说："嘿！看你，跟个泥菩萨似的！"双喜说："大哥别说二哥，两个差不多！"说着都笑了起来，嘻嘻哈哈地回村公所去了。

All praised the untiring labour of the cadres — how they had fought the flood for three days and three nights without sleep and nearly nothing to eat. The peasants urged them to go home and get some rest. Ta-shui and Shuang eyed one another. "Hy," said Ta-shui, "you look like a mud Buddha." "The pot shouldn't call the kettle 'black,'" Shuang retorted. "We're two of a kind." Laughing, the cadres slowly walked back to the village.

老爹常想给大水娶个媳妇，可是大水说："咱们使什么娶呀?"老爹说："没办法，再跟申耀宗借些钱儿吧。"——听说借钱，大水就急了。自从娘死那一年，指着五亩苇子地，借了申耀宗六十块现大洋，年年打利打不清，就像掉到井里打扑腾，死不死，活不活的。大水说："唉，还不够瞧的! 要再借，剩下这可怜巴巴的五亩地，也得戴上笼头啦!"老爹说："小子，不给你娶媳妇，我死也不合眼! 咱们咬咬牙，娶过媳妇来，再跳打着还账不行啊?"大水可不同意。这好小伙，长得挺壮实，宽肩膀，粗胳膊，最能干活;总是熬星星，熬月亮，想熬个不短人、不欠人的，松松心儿再娶媳妇。

Tieb wanted Ta-shui to take a bride and was willing to borrow more money from Shen to finance the marriage. Since their financial status was already precarious, Ta-shui was more concerned about the marriage question than the news that the Japanese were advancing on Peking, a hundred miles to the north. "Things are bad enough as it is," he protested. "If we keep borrowing, we'll end up by losing our miserable little plot of ground too." Tieb felt that the house was really much too hard to manage without a woman around to run things. He insisted that they could assume the additional burden. Ta-shui didn't agree. Powerfully built, with broad shoulders, brawny arms, Ta-shui was a hard worker. He thought that if he would put his back to it, and labour day and night, they could get rid of the debt. Then he would feel free to marry.

Tieb is a familiar term for "father"

开辟地区的同志们，这一天晚上统统出发了。大水接受双喜的经验，准备晚一点去，免得碰见敌人。半夜里，他要出发了，事先约好送他的老乡可还不见来，大水很着急。小梅说："别等了，船有的是。这会儿人们都睡了，临时找也很麻烦，就我送你去吧!"大水笑着说："得了吧! 去的时候好办，回来你一个人怎么着? 这白洋淀可容易失迷呢。"小梅怪他说："看你! 隔着门缝儿瞧人，把人看扁啦。我也是河边生，河边长，这一条路，船来船往也不知道走过多少遭儿,还有个错呀?"

That night, the guerrillas set out for the occupied villages. Profiting by Shuang's experience, Ta-shui planned to start later to avoid running into enemy patrols. At midnight he was ready to leave, but the peasant who had agreed to row him to Shenchai still hadn't appeared. Ta-shui fretted impatiently. "Don't wait any longer," said Mei. "There are plenty of boats. Everybody's asleep and it'd be hard to find a boatman, but I can take you." "No, thanks. I could help you get me over, but how would you find your way back alone? It's easy to get lost on Paiyang Lake." "Humph! If you peer at a person through a crack, he looks flat. Don't be so prejudiced. I was born and brought up here; I don't know how many times I've crossed the lake in a boat. How can I go wrong?"

小梅想了半天,皱着眉头说:"唉,这个人,真拿他没办法!"双喜给她鼓劲儿,笑着说:"能拔出脓来,才是好膏药呢。"小梅说:"狗皮上贴膏药,怕不粘哩!我说说试试看吧。"小梅一连劝了好几天,一阵软,一阵硬,好说歹说,总算把张金龙又说转了。最后他答应:"好!我就瞧着你的面子,在这儿干吧!"他就在区小队当了个班长。

Mei thought for a long time, her brow wrinkled in a frown. "Ai, that one," she sighed. "I don't know what to do with him." With an encouraging smile Shuang said, "The pus can be drawn out with a good poultice." Mei shook her head. "I'm afraid the poultice won't stick on the skin of a dog. Anyhow, I'll try and talk to him." She argued with Chin-lung for several days, now softly, now harshly, now with threats, now with cajolery, until he reluctantly gave in. "All right, I'll work here in the district — but it's only for your sake." He was appointed a lieutenant in the district militia.

张金龙骄傲地喊:"看我的准头怎么样?这回瞧你的吧!"说着他拿一块砖立在岗楼的垛口上,刚一放就一声枪响,连他的手都打穿了。听得见张金龙骂:"你妈的王八蛋!你打老子的手,你不算好汉!"牛大水愤恨地喊:"张金龙!你狗熊耍把戏,混充人形儿呢。你是个屁英雄好汉!"

"Not bad, eh?" he crowed. "Now it's your turn!" As he spoke he raised his hand to place a tile on the parapet. Before he could let go, a rifle cracked and a bullet tore through the tile and his hand together. Cheers and

— 227 —

laughter from the regional troops drowned the sound of Chin-lung's savage swearing. But the time for serious business had come.

他瞧见墙角落里立着个衣架,衣架上面挂一件黄呢子大衣,他满心欢喜,赶忙脱了花缎子旗袍,就去拿大衣,没想到那大衣自个儿在咕容咕容地动呢。小水吓了一跳,拿枪头子把大衣往起一挑,见里面藏着个鬼子,猴儿爬竿似的抱着衣架,簌簌地发抖。小水喝一声:"快下来!"鬼子一害怕,连人带衣架倒在地上,小水忙把他按住。米保长跑来一看,原来就是跳舞的那个"狗牙子伤",也给活捉了。

When he spied a good overcoat hanging on a coat rack in a corner, he decided to put it on. But as he reached the garment, it distinctly moved. Hsiao-shui nearly jumped out of his skin. Cautiously, he poked the coat open with the point of his gun. There, wrapped high around the pole of the clothes rack like a monkey on a stick, was a Japanese soldier, shivering violently. "Come down off there," shouted Hsiao-shui. Scared to death, the Japanese brought himself and the rack crashing to the floor together.

他们不管听懂听不懂,都哼呀哈地点头。末了,大水对申耀宗说:"老申,你看我讲得对不对?"申耀宗忙说:"这可句句都是实话!"大水说:"好。咱们都是中国人,都抱成堆儿,团成个儿跟日本人干。你在大乡上办事,我想知道岗楼上的情形,你敢跟我说吗?"申耀宗是个猫儿眼,看时候变。他说:"咱们都是中国人,怎么不敢说?我吃这碗饭也是好吃难消化。一个中国人,还能跟日本人一条心?"就把岗楼上的人数、枪支、军官的姓名、特务活动的办法……都说了。又问大水:"你看,我说的有虚吗?"

Whether they understood or not, they nodded their heads in approval at the proper intervals. When he finished, Ta-shui turned to his host. "Do you think I'm right, old Shen?" "Every word is absolutely true," replied Shen fervently. "Good. We're all Chinese and we have to stick together as one and fight the Japanese. You're in the puppet administration. I want to know what the situation is in the fortress. Do you have the courage to tell me?" Shen's attitude was as adaptable as a cat's eyes to light. "We're all Chinese, why shouldn't I dare to speak?" he replied staunchly. "I find the puppets' food good to eat but hard to digest. How can a Chinese feel the same as a Japanese?" He itemized the number of men in the fortress, the number of weapons, tha names of the officers, the methods used by the spies — Shen told everything he knew. "I haven't held anything back，have I?" he asked.

　　崔骨碌拉着兰女说:"你到底愿意跟谁好呀?"兰女把嘴撇得个瓢儿似的，说:"哼! 他啊,那么个麻脸儿,我八辈子也看不上!"崔骨碌涎着脸儿说:"我呢?"兰女斜眼瞟着他说:"你呀,我就怕你是一个没骨头的伞,支撑不开。将来闪得我没下场,倒不如趁早拉倒呢!"崔骨碌搂着她说:"拉倒可不成,不是要我的命啦!"兰女嗤地一笑,用手指头点着他的头说:"要不了你的命,可要我的命呢!"

Kulu urgently grasped her arm. "Who do you love?" "Humph! That guy," Orchid pouted. "I've never seen such a face full of pockmarks." "What about me?" persisted Kulu hungrily. "You?" she mused，looking at his sideways out of half-colsed eyes. "I afraid you're a ribless umbrella — you won't be able to stand up in the storm. We ought to part now before I become too mad about you." "Do you want me to die of love?" murmured Kulu，passionately wrapping her in his arms. Orchid giggled and pressed the tip of her finger against his forehead. "I'm more worried that you'll kill me with it."

　　大水气坏了,又着腰说:"这还了得! 在外面打人,回来又打人!"张金龙窜着跳着骂:"牛大水,你王八蛋! 我打我的老婆,干你什么事? 你他妈的暗箭伤人,你安的什么心眼儿?"双喜冷冷地喝道:"张金龙,你还敢撒野! 蔡大队长下来了,正要找你谈话,你马上跟我们走!"张金龙翻着白眼说:"他找我干吗?"双喜说:"哼,牛皮灯笼肚里亮,你心里还不明白?"张金龙偷眼一看,双喜脸上冷得像下了霜,口气又这么硬,知道搪不过去,就顺水推舟地说:"他要找我? 那正好,我正想找他算算账呢。"说完,一撅屁股先走了。双喜、高屯儿怕他溜,也紧跟着走出去。这儿,大水把小梅扶到炕上,小梅手上、身上都染红了。

panting，his hands on his hips，Ta-shui shouted，"That's fine. On the job you hit people，then come home and hit your wife!" "What business is it of yours if I want to hit my wife!" screamed Chin-lung，hopping with rage. "What do you mean by stabbing me in the back!" Blacky and Shuang dragged him out，still raving. Ta-shui helped Mei up. Her hands and clothes were stained with blood.

　　路上,代表们又说笑开了。大水对小梅说:"哈,黑老蔡真来得巧! 他要不来检查工作,咱们不定闹成什么样儿咧!"小梅笑着说:"嘿! 你那会儿凶成什么啦？指着我的鼻子，尽给我扣帽子！反正我也没有招儿，你给我扣什么帽子，我也给你扣什么帽子！"大水好笑地说："那会儿我是屁股上挂镜子，照见别人照不见自己，心里可实在生你的气呢。"小梅说，"我还不是气得要命！心里说，这人怎么这样不讲理，真是个牛脾气，以后再不跟他好啦。"说着转过头来，对大水笑了。大水说："你以后还跟我好不？"小梅腾的一下脸红了，说："看你还问这个话儿！"

During the trip back to Shenchai，the atmosphere was friendly and gay. Ta-shui and Mei walked together. "Blacky came just in time," said Ta-shui. "If hehadn't shown up for inspection，who knows where our quarrel would have ended?" Mei laughed. "You certainly were terrible — pointing your finger right at my nose and pinning all sorts of labels on me. And I was just as bad — whatever you called me I came back at you with more. " "I was wearing a mirror on my backside — it reflected others but I couldn't see myself. I was really mad at you. " "And I was furious. I thought to myself — how can he be so unreasonable? He's got a temper like a bull. I'm through with him!" "You didn't mean it，did you?" "How can you ask that?" replied Mei，her face scarlet.

立时，鬼子伪军都出动了，来了足又七八十人，四面房上都压了顶，对面房顶上还架了一挺机枪。郭三麻子叫崔骨碌几个在房顶上喊："快出来！四面都团团围住啦，你还能往哪儿跑？""把枪扔出来！投降了，给皇军干事儿，不比穷八路强啊？"崔骨碌还直着脖子喊："喂，我说里面的人，你听着！机关枪就在你脑袋上瞄着呢！你屁股下面坐着什么橛子，根儿还那么硬呀？八路军的饭我也吃过，有什么香的，又什么甜的？又管得紧，又没有钱儿花，还值当你那么拼命啊？我过到这边来，手里的票子大把抓，吃喝玩乐儿，可自在多啦。你还是快快归顺了吧！"

About eighty Japanese and puppet soldiers arrived and took up positions on the roofs of the buildings surrounding the compend. On the building directly opposite the ruins in which Shuang was hiding，a machine-gun was set up. From that vantage point，acting on Kuo's instructions，Kulu and a couple of other puppets shouted enticements. "Come out quickly. You're surrounded. Where can you run to?" "Throw away your gun and come out. Surrender and join the Imperial Forces. It's much better than that poor Pa Lu!" Kulu tried a long speech. "Wey! You，inside there — listen. There's a machine-gun pointing at your head. I've eaten the food of the Pa Lu. What's so fragrant and sweet about it? They're very strict with you; you get no money. Why should you give your life for them? Now that I'm no this side, I've always got a big roll of bills; I eat, drink and play — it's a much better way to live. The best thing for you is to surrender."

回到村里,老排长就找双喜,很生气地嘟囔说:"我不干了! 这是闹着玩儿,还是打仗呀? 简直是乱七八糟。我当了十几年的排长,没见过这样的兵! ……我……唉! 我干不了啦!"双喜问明了情由,就安慰他说:"你老人家别着急,咱们这些兵是什么兵呀,都是拿锄把子的手,猛不乍地拿起枪就会打仗啊? 这可是'瘸子担水'——得一步步来么! 赶明儿咱们开个检讨会,你老人家多点拨点拨吧!"老排长听了这最后一句话,笑开了脸儿,一连应着:"没说的,没说的。"双喜就找大水去了。

Back at the village, the old captain was so angry he could hardly talk. "I quit," he fumed to Shuang. "These guys aren't fighting, they're playing some kind of a game. I've been in the army over ten years, but I never met such a messed-up bunch.... I - hell! I quit!" "Take it easy, old-timer," soothed Shuang. "Until a few days ago, the only thing these fellows ever held in their hands was a hoe. You can't suddenly switch to a gun and expect them to know how to fight. They're like cripples carrying water — you've got to lead them slowly — step by step. We'll call a meeting the first thing tomorrow, and you can 'enlighten' them." Shuang's last phrase brought a grin to the old captain's face. "All right, all right." He didn't say any more about resigning.

大金牙走到大门口,回头啐了一口,说:"哼! 三个鼻窟窿眼儿,多出你这口气!"就扭着屁股出去了。大水回到屋里,小梅站起来迎他,眼里还带着泪花儿呢,可笑着说:"大水! 你把她老底子翻出来,可给我出了一口气。我叫这臭娘们儿真欺负苦啦!"大水笑着问:"你不是不干啦?"小梅说:"为什么不干? 不干,出来是干吗的呀!"大水笑着说:"着哇! 干工作免不了碰钉子,谁还不是一样! 咱们共产党员就不怕碰钉子,越碰越硬梆,碰成个铁头,就什么也不怕啦!"

At the door, Goldy fired her final shot. "You ought to learn to keep your big nose out of other people's business!" She left with an indignant swish of the hips. Mei, smiling through her tears, welcomed Ta-shui back into the house. "You certainly showed her up. That bitch has been making life hell for me. " "Are you still going to quit?" laughed Ta-shui. "What for? It's my job!" With an approving nod Ta-shui passed on the lesson he himself had recently learned. "Everybody, at some time or other, has difficulty in his job. We communists mustn't be afraid of trouble. The harder things go, the tougher we must become, until we're like steel and afraid of nothing. "

大水心里难过得吃不下。问福海,张金龙常到哪儿去。老头儿抢着说: "他没个准地点,福海也不知道。"大水告辞出来。福海送他到门口,小声说: "他哪一天晚上都去高财主家泡着,睡人家闺女,谁不知道! 你到那儿去瞧瞧吧。哼,没见过这号八路军! 他别以为屎壳郎掉在白面里,就显不出黑白!" 他指了地点,大水去了。到了高财主家,门房挡住不让进。大水解释半天,才得进去。他进到里院,掀开门帘,满屋亮堂堂的,当间一桌麻将,打牌的都穿绸着缎,就不见张金龙。

In no mood for eating, Ta-shui asked the mayor where Chin-lung spent his time. Again, the old man interrupted: "He has no definite place. My son doesn't know. " But as Ta-shui was leaving, the mayor saw him to the door. "Every night he goes to the home of the rich landlord, Kao," he whispered. "The whole village knows that he's sleeping with the landlord's daughter. You go see for yourself. I never met that kind of a Pa Lu before. He's as easy to pick out from the others as a black dung beetle in white flour. " He gave directions how to reach Kao's house, and Ta-shui set out. Kao's gatekeeper required considerable persuasion before he would let Ta-shui enter the compound. At last, Ta-shui crossed the courtyard and stood in the doorway of a brilliantly lighted room. He found richly dressed people absorbed around a mahjong game. But at first he didn't see anyone who looked like Chin-lung.

谷子春又高声地喊:"新郎新娘——报告恋爱经过!"这更热闹了,人们乱哄哄的。牛大水先给拉了起来,站在前面。他穿了一身灰布的新制服,头上戴着新军帽,一朵红花别在胸前。他满面红光,笑呵呵地说:"这可叫我说什么呀? 我跟她没个什么恋爱经过!"大伙儿嚷:"不说不行!"大水说:"可当真没有嘛!"有人问:"你说说,你们俩亲过嘴儿没有?"大水满脸是笑,可又皱着眉头说:"这话可太不像问题啦! 我两个一块儿工作这么些年,真是小葱拌豆腐——一清二白；别说亲嘴，就连个手也没有拉过呀！"

Again the master of ceremonies took the floor. "Bride and groom - report on how you made love." A veritable riot of cheers, applause and stamping of feet enthusiastically seconded this proposal. Ta-shui was hauled to his feet and dragged to the center of the room. Wearing a new army cap and a new grey cloth uniform, his face was redder than the big paper chrysanthemum pinned on his chest. "What can I say?" he asked with a laugh. "We didn't make love." "Confess," shouted the crowd. "You must speak!" "Really we didn't," insisted Ta-shui. "Let's hear it," yelled someone. "Did you kiss?" "That's a fine question. We worked together for years like brother and sister. Not only didn't we kiss, we never even held hands."

喝酒中间，郭三麻子想起李兰女，就打发护兵去找她来玩。护兵去了两趟，兰女推说有病，只是不来。三麻子很着恼，射了一眼崔骨碌，冷笑说："哼，这两天我没顾上去，早知道有人鞋底上抹了油啦！他妈的，不定在背后搞什么鬼呢！"崔骨碌只是闷着头儿喝酒，假装没听见。张金龙瞅着他俩，嬉皮笑脸地说："哈呀，今天这个菜，可有点儿酸溜溜啊！"三麻子有些醉了，麻脸儿通红，拍着桌子说："他妈的！什么酸不酸！我给他搁上些辣子，再换上写黄连，叫他瞧瞧我姓郭的厉害！"

After they had been drinking steadily for about half an hour, Kuo thought of Orchid. He sent his bodyguard to fetch her, but she begged off, saying she wasn't feeling well. Kuo shot a nasty glance at Kulu. "I've been busy the past couple of days," he laughed coldly. "I might have known some guy would go sneaking around behind my back. Who knows what the bastard's been up to." Kulu kept his nose in his wine cup and pretended not to have heard. Always glad to stir up trouble, Chin-lung added fuel to the flames. "I think your wine must be a little bitter, Kuo old man," he sniggered. Kuo's face was flushed with drink. "Bitter, my eye," he roared, pounding the table. "I'll show him what it is to eat bitterness!"

张金龙心里很活动，就问："现在郭团副在哪儿?"何世雄说："老郭和李六子这一伙，先进城了。咱上头早跟城里接洽好，就等着我去呢。"又笑着说："还不就是咱们这一把子，大大小小都是官儿啦。"张金龙喝得筋都暴起来了，他放下酒杯，说："何团长，我这个人你也知道，说话向来是'袖筒里入棒槌'——直

<u>出直入</u>！要是有郭三麻子在，我反正不去！"何世雄笑着，说老郭走火绝不是故意的。旁边何狗皮也劝张金龙。最后，张金龙马马虎虎答应了。临走，何世雄给了他十两大烟土，说："这事儿你可一个字儿别露！我走的时候再叫你。"张金龙就回去了。

Chin-lung was very taken by the prospect, but he still hesitated. "Where is Kuo?" "Old Kuo and Li and the others are already in the city, waiting for me," said Ho, and added with a laugh, "I made all the arrangements with the Japanese. Everyone of us, big and small, will be an official." Chin-lung was so drunk that the veins stood out on his forehead. He put down his wine cup. "Commander Ho," he said solemnly, "you know me — I <u>speak frankly and to the point</u>.... If Kuo is in... I'm out!" Ho and his son made light of Kuo having shot Chin-lung, and said of course he hadn't done it purposely. Finally, after much soothing and persuasion, Chin-lung muzzily gave his consent. As he was leaving, Ho gave him ten ounces of opium. "Don't breathe a word of this to anyone!" he warned. "I'll notify you when we're to go." Chin-lung staggered home.

他们大部分都是共产党员。大水见他们挺有精神地守在岗位上，心里很高兴。说："你们真不错呀！都不怕淋？"大伙儿说："嗨，都是庄稼人，怕什么淋！"柳喜儿滑稽地说："这才好呢，叫这雨一淋，就长得旺啦！"大伙儿都笑了。一个民兵说："这雨还有个好处，一张嘴就喝上水啦！"柳喜儿笑着说："可不！雨水煎茶，天上的味儿呢。"

大水心里想："这小伙子，可像双喜咧。"他满心欢喜，对大伙儿说："你们可注意点，别病了，完不成任务。"他们说："病不了！常挨淋，这点雨还怕，身子骨就太娇贵啦。"

Most of them were Party members; Ta-shui swelled with pride to find them so steady. "You're really all right!" he commended them. "Aren't you bothered by the rain?" "We're farmers," they chorused. "We like the rain." "It's good for us. It makes us grow," said Hsi comically. The others laughed. "The nice thing about rain," joked a militiaman, "is that when you're thirsty, you just open your mouth and there's your drink." "<u>And when you make tea out of it, it has a heavenly flavour</u>," punned Hsi. With a wrench at his heart, Ta-shui thought how much Hsi resembled Shuang. He turned to serious business. "Be careful not to get sick," he urged the peasant soldiers. "You won't be able to do this job if you're ill." "We're used to the rain," they assured him. "We'd have to have soft bones for a little shower like this to hurt us."

附录三 文学作品中歇后语的俄语翻译

(1)徐庶入曹营——一语不发。

李老太太听了一片奖励自己的话,不由得高兴起来,觉得自己到底是比丈夫大着两岁,应当容让他,虽然想起丈夫的一天到晚撅着嘴,徐庶入曹营一语不发,也确是心里堵得慌。(老舍《离婚》一九)

Перевод: Услышав бесчисленные похвалы в свой адрес, госпожа Ли так возрадовалась, что ощутила вдруг свое превосходство над мужем и решила быть снисходительной, хотя он все время молчал и хмурился, словно Сюй Шу, входящий в лагерь Цао Цао①.

Молчал и хмурился, словно Сюй Шу, в ходящий влагерь Цао Цао. — Цао Цао и Сюй Шу — герои классического романа Ло Гуаньчжуна 《Троецарствие》(XV в.).

(2)乌龟不笑鳖——都在泥里歇。

(胡玉音说:)"你这个坏人,你是想吓我,吓我?"(秦书田说:)"不是吓你,我讲的是真话,铁板上钉钉子,一点都不假。""不假?乌龟不笑鳖,都在泥里歇。都是一样落难,一样造孽。"(古华《芙蓉镇》)

Перевод: — Ты что, пугать меня решил, пугать? — Я не пугаю тебя. Это чистая правда. Что называется, на железной доске вырезана и гвоздями прибита... — Ты не смеешься? — Простая черепаха не смеется над съедобной — обе копошатся в грязи! Мы с тобой оба в беде...

(3)癞蛤蟆想吃天鹅肉——异想天开。

平儿说道:"癞蛤蟆想吃天鹅肉,没人伦的混账东西,起这个念头,叫他不得好死!"(《红楼梦》)

Перевод: — Паршивая лягушка захотела полакомиться мясом небесного лебедя! — возмутилась Пинъэр. — Негодяй, позабывший правила приличия! Раз он такое задумал, издохнуть бы ему, как собаке!

---

① 注:解释徐庶入的军营。

（4）三钱银子买个老驴——自夸骑得。

沙僧上前,把他脸上一抹道:"不羞,不羞!好个嘴巴骨子!**三钱银子买了老驴,自夸骑得!**"(吴承恩《西游记》)

Перевод: — И не стыдно тебе? — закричал Шасэн, подскочив к Чжу Бацзе и махнув его рукой по лицу. — Ишь ты морда! 《Купил себе старого осла за три гроша и хвалится!》.

（5）蛇头上的苍蝇——自来的衣食。

那妖闻言,呵声笑道:"这叫作个蛇头上苍蝇,自来的衣食。你众小的们,急忙赶上去,与我拿将来,我这里重重有赏!"(《西游记》)

Перевод: Услышав это, волшебник рассмеялся от удовольствия. — 《Когда мухи садятся змее на голову, это все равно, что пища сама лезет в рот》, — сказал он. — Вы вот что, ребятки· схватите его да тащите сюда поскорее. А я уж вас поблагодарю как следует.

（6）掩耳盗铃——哄人。

贾政也撑不住笑了。因说道:"哪怕再念三十本《诗经》,也都是掩耳盗铃,哄人而已。"(吴承恩《红楼梦》)

Перевод: Цзя Чжэн тоже не сдержал улыбки и промолвил: — Он может выучить еще тридцать разделов 《Шицзина》. Это будет все равно что, 《заткнув уши, красть колокол》, — толку никакого, один обман!

（7）狗咬吕洞宾——不识好人心。

彩霞咬着牙,向贾环头上戳了一指头,说道:"没良心的!狗咬吕洞宾,不识好人心。"(曹雪芹《红楼梦》)

Перевод: Возмущенная Цайсй, тыча ему в лоб пальцем, вскричала: — Бессовестный вы! Как собака, которая кусала Люй Дунбиня①, не ведая, что творит!

Люй Дунбинь — имя одного из восьми даосских святых.

（8）商鞅变法——自作自受。

她的坏招数也许就是马少奶奶教给的,而马少奶奶是商鞅制法,自作自受。(老舍《离婚》)

Перевод: Быть может, именно это и дало повод госпоже Ма младшей

---

① 是用俄语解释商鞅、吕洞宾等形象。

меня поучать. Она действует по законам Шан Яна①: <u>каждый получает по заслугам.</u>

Шан Ян — одни из первых законодателей Китая (IV в. до н. э.).

(9)铁刷帚刷铜锅——家家挺硬。

且不言唐长老困苦,却说那三个魔头齐心竭力,与大圣兄弟三人,在城东半山内努力争持。这一场,正是那铁刷帚刷铜锅,家家挺硬。(吴承恩《西游记》)

Перевод: Не будем пока рассказывать вам о страданиях и мучениях Танского монаха. Обратимся к трем дьяволам, которые дрались не на жизнь, а на смерть с тремя монахами — Сунь Укуном и его духовными братьями. Они бились с одинаковой яростью, не щадя сил своих. Видно, про них говорится в пословице: «<u>Нашла коса на камень</u>». Бой происходил на пригорке к востоку от города. Вот послушайте, что это был за бой!

(10)可着头做帽子——一点儿富余也不能。

鸳鸯道:"如今都是可着头做帽子了,要一点儿富余也不能的。"(曹雪芹《红楼梦》)

Перевод: — Мы теперь лишнего не готовим, — промолвила Юаньян, — <u>сколько едоков, столько и еды.</u>

(11)猪八戒掉在泔水桶里——得其所哉。

孙先生虽然心里也吃了凉柿子似的,可是不招大家妒恨,人家孙先生走哪路门子,自己就和大家声明,不像老李那么骄傲厉害,听人家孙先生:"哎呀,新市长儿是乡亲哟!老孙是猪八戒掉在泔水桶里,得其所哉!说不定,还来个秘书儿当当。"(老舍《离婚》)

Перевод: Вот господин Сунь ни в ком не вызывал ненависти, потому что с каждым делился своими соображениями, не то что этот зазнайка Лао Ли. — О! Новый мэр — мой земляк, — говорил господин Сунь. — Теперь я получу все, что пожелаю, буду кататься <u>как сыр в масле</u>, а может, еще и секретарем стану.

(12)黄梅不落青梅落——老天偏害没儿人。

三藏闻言,止不住腮边泪下道:"这正是古人云,黄梅不落青梅落,老天偏害没儿人。"(吴承恩《西游记》)

---

① 同上。

Перевод: Выслушав эту печальную историю, Трипитака не удержался и заплакал.

— Еще древние люди говорили: «Слива Хуан-мэй не опадает, а опадает слива Цин-мэй. Небо наказывает тех, у кого нет детей».

(13) 仓老鼠问老鸹去借粮——守着的没有，飞着的倒有。

柳氏啐道："…可是你舅母姨娘两三个亲戚都管着,怎不和他们要的,倒和我来要。这可是'仓老鼠问老鸹去借粮——守着的没有,飞着的倒有'。"（曹雪芹《红楼梦》）

Перевод: — Ты что, рехнулся! — разозлилась тетка Лю. — Попросил бы своих теток, они присматривают за садом, так нет, ко мне пристал! Как говорится, просила крыса зерна у журавля! Крыса в амбаре живет, где хранится зерно, а журавль в небе летает! Где ему взять!

(14) 喝了红薯烧酒——讲酒话。

"什么？什么？你老伯喝了红薯烧酒讲酒话,怎么拿唐僧上西天取经来打比,那是封建迷信,我们这是农业革命！你这话要叫上级听去了,嘿嘿……"（古华《芙蓉镇》）

Перевод: — Что, что? Ты, старик, видно, выпил много, невесть что болтаешь! Как можно сравнивать мое путешествие с паломничеством Танского монаха? Там — феодальные суеверия, а у нас — аграрная революция! Если б тебя начальство услышало то...

(15) 丈八的灯台——照见人家,照不见自家。

那宝玉是个丈八的灯台——照见人家,照不见自家的。只知嫌人家脏,这是他的屋子,由着你们糟蹋。（曹雪芹《红楼梦》）

Перевод: Это все Баоюй, он как фонарь на длинном шесте, на других светит, а сам в темноте; думает, все плохие, один он хороший. Смотрите, что вы натворили у него в комнате, все перевернули вверх дном!

(16) 鸡飞蛋打———一场空。

"祥子你等等走！"虎妞心中打了个闪似的,看清楚:自己的计划是没多大用处了,急不如快,得赶紧抓住祥子,别鸡也飞蛋也打了！（老舍《骆驼祥子》）

Перевод: — Погоди! — крикнула Хуню, когда Сянцзы направился к воротам. План ее провалился. Теперь главное удержать Сянцзы, а то она останется ни с чем.

(17) 狗熊的舅舅——猩猩儿。

小赵儿,官话有的说,狗熊的舅舅,猩猩儿,精的咧。(老舍《离婚》)

Перевод: Сяо Чжао, как говорят на официальном языке, — хитер, как лиса, ловок, как обезьяна.

(18)一条绳拴着两蚂蚱——谁也跑不了。

"咱们俩的事,一条绳拴着两蚂蚱,谁也跑不了！你等等,等我说明白了!"(老舍《骆驼祥子》)

Перевод: — Нас бог связал одной веревочкой, — уговаривала она парня. — Не уходи, я все улажу!

(19)皮笊篱——一捞个罄尽。

行者道:"老官儿,既然晓得老孙的手段,快把金丹拿出来,与我四六分分,还是你的造化哩。不然,就送你个皮笊篱,一捞个罄尽。"(吴承恩《西游记》)

Перевод: — Почтенный учитель, — отвечал на это Сунь У-кун. — Вы знаете мои способности. Давайте сюда ваши пилюли, да поживее. Мы их поделим. Четыре части моих, а шесть ваших. Скажите спасибо, что счастливо отделались. Ведь я мог пустить в ход волшебство, и все пилюли мигом очутились бы у меня.

(20)见提着影戏人子上场——好歹别戳破这层纸儿。

尤三姐听了这话,就跳起来,站在炕上,指贾琏笑道:"你不用和我花马吊嘴的,清水下杂面,你吃我看见。见提着影戏人子上场,好歹别戳破这层纸儿。"(曹雪芹《红楼梦》)

Перевод: Тут девушка вскочила и возмущенно произнесла: — Хватит молоть чепуху! Мы с сестрой для тебя слишком грубая пища, смотри не подавись! А меня лучше не задевай!

(21)牛栏里伸进张马嘴——有你说的。

"她摆她的摊子,你还你的店子,井水不犯河水,她又没踩着哪家的坟场!""今天日子好,牛槽里伸进马脑壳来啦!哈哈哈……"(古华《芙蓉镇》)

Перевод: — Она своим лотком занимается, а ты занимайся своей столовой! Колодезная вода речной не помеха. Можно подумать, она на чужую могилу наступила! — Ну и денек сегодня! В коровьем хлеву лошадиная морда объявилась! — Ты лучше своей столовой займись, чтоб в лапше мышиного помета не было! Ха ха ха...

参 考 文 献

[1] КРОПВ Ю. Л. Опыт описания структуры и классификации пекинских поговорок сехоуюй[M]. Жанры и стили литератур Дальнего Востока. Тезисы докладов научной конференции. Ленинград, 1966.

[2] ПРЯДОХИН М. Г. Китайские недоговорки : иносказания [M]. Москва：наука，1977.

[3] ROHSENOW J S. A Chinese-English Dictionary of Enigmatic Folk Similes[M]. The University of Arizona Press，1991.

[4] CHRISTIANE N. Text Analysis in Translation [M]. GA：Amsterdam Atlanta，1991.

[5] NIDA E A. From One Language to Another：Functional Equivalence in Bible Translating[M]. Scotland：Thomas Nelson Publishers，1986.

[6] WILSS W. The Science of Translation：Problems and Methods[M]. Shanghai：Shanghai Foreign Language Education Press,2001.

[7] HOUSE. J. Quality of Translation [C]//Baker. M. Routledge Encyclopedia of Translation Studies[M]. Shanghai：Shanghai Foreign Language Education Press,2004.

[8] HOUSE J. Translation quality assessment：Linguistic description versus social evaluation[C]. Meta. XLVI,2004

[9] NEWMARK P A. Textbook of Translation[M]. Shanghai：Shanghai Foreign Language Education Press，2001.

[10] CHRISTIANE N. Translating as a Purposeful Activity：Functionalist Approaches Explained[M]. Shanghai：Shanghai Foreign Language Education Press,2001.

[11] ANDRE L. Translation，Rewriting and the Manipulation of Literary Fame[M]. Shanghai：Shanghai Foreign Language Education Press,

2004.

[12] FORSTER L. Translation：An Introduction，In Aspects of Translation[M]. London：Secker and Warburg,1958.

[13] CATFORD J C. A Linguistic Theory of Translation[M]. London：Oxford University Press,1965.

[14] BAKER M. Routledge Encyclopedia of Translation Studies［M］. Shanghai：Shanghai Foreign Language Education Press，2004.

[15] GIDEON T. Descriptive Translation Studies and Beyond［M］. Shanghai：Shanghai Foreign Language Education Press，2001.

[16] LAWRENCE V. The Translator's Invisibility：A History of Translation[M]. Shanghai：Shanghai Foreign Language Education Press，2004.

[17] CHRISTIANE N. Translation as a Purposeful Activity Functionalist Approaches Explained［M］. Shanghai：Shanghai Foreign Language Education Press，2001.

[18] 包惠南. 文化语境与语言翻译[M]. 北京：中国对外翻译出版公司，2001.

[19] 谭永祥. 歇后语新论[M]. 济南：山东教育出版社,1984.

[20] 温端正. 歇后语[M]. 北京：商务印书馆,2000.

[21] 汉英词典（修订版）[M]. 北京：外语教学与研究出版社,1996.

[22] 范家材. 英语修辞赏析[M]. 上海：上海交通大学出版社,1992.

[23] 牛津高级英汉双解词典[M]. 北京：商务印书馆,1997.

[24] 金惠康. 跨文化交际翻译[M]. 北京：中国对外翻译出版社,2003.

[25] 刘宓庆. 当代翻译理论[M]. 北京：中国对外翻译出版社,1999.

[26] 陈金荣. 英语谚语民族特点分析[J]. 云南学刊,1992(2):83－85.

[27] 王佐良. 翻译:思考与试笔[M]. 北京：外语教学与研究出版社,1989.

[28] 叶舒宪. 诗经的文化阐释·自序[J]. 武汉：湖北人民出版社,1994.

[29] 华莉. 对翻译等值理论的再思考[J]. 四川外语学院学报，2000,16(4):77－80.

[30] 蔡毅,段京华. 苏联翻译理论[M]. 武汉：湖北教育出版社,2000.

[31] 杨仕章. 苏俄翻译理论中等值思想的演变[J]. 中国俄语教学,2001,20(1):46－52.

[32] 何自然. 语用学与英语学习[M]. 上海：上海外语教育出版社,1997.

[33] 杜诗春,宁春岩.语言学方法论[M].北京:外语教学与研究出版社,1997.

[34] 杨永林.社会语言学研究[M].北京:高等教育出版社,2004.

[35] 许渊冲.中国古诗精品三百首[M].北京:北京大学出版社,2004.

[36] 罗新璋.中外翻译观之"似"与"等"[M].武汉:湖北教育出版社,1996.

[37] 杨晓荣.翻译批评导论[M].北京:中国对外翻译出版公司,2005.

[38] 司显柱.论功能语言学视角的翻译质量评估模式研究》[J].外语教学,2006,27(2):63－67.

[39] 王宏印.参古定法,望今制奇:探寻文学翻译批评的评判标准》[J].天津外国语学院学报,2002,9(3):25－28.

[40] 李晓敏,杨自俭.译文评价标准新探索[J].上海科技翻译,2003(3):17－20.

[41] 司显柱.功能语言学视角的翻译标准再论[J].外语教学,2006,27(2):63－67.

[42] 罗选民,董娜,黎土旺.语料库与翻译研究[J].外语与外语教学,2005,32(5):380－384.

[43] 司显柱.功能语言学与翻译研究:翻译质量评估模式建构[M].北京:北京大学出版社,2007.

[44] 许建平,张荣曦.跨文化翻译中的异化与归化问题[J].中国翻译,2002,23(5):36－39.

[45] 李照国.中医翻译导论[M].西安:西北大学出版社,1993.

[46] 许钧."创造性叛逆"和翻译主体性的确立[J].中国翻译,2003,24(1):7－11.

[47] 赵宁.论充分翻译[J].外语教学,2003,24(5):43－46.

[48] 许钧.文学翻译的理论与实践:翻译对话录[M].南京:译林出版社,2001.

[49] 查明建,田雨.论译者主体性:从译者文化地位的边缘化谈起[J].中国翻译,2003,24(1):19－24.

[50] 谢天振.译介学[M].上海:上海外语教育出版社,1999.

[51] 李运兴.语篇翻译引论[M].北京:中国对外翻译出版公司,2001.

[52] 屠国元,朱献珑.译者主体性:阐释学的阐释[J].中国翻译,2003,24(6):8－14.

[53] 潘文国.当代西方的翻译学研究:兼谈"翻译学"的学科性问题[J].中国

翻译,2002,23(1):31-34.

[54] 孙艺风.翻译规范与主体意识[J].中国翻译,2003,24(3):3-9.

[55] 李建忠.文化差异与翻译语言文学与文化[M].北京:知识产权出版社,2001.

[56] 袁晓宁.关于翻译中归化和异化的哲学思考[J].外语与外语教学,2003(1):26-28.

[57] 韩子满.文化失衡与文学翻译仁[J].中国翻译,2000(2):39-43.

[58] 沈育英.论译者作为文化操作者[J].外语教学,2003,24(1):83-86.

[59] 中国社会科学院语言研究所词典编辑室编.现代汉语词典[M].北京,商务印书馆,1984.

[60] 郭建中.汉语歇后语翻译的理论与实践[J].中国翻译,1996(2):12-15.